p 137 Atticus' most pe—
"to challege stere
people as types.
shoes + see them

p 139 one of central themes
steriotype / community re: Boo — they become sympathetic
toward him + no longer see him as a witch) or monster

p 169 Calpurnia was no "mammy"
p 179 outcasts = scapegoats

MW01071013

Understanding
To Kill a Mockingbird

UNDERSTANDING
To Kill a Mockingbird

A STUDENT CASEBOOK TO ISSUES, SOURCES, AND HISTORIC DOCUMENTS

Claudia Durst Johnson

The Greenwood Press
"Literature in Context" Series

GREENWOOD PRESS
Westport, Connecticut • London

Library of Congress Cataloging-in-Publication Data

Johnson, Claudia D.
　　Understanding To kill a mockingbird : a student casebook to
　issues, sources, and historic documents / Claudia Durst Johnson.
　　　　p.　cm. — (The Greenwood Press "Literature in context"
　series, ISSN 1074–598X)
　　Includes bibliographical references and index.
　　ISBN 0–313–29193–4
　　1. Lee, Harper. To kill a mockingbird.　2. Literature and
　history—United States—History—20th century.　3. Afro-Americans in
　literature.　4. Civil rights in literature.　I. Title.　II. Series.
　PS3562.E353T6338　1994
　813'.54—dc20　　　　94–4793

British Library Cataloguing in Publication Data is available.

Library of Congress Catalog Card Number: 94–4793
ISBN: 0–313–29193–4
ISSN: 1074–598X

First published in 1994

Greenwood Press, 88 Post Road West, Westport, CT 06881
An imprint of Greenwood Publishing Group, Inc.

Printed in the United States of America

The paper used in this book complies with the
Permanent Paper Standard issued by the National
Information Standards Organization (Z39.48–1984).

10 9 8 7 6 5 4 3

Contents

Introduction

To Kill a Mockingbird is unquestionably one of the most widely read, best-selling, and influential books in American literature. It has made a significant difference in the lives of individuals and in the culture as a whole. An indication of the novel's impact on its readers is found in a "Survey of Lifetime Reading Habits" conducted by the Book-of-the-Month-Club and the Library of Congress's Center for the Book in 1991. Using 5,000 respondents, the researchers found that one of the three books "most often cited as making a difference" in people's lives was Harper Lee's *To Kill a Mockingbird* (it was second only to the Bible).

How and why has Lee's novel made a difference? Part of its immediate appeal can be explained by its sensitive and insightful portrayal of race relations in Alabama at a time when the battle for integration and equal rights was at its height in America, and when much of the action was centering on Alabama. But the novel's impact has not been restricted to the period in which it emerged. Its influence has been enduring because it allows the reader, through the lives of children, "to walk around in the shoes" (as its main character says) of people who are different from ourselves. The novel challenges our stereotypes—of the Southerner, the African-American, the eccentric, the child, the young lady. At the same time that many people see characters and social situations in different ways after reading the novel, they also recapture some part of their own youth in the story of its characters. The novel's universal and lasting appeal comes in part from the reader's nostalgia for the time of innocence in which children live before harsh truths enter their lives.

One year after its publication in 1960, *To Kill a Mockingbird* had gone through 500,000 copies and had been translated into ten languages. In a study of best-sellers, Alice P. Hackett and James H. Burke found that in the eighty-year period 1895–1975, *To Kill a Mockingbird* was the seventh best-selling book in the nation and the third best-selling novel. By 1975, fully 11,113,909 copies of the book had been sold; by 1982, over 15 million. By 1992, Popular Library and Warner Books had sold 18 million in paperback books alone. *Books in Print* and the On-Line Catalog of the Library of Congress indicate that *To Kill a Mockingbird* has never been out of print since 1960 in either hardcover or softcover, and it remains popular in languages other than English.

To illustrate the enduring pertinence of the novel, in the fall of 1993—some thirty-three years after the publication of *To Kill a Mockingbird*—two headlined stories in national newspapers addressed issues central to the novel: censorship in the public schools and the stereotyping of African-Americans. *To Kill a Mockingbird* continues each year to be prominently displayed as a frequently challenged book in the windows of bookstores throughout the nation. In early spring of 1993, the novel provoked a heated debate among nationally prominent attorneys over the nature of heroism. As a less profound indication that the book endures, the *Village Voice* in New York City ran a movie advertisement in the fall of 1993 crediting a musical group called the Boo Radleys. At the same time in Boston, a band called Tequila Mockingbird was playing in local night spots!

During the course of this study of *To Kill a Mockingbird*, numerous questions will be posed for the reader to think through; so it is appropriate to begin by contemplating a fundamental issue in an ongoing debate about how this type of literature should be studied:

- Should a work of literature (Mark Twain's *The Adventures of Huckleberry Finn* or Edgar Allan Poe's "The Fall of the House of Usher," for example) be studied as a self-contained unit?

Harper Lee. Photo courtesy of University of Alabama Alumni
Publications.

- In other words, does the author provide within the work all the information the reader needs for a study of the work?
- More specifically, should a reader of Mark Twain's *Huckleberry Finn* confine himself or herself to a searching analysis of the novel only?
- Would it enhance a student's understanding of the work to go beyond the author and the story (in this example, Twain's *Huckleberry Finn*) to learn more about slavery, the religious and moral climate of the time, or the reading habits and other entertainment of the nineteenth century? Maybe using the example of an obviously social work like *Huckleberry Finn* loads the argument in favor of including background information. Maybe some works are more readily studied as self-contained entities than others.
- Are there certain short stories, novels, plays, poems, or film scripts that could or should be considered without reference to issues and information outside the work itself?

Frequent exposure to literature and studies of literature can cause one's initial impressions about such issues to change. With more experience, finding the "best" way to approach a work of literature becomes fairly simple to determine, as the long-standing debates among literary scholars suggest.

In this study, we begin with a literary analysis that makes no reference to matters outside the form and themes of Harper Lee's novel. Subsequently, however, we broaden the traditional literary approach to include issues and historical background that are external to the novel itself, as a means of deepening our understanding of the novel.

The approach can be described as interdisciplinary. That is, the materials we provide to accompany our study of the novel come from a variety of disciplines: history, popular culture, sociology, and legal studies—not just literary criticism, the discipline that merely opens the inquiry at hand. The assumption on which this volume rests is that in the social and historical background of the novel, one can find useful issues for analysis of a literary text.

Besides, such a broad approach to the literary text enlarges our understanding of both past and present—the history out of which the fiction emerges as well as the enduring issues that are part of the fabric of the fiction.

The broad questions raised about the novel by the documents in this collection are as follows:

- How can the form and themes of *To Kill a Mockingbird* be viewed independently of all other considerations?
- How does information about the climate of opinion in the South of the 1930s (the time of the novel's setting) shed light on the trial in the novel in particular?
- How does information about the civil rights struggle taking place in Alabama while the novel was being written deepen our understanding of race relations in *To Kill a Mockingbird* and explain the response to it?
- How does a grasp of commonly held social types and stereotypes— particularly Southerners, African-Americans, poor whites, little girls, eccentrics, and the ideal family—lead us to an appreciation of character portrayal in the novel?
- How does the legal controversy over the character of Atticus Finch bring into keen focus the questions raised by the novel over the conflict between the good man and the good lawyer? Is it possible to be both?
- How does information about censorship in schools and libraries in general, and censorship of this novel in particular, throw light on the theme, tone, and language of the novel?

A variety of different records are excerpted here as source material for our study of *To Kill a Mockingbird*:

- a literary article
- transcripts from a county court case
- a transcript of a Supreme Court opinion
- newspaper articles
- "letters to the editor"
- an interview
- editorials
- position papers from national organizations
- a memoir
- photographs
- an informal debate between two lawyers
- historical and sociological studies
- magazine articles

In a very real sense, all the source materials contained in this volume are as much works of literature as is *To Kill a Mockingbird*.

Some excerpts provided here are actually from other narrative fiction, but other nonfiction is as carefully shaped in the form of argumentation or recreations of history. In each instance, the source materials have been selected to work with the fictional creation, the novel, to bring past and present issues into sharper focus.

In addition to the documents, each section of the text contains (1) introductory discussion, (2) study questions, (3) topics for written or oral exploration, and (4) a list of suggested readings.

Understanding
To Kill a Mockingbird

1

Literary Analysis: Unifying Elements of *To Kill a Mockingbird*

UNIVERSAL THEMES

The success of *To Kill a Mockingbird*, one of the most frequently read novels of the last hundred years, can be attributed to its powerful, universal themes. One central theme, encompassing both Part One (which is primarily Boo Radley's story) and Part Two (which is primarily Tom Robinson's story), is that valuable lessons are learned in confronting those who are unlike ourselves and unlike those we know best—what might be called people of difference. In the story, the children must grow up, learn civilizing truths, and rise above the narrowness of the place and time in which private codes and even some legal practices contradict the idealistic principles that the community professes: "Equal rights for all, special privileges for none," as Scout says. In practice, however, equal justice was not available to Boo Radley at that turning point in his life; nor is it available to the Tom Robinsons of this world.

Within such a social climate, the children learn how citizens of their community, which is made up of different races, classes, and temperaments, interact in times of crisis. The "outsiders" in this novel are primarily represented by the unseen eccentric, Boo Rad-ley, and by the African-American, Tom Robinson. They are clearly outside the mainstream of Maycomb society, even though they have lived in the community for as long as most can remember. Because of their position in society, they are at first regarded by the children as demonic and witchlike. But in the process of ma-turing, the children come to embrace the outsiders among them. Even more, they come to acknowledge their kinship with the out-siders—in a sense, the outsider within themselves.

During the course of the novel, the children pass from inno-cence to knowledge. They begin to realize their own connection with the community's outsiders, and they observe one man's hero-ism in the face of community prejudice. One overarching theme of the novel—which brings Part One, the story of Boo Radley and the children, in union with Part Two, the trial of Tom Robinson—can be stated in this way: the mark of virtue, not to mention ma-turity and civilization, involves having the insight and courage to value human differences—people unlike ourselves and people we might label as outsiders.

In this novel the emphasis is on people of a race and culture different from that of the Finch children, but it also includes the eccentric Boo Radleys of the world who are so different from the people we are and know that they become witchlike and demon-like in the homogeneous community's consciousness. After all, dif-ference is unsettling, even frightening. As the children learn, it takes a strong mind and a big heart to come to love Boo Radley, of whom they are at first so terrified; and it takes immense courage to defend another human being, one who is different from them-selves, against community injustice borne of fear.

Certainly, as Atticus says in his final summation to the jury, not all outsiders are necessarily good people. Bob Ewell is an example. But the children learn that some outsiders they encounter (like Mayella Ewell) deserve their pity, and that others (like Mrs. Du-bose) may be more complex than they at first discern. However, as Atticus also says, they all are human beings. They are also, in some way, victims.

Another element of this same theme, an element that incorpo-rates numerous other characters, is the sympathetic bond that the children begin to acknowledge between themselves and the peo-ple who are so different from them. Part of the process of Scout's

Why Scout Outsider)

learning to know Boo Radley and the black people in Maycomb is Scout's coming to feel just how much of an outsider she is herself. As an avid reader, she is a freak in her first-grade class. As a tomboy, she is without little girl friends. As an independent-minded daughter of Atticus Finch, she is the object of brutal ridicule in the genteel ladies' missionary society.

A second theme that runs throughout the novel is that the laws and codes the town of Maycomb professes and lives by are always complex and often contradictory. The idea of law is raised at the start of the novel in the epigraph from Charles Lamb: "Lawyers, I suppose, were children once." The main adult character is a lawyer, and his two children seem destined to be lawyers. They are already at an early age familiar with legal terms. Their African-American housekeeper knows that things are different in the household of a lawyer, and she herself has learned to read from a classic book of law. Part One of the book, which develops the children's initiation into a world much uglier than the one they knew within the protective boundaries of their father's house, is built on legalities and social codes, both law-abiding and law-breaking: Scout's "crime" of entering the first grade already knowing how to read, the long-ago arrest of Boo Radley and his friends for their loud behavior in the public square and Boo's second arrest for stabbing his father in the leg, the threat of lynching Tom Robinson, the charge of rape against him, the "entailments" of Mr. Cunningham, the illegal trespassing of the children on the Radley property, and the breaking of the hunting and truancy laws by the Ewells.

Most of Part Two is concerned with a trial and takes place in a courtroom. Here, most conversation is about legal matters concerning the constitution of juries and the penalty of death for rape. Finally, at the end of the story, Atticus and the sheriff break the law to protect Boo Radley from jail and from the community's attention after he has saved the children's lives by killing Bob Ewell.

A complication of this second theme is that even though the law should protect from evil and injustice the "mockingbirds" like Tom Robinson and Boo Radley and all those people of difference who are often victims of a homogeneous society, it has finally not been able to do so, mainly because hidden social codes contradict their stated legal and religious principles. For whatever reason, the law has been inadequate to protect Tom, who is sent to prison and gets shot. It has also been inadequate to protect Boo, who is imprisoned by his father after a minor youthful skirmish with the law. And it is not the law that protects the children from Bob Ewell. Ironically, although the novel leads us to deplore the violence of the lynch mob that disrupts law, it is only an act of violence rather than law that protects the children from a literal mad dog and a human mad dog, Bob Ewell.

In summary, the two parts of the novel, which focus on the stories of two "mockingbirds" who are considered outlaws, are brought together through the various elements of the fiction to merge in a central theme of growing up to acknowledge the human bonds between ourselves and those so different from us.

ELEMENTS OF FICTION

The novel is also successful because the multiple elements that make up the fiction support its themes. These elements consist of (1) point of view (or voice) and language, (2) tone, (3) time and place of setting, (4) characters, (5) plot structure, and (6) images and symbols.

In terms of the first element, it is clear that the author has developed a complex, first-person *point of view*. At the beginning and end of the novel, framing the story, is the point of view of the grown-up Scout (Jean Louise) looking back on the events of her childhood. Very quickly, however, another dimension is introduced, as we realize that the mature Scout is not simply recalling and interpreting the past but recalling it *as she had seen it as a child*. Much of the dialogue and narrative, for example, preserves the very young Scout's speech: it is told with the simple vocabulary and simple sentences of a young child, often fusing ungrammatical language and children's slang that we can't imagine the adult Scout using. For example, she says, "Miss Caroline was no more than twenty-one. She had bright auburn hair, pink cheeks, and wore crimson fingernail polish. She also wore high-heeled pumps and a red-and-white striped dress. She looked and smelled like a peppermint." There are, then, two levels of perception: the innocent view of the child, and the memory of the more knowing adult.

The *language* also combines (1) the rough dialogue of the boisterous children playing and fighting, with (2) the simple eloquence of Atticus's summation to the jury. Despite the characters' love of the written word, the novel seems to come out of a spoken rather than a written tradition. Just flipping through the pages reveals how much of it is conversation; for example, rather than having the adult narrator describe or explain a matter, we find that Atticus explains it in conversation with his brother or the children.

The second element of the novel's structure, closely related to voice, is tone. The *tone* of any work can range from flippant to ponderous. The tone of this novel, in keeping with the child's point of view, is simple rather than grandly eloquent. It is honest and direct rather than suggestive and secretive. As action involves the children's antics and perceptions, the tone is often comic. Descriptions of Scout's first day of school and her first snowman (or woman?) are good examples. At times, however, with simple, direct, and unemotional language, the tone soars into lofty, emotionally moving profundity—as when the Reverend Sykes instructs Scout to join the black people in the balcony in standing up in homage to her father. The lines are simple: "Miss Jean Louise, stand up. Your father's passin'." But the moment it creates is a highly charged one. The same is true of Atticus's discovery that the African-American community has brought a kitchenful of food to his house in appreciation of his efforts to help Tom Robinson, and of the moment when Scout turns to see Boo Radley in Jem's room and later as she looks down her street from the Radley porch and realizes that Boo has been looking out for them.

One of the most important elements in this fiction is the third one: *the time and place of its setting.* The setting of *To Kill a Mockingbird* is so vivid and exact that it seems at times to be a separate character. The time is the 1930s, when, the reader is told, massive unemployment and poverty plague the country. Franklin Roosevelt has just become President of the United States and, we are told, has given the nation some hope that the economic depression will be over. Part of the community has begun to take advantage of programs created by Roosevelt for economic relief. Everyone seems to be poor. Many have lost or are losing their land. Professional people like lawyers and doctors are paid in services and produce rather than cash. It is also a time, the novel reveals, when Adolf Hitler is rising to power in Europe, and it is already generally known that the persecution of Jews in Germany has begun.

This is the time of the setting. The place is the South, specifically southern Alabama—distinct not only from the northern United States but even from northern Alabama, which has industry, the state university, and a geographic/political element that did not secede from the Union during the Civil War. The South in this novel has been strongly influenced by the antebellum, cotton-growing plantation system and by defeat in the Civil War. The continuing influence of the plantation system and the war reveal themselves most decidedly in the attitudes toward race, the glorification of the past, the community's suspicion of outsiders, the lingering paternalism of some members of the more privileged class, and its tradition (on the surface) of polite and gentle manners. The South's defeat in the Civil War has contributed to the economic standstill of growth in the community and its removal from the rest of the world.

Typical attitudes toward race are especially evident in the town's reaction to Atticus's defense of Tom Robinson and in the views of the missionary society. Glorification of the past can be seen in Aunt Alexandra's somewhat ridiculous pride in her ancestors, even a relative who took a shot at the president of the University of Alabama. Suspicion of outsiders extends not only to the U.S. President's wife, Eleanor Roosevelt, but to the new young teacher from northern Alabama. Class snobbery is seen in Aunt Alexandra's obsession with what she regards as "good" or "old" families and her refusal to approve of Scout's playing with lower-class children. The tradition of paternalism, which seems a throwback to plantation days, is apparent in Atticus's assistance not only to Tom Robinson but also to Walter Cunningham, the dirt-poor farmer. Finally, typical southern courtliness is seen in the polite use of "Ma'am" and "Sir," in Atticus's gracious demeanor toward Mrs. Dubose, and in the attitude of respect adopted by children in the presence of adults.

Within the general setting of a small southern town are several arenas in which the action occurs: the house and yard of the Finch family, the elementary schoolhouse, the grounds around the Radley house, the Dubose house, Miss Maudie's yard, the street onto which these houses front, an African-American church, a courthouse, the street in front of the county jail, the house and yard of the Ewell family, and the yard in front of the Robinson family house. These arenas encompass particular institutions within the community: the family, the neighborhood, the public educational institution, the justice system, and the religious institution. Yet most are in some essential way corrupted or weakened and removed from the institutional ideal.

The fourth consideration is the *characters*, all of whom are Southerners. The major characters include the Finch family (the father Atticus, his daughter Scout, his son Jem, and his African-American housekeeper Calpurnia). Beyond the immediate Finch family, an equally important character is Dill, the young friend of the Finch children who spends his summers with relatives in Maycomb. These are the most important acting characters. In the next level of importance are the two characters who are chiefly acted upon: Tom Robinson, an African-American man accused of rape, and Boo Radley, whose presence is felt more in the children's minds than in actuality. Next are members of the extended Finch family and neighbors: Miss Maudie, a sympathetic, older friend of the children; the terrifying Mrs. Dubose; the ne'er-do-well Bob Ewell and his daughter Mayella; and Atticus's sister, the children's Aunt Alexandra.

The characters are at times divided into opposing camps, according to age or race or social status. At times, for example, the children seem to be opposed to the adults, the African-American characters at odds with the white characters, and the lower-class Old Sarum characters set apart from the townspeople.

At the same time, boundaries between these categories are often broken down momentarily, as when the children feel a kinship with the once-feared adult, Boo Radley, and when the adult Dolphus Raymond sympathizes with the children's disgust at the trial. Barriers between classes are broken down when an Old Sarum child is a luncheon guest in the Finch household; and lines between the races are broken down when the children attend a black church, when they later sit with the black spectators in the courthouse balcony, and when Scout asks to visit Calpurnia's house.

The common denominator in all the white characters is their southernness and their eccentricity. The classic eccentric is Boo Radley, who has been locked up by his father for most of his life and who, gossip has it, lurks about at night feeding on raw animals. But actually each one of the major white characters can be described as "peculiar" in some essential way. Scout Finch is a precocious little girl who dresses in overalls, curses, and beats up little boys. Her brother, Jem, is a loner who, like Scout, calls his father by his first name. Atticus, their father, is also an eccentric in that he does not hunt or fish or participate in sports, as other men in this community do. Dill, the children's friend, is a child sent away by his mother to live much of the year with distant relatives. He lives largely in an imagined world, spinning fantastic tales about being kidnapped, for example, which he relates to his two friends. All the neighbors who live on the street are eccentric. Miss Maudie hates her house, spends most of her time gardening with overalls on, amuses the children by sticking out her false teeth, and is not above shouting rejoinders to some churchgoers who claim she loves flowers too much. Mrs. Dubose is a drug addict who screams insults at the children when they pass her house. Dolphus Raymond, who lives in the country, pretends to be drunk all the time to give the community a reason for his decision to live with an African-American wife and children. Bob Ewell lives on welfare, whatever he scavenges from the garbage dump near his house, and the game he kills out of season.

Plot structure is the fifth element of fiction that embodies the major ideas of the novel. The novel is framed by the comments of the adult narrator, but the story within that frame is chronologically developed; it covers a period of two and a half years, from the time Scout is six until the fall of her eighth year. The action is divided into two main parts. The first primarily develops the children's approach to Boo Radley, their unseen neighbor. The second part is the story of the trial of Tom Robinson for rape. Each part consists of distinct episodes.

Part One offers the following episodes:

1. Scout, Jem, and Dill spend their first summer together, when they begin approaching Boo Radley.

2. Scout is able to endure her first year at school when Boo Radley contacts the children through the hole in the tree.

3. During the second summer Scout rolls in a tire against the Radley house, the children begin the Radley drama, and Jem tries to see in the Radleys' windows at night.

4. In the fall of the next school year, Mr. Radley plasters up the hole in the tree, it snows, and Boo puts a blanket around Scout's shoulder during the fire.

5. During Christmas of that year, Scout beats up her cousin Francis and the Robinson theme is introduced.

6. In February Atticus shoots a mad dog.

7. In the spring Jem is forced to read to Mrs. Dubose.

Part Two has fewer distinct episodes:

1. The children visit Calpurnia's church.

2. Aunt Alexandra's arrival causes conflict.

3. During the next summer Atticus faces a lynch mob.

4. Tom Robinson is tried for rape.

5. Scout has to face the missionary society and the death of Tom Robinson.

6. The children are attacked on the way home from a Halloween party in the fall.

The action of the novel is unified by the fact that it opens and closes with Boo Radley. Furthermore, the Tom Robinson and Boo Radley sections are integrally connected, in that two characters and what they represent are united in their identification with the mockingbird of the title. Like the mockingbird, they are vulnerable and harmless creatures who are at the mercy of an often unreasonable and cruel society.

The mockingbird brings us to the sixth consideration in a discussion of the elements of fiction: the novel's *imagery and symbolism*, the central figure of which is the mockingbird. Atticus and Miss Maudie explain that to kill a mockingbird is a sin because it is a harmless creature that gives others its song. Tom Robinson and Boo Radley are clearly identified with the mockingbird: Mr. Underwood, the Maycomb newspaper editor, "likened Tom's death to the senseless slaughter of songbirds by hunters and children" (241); and when Atticus and Sheriff Tate contemplate the effect of arresting Boo Radley for murder, Scout interjects, "Well, it'd be sort of like shootin' a mockingbird, wouldn't it?" (276).

Other, less prominent symbols are interwoven in the text. Mrs. Dubose's camellias, for example, appear to be images of an old southern frame of mind that defies defeat. Although the flowers are beautiful, they are clearly associated with the insane racism and cruelty spewed out by Mrs. Dubose, an aged southern aristocrat who supposedly keeps a Confederate gun close at hand. When Jem destroys her camellias, he is lashing out at the attitudes she represents.

The columns or pillars, looking somewhat out of place on the courthouse, also exemplify an outmoded, antebellum, plantation way of life and attitudes that continue to surface.

The rabid dog that Atticus shoots is a symbolic foreboding of his attempt to save the community from committing an act of madness. And guns themselves in the novel represent a kind of violence and savagery, an abuse of power, that Atticus has tried to avoid even though he is a sharpshooter. Miss Maudie believes that Atticus decided to lay down his gun when he realized it gave him an unfair advantage over dumb animals.

Each element of the fiction—point of view, tone, setting, characterization, plot structure, and imagery—plays an integral part in the advancement of the novel's major themes.

STUDY QUESTIONS

1. Consider the point of view of the novel. Do you find it to be simple or complex? Consistent or inconsistent? Does the point of view contribute positively to the novel or detract from it?

2. After reading the novel, consider the origins of the story that the narrator and her brother argue about in the first few paragraphs. Which of the reasons given for what "started it all" makes the most sense?

3. Critics have disagreed about the relationship of Part One to Part Two; some declare that there is no convincing link between the two parts. Would you agree, or do you see a viable relationship between them?

4. To get a sharper view of Maycomb, compare and contrast it with the town where you grew up.

5. Review the various things the children find in the tree. Can meanings be attributed to each? Discuss.

6. Is Mrs. Dubose completely unsympathetic in your view? Are you convinced by Atticus that she has qualities to be admired?

7. Characterize the group that visits the Finch house shortly before Tom's trial. In your view, are they well-meaning or threatening? Explain.

8. The reader is never told precisely why Bob Ewell continues to cause trouble after Atticus loses Tom Robinson's case. Interpret Ewell's motives.

9. In failing to arrest Boo Radley at the end, Sheriff Tate is breaking the law, as is Atticus, who knows the truth of Ewell's murder. Do you agree with some critics that Atticus's actions are "wrong" as well as illegal? Support your position.

TOPICS FOR WRITTEN OR ORAL EXPLORATION

1. Write a paper on other works of literature that are mentioned throughout the novel. Trace these references, making note of when and where they occur in the narrative. What parts do each play in the action or major ideas of the novel?

2. Present a legal defense of Boo Radley at the time of his first arrest. Make sure that you are prepared to bring up any points by the other side and offer your own rejoinders.

3. Write a paper analyzing the theme of superstition in the novel. Trace all accounts of it and indicate how the idea of superstition fits the theme of the novel.

4. Write characterizations of three or four of the Finchs' neighbors. How do they reflect the theme of race and difference in the novel?

5. Descriptions of buildings are extremely important in the novel—both public buildings and private residences. Write a paper analyzing these carefully. How does the look of a building reflect something of what goes on inside?

6. Prepare a careful written analysis of Dill, taking into account his physical appearance, his family background, and his characteristics. In light of these elements, isn't it especially fitting that it is Dill who sets the other children on the trail of Boo Radley? Why or why not?

7. The theme of literacy—both reading and being unable to read—is intricately woven into much of the plot and conversation. Trace these references and analyze them in a paper. Is the author making a point in returning to the idea repeatedly?

8. Write an analysis of the frequent mention of particular flowers in the novel. With whom are these flowers associated, and how? In each case, what meaning do the flowers seem to have?

9. Write a comparison and contrast of Scout and Mayella.

10. Write a comparison and contrast of Atticus Finch and Bob Ewell.

11. Write an analysis of the scene of the missionary society. Put your generalized characterization of the scene in the form of one thesis sentence, which you can then support with details.

12. Write a comparison and contrast of Aunt Alexandra and Miss Maudie.

13. The idea of actual and symbolic prisons and imprisonment runs through most of the novel. Analyze both in a paper.

14. In a paper, trace the theme of insanity in the novel.

15. Harper Lee called her novel "a love story." Write or discuss this as an accurate characterization of the novel.

16. Discuss the implicit ideas and practices of child rearing that emerge in the novel.

17. The novel reveals many unwritten social codes. Formulate a paper or discussion on this idea.

18. Write a paper or discuss the role of imagination and creativity in the children's lives.

19. Write a comparison and contrast of two of the novel's "dramas": the Radley plays and the Halloween pageant.

20. In a paper, trace the children's habit of learning by observing and spying, rather than "doing." If you discern any pattern here, explain it.

21. Discuss eccentricity as a theme in the novel. Consider adults other than Boo Radley.

SUGGESTED READINGS

The following works of fiction by Truman Capote draw heavily on a child's experiences in Monroeville, Alabama, and in Mississippi and Louisiana during the same time period as that in which *To Kill a Mockingbird* is set:

Capote, Truman. *A Christmas Memory*. New York: Random House, 1956.
———. *The Grass Harp*. New York: Penguin Books, 1951.
———. *Other Voices—Other Rooms*. New York: Random House, 1968.

The following works include all of the very few literary articles written about Harper Lee's highly successful novel:

Dave, R. A. "*To Kill a Mockingbird*: Harper Lee's Tragic Vision." In *Indian Studies in American Fiction*, ed. M. K. Naik, 311–23. Dharwar: Karnatak University and the Macmillan Company of India, 1974.
Erisman, Fred. "Literature and Place: Varieties of Regional Experience." *Journal of Regional Cultures* 1 (Fall/Winter 1981): 144–53.
———. "The Romantic Regionalism of Harper Lee." *Alabama Review* 26 (1973): 122–36.
Going, William. "Store and Mockingbird: Two Pulitzer Novels about Alabama." In *Essays on Alabama Literature*, 9–31. Tuscaloosa: University of Alabama Press, 1975.
Johnson, Claudia D. "The Secret Courts of Men's Hearts: Code and Law in Harper Lee's *To Kill a Mockingbird*." *Studies in American Fiction* 19 (Autumn 1991): 129–39.
———. *Threatening Boundaries*. New York: Twayne Publishers, 1994.
Stuckey, W. J. *The Pulitzer Prize Novels: A Critical Backward Look*. Norman: University of Oklahoma Press, 1981.

Another source of material on *To Kill a Mockingbird* is the body of magazine and newspaper reviews that appeared just after the novel's publication:

"About Life and Little Girls." *Time*, vol. 76 (August 1, 1960): 70, 71.
Adams, Phoebe. "Summer Reading." *Atlantic*, vol. 206 (August 26, 1960): 98, 99.
Bradbury, Malcolm. "New Fiction." *Punch*, vol. 239 (October 26, 1960): 611, 612.
Bruell, Edwin. "Keen Scalpel on Racial Ills." *English Journal* 53 (December 1964): 660.
"Fiction: Three to Make Ready." *Kirkus Review*, May 1, 1960: 360.
Haselden, Elizabeth Lee. "We Aren't in It." *Christian Century*, vol. 78

(May 24, 1961): 655. (One of the few unfavorable reviews of the novel.)

Henderson, Robert W. "Lee, Harper: *To Kill a Mockingbird.*" *School Library Journal* 85 (May 15, 1960): 44.

Hicks, Granville. "Three at the Outset." *Saturday Review*, vol. 43 (July 23, 1960): 15–16.

Jackson, Katherine Fauss. "Books in Brief." *Harpers*, August 1960: 101.

Lemay, Harding. "Children Play; Adults Betray." *New York Herald Tribune*, July 10, 1960: 5.

Lyell, Frank H. "One-Taxi Town." *New York Times Book Review*, vol. 65 (July 10, 1960): 5, 18.

McMillan, James B. "*To Kill a Mockingbird.*" *Alabama Review*, July 1961: 233.

Mitgang, Herbert. "Books of the Times." *New York Times*, vol. 109 (July 13, 1960): 33.

Schumach, Murray. "Prize for Novel Elates Film Pair." *New York Times*, vol. 110 (May 19, 1961): 26.

"Sheer Purgatory." *Times Literary Supplement*, vol. 59 (October 28, 1960): 697.

Sullivan, Richard. "Engrossing First Novel of Rare Excellence." *Chicago Sunday Tribune*, July 17, 1960: 15.

"*To Kill a Mockingbird.*" *Commonweal*, vol. 73 (December 1960): 289.

"*To Kill a Mockingbird.*" *New Yorker*, vol. 36 (September 10, 1960): 203, 204.

Waterhouse, Keith. "New Novels." *New Statesman*, vol. 60 (October 15, 1960): 580.

2

Historical Context: The Scottsboro Trials

Tom Robinson's trial bears striking parallels to the "Scottsboro Trial," one of the most famous—or infamous—court cases in American history. Both the fictional and the historical cases take place in the 1930s, a time of turmoil and change in America, and both occur in Alabama. In both, too, the defendants were African-American men, the accusers white women. In both instances the charge was rape. In addition, other substantial similarities between the fictional and historical trials become apparent.

A study of the Scottsboro trials will sharpen the reader's understanding of *To Kill a Mockingbird*. Both the historical trial(s) and the fictional one reflect the prevailing attitudes of the time, and the novel explores the social and legal problems that arise because of those attitudes.

First, it is essential to understand the social and economic climate of the 1930s. The country was in what has been called the Great Depression. Millions of people had lost their jobs, their homes, their businesses, or their land, and everything that made up their way of life. In every American city of any size, long "bread lines" of the unemployed formed to receive basic foodstuffs for themselves and their families, their only means of subsistence.

Many people lived in shanty towns, their shelters made of sheet metal and scrap lumber lean-tos. All over America it was common to see unemployed men and women riding the rails, looking for work, shelter, and food—for anything that offered some means of subsistence, some sense of dignity. It was a time when even a full-time employee, such as a mill worker, earned barely enough to live on. In fact, in 1931 a person working 55 or 60 hours a week in Alabama and other places would earn only about $156 annually.

The economic collapse of the 1930s resulted in ferocious rivalry for the very few jobs that became available. Consequently, the ill will between black and white people (which had existed ever since the Civil War) intensified, as each group competed with the other for the few available jobs. One result was that incidents of lynchings—primarily of African-Americans—continued. Here, lynching should be defined as the murder of a person by a group of people who set themselves up as judge, jury, and executioner outside the legal system.

It was in such a distressing social and economic climate that the Scottsboro case (and Tom Robinson's case) unfolded.

On March 25, 1931, several groups of white and black men and two white women were riding the rails from Tennessee to Alabama in various open and closed railroad cars designed to carry freight and gravel. At one point on the trip, the black and white men began fighting. One white man would later testify that the African-Americans started the fight, and another white man would later claim that the white men had started the fight. In any case, most of the white men were thrown off the train. When the train arrived at Paint Rock, Alabama, all those riding the rails—including nine black men, at least one white man, and the two white women— were arrested, probably on charges of vagrancy. The white women remained under arrest in jail for several days, pending charges of vagrancy and possible violation of the Mann Act. The Mann Act prohibited the taking of a minor across state lines for immoral purposes, like prostitution. Because Victoria Price was a known prostitute, the police were tipped off (very likely by the mother of the underaged Ruby Bates) that the two women were involved in a criminal act when they left Tennessee for Alabama. Upon leaving the train, the two women immediately accused the African-American men of raping them in an open railroad car (referred to as a "gondola") that was carrying gravel (or, as it was called, "chert").

The trial of the nine men began on April 6, 1931, only twelve days after the arrest, and continued through April 9, 1931. The chief witnesses included the two women accusers, one white man who had remained on the train and corroborated their accusations, another acquaintance of the women who refused to corroborate their accusations, the physician who examined the women, and the accused nine black men. The accused claimed that they had not even been in the same car with the women, and the defense attorneys also argued that one of the accused was blind and another too sickly to walk unassisted and thus could not have committed such a violent crime. On April 9, 1931, eight of the nine were sentenced to death; a mistrial was declared for the ninth because of his youth. The executions were suspended pending court appeals, which eventually reached the Supreme Court of the United States.

On November 7, 1932, the United States Supreme Court ordered new trials for the Scottsboro defendants because they had not had adequate legal representation.

On March 27, 1933, the new trials ordered by the Court began in Decatur, Alabama, with the involvement of two distinguished trial participants: a famous New York City defense lawyer named Samuel S. Leibowitz, who would continue to be a major figure in the various Scottsboro negotiations for more than a decade; and Judge James E. Horton, who would fly in the face of community sentiment by the unusual actions he took in the summer of 1933.

In this second attempt to resolve the case, the trial for the first defendant lasted almost two weeks instead of only a few hours, as it had in 1931. And this time the chief testimony included the carefully examined report of two physicians, whose examination of the women within two hours of the alleged crime refuted the likelihood that multiple rapes had occurred. Testimony was also given by one of the women, Ruby Bates, who now openly denied that she or her friend, Victoria Price, had ever been raped. As a result of this, as well as of material brought out by investigations and by cross-examinations of the witnesses of Samuel Leibowitz, the character and honesty of accuser Victoria Price came under more careful scrutiny.

On April 9, 1933, the first of the defendants, Haywood Patterson, was again found guilty of rape and sentenced to execution. The execution was delayed, however; and six days after the original date set for Patterson's execution, one of the most startling events

Defense attorney Samuel Leibowitz (far left) and seven of the Scottsboro defendants in 1933. Photo courtesy of AP/Wide World Photos.

of the trial took place: local judge James Horton effectively over-turned the conviction of the jury and, in a meticulous analysis of the evidence that had been presented, ordered a new trial on the grounds that the evidence presented did not warrant conviction. (It is probably not a coincidence that Judge Horton lost an election in the fall following his reversal of the jury's verdict.)

Despite Judge Horton's unprecedented action, the second de-fendant, Clarence Norris, was tried in late 1933 and was found guilty as charged; but his execution was delayed pending appeal.

During this time all the defendants remained in prison, and not for two more years was any further significant action taken as At-torney Leibowitz filed appeals to higher courts. Finally, on April 1, 1935, the United States Supreme Court reversed the convictions of Patterson and Norris on the grounds that qualified African-Americans had been systematically excluded from all juries in Al-abama, and that they had been specifically excluded in this case.

However, even this decision by the Supreme Court was not the end of the trials, for on May 1, 1935, Victoria Price swore out new warrants against the nine men.

Primary documents related to the case afford several avenues of comparison between the Scottsboro trials and Tom Robinson's trial in *To Kill a Mockingbird*. This is in addition to the more obvious parallels of time (1930s), place (Alabama), and charges (rape of white women by African-American men). First, the threat of lynching is common to both cases. Second, there is a similarity between the novel's Atticus Finch and the real-life Judge James E. Horton, both of whom acted in behalf of black men on trial in defiance of their communities' wishes at a time of high feeling. In several instances, the words of the Alabama judge remind the reader of Atticus Finch's address to the jury and his advice to his children. Third, the accusers in both instances were very poor, working-class women who had secrets that the charges of rape were intended to cover up. Therefore, the veracity or believability of the accusers in both cases became an issue.

In order to keep straight the people and events in this compli-cated case, a brief list of the main characters and a brief chronology of main events follow.

MAJOR FIGURES IN THE SCOTTSBORO CASE

Defendants: Charley Weems, Clarence Norris, Haywood Patterson, Andy Wright, Willie Roberson, Eugene Williams, Ozie Powell, Olen Montgomery, and Roy Wright.

Accusers: Victoria Price and, at first, Ruby Bates.

Chief Defense Attorney: Samuel Leibowitz.

Prosecuting Attorney: Thomas Knight, Jr.

Judges: A. E. Hawkins (spring of 1931), James E. Horton (spring of 1933), William W. Callahan (winter of 1933/34).

Chief Witnesses other than the accusers and defendants: Jack Tiller, friend of Price and Bates; Lester Carter, friend of Price and Bates; Dr. R. R. Bridges, examining physician.

CHRONOLOGY OF EVENTS

March 25, 1931	Arrest of nine Scottsboro "boys."
April 6–9, 1931	First trials in Scottsboro, Alabama. Appeals begin and continue for a year and a half.
November 7, 1932	United States Supreme Court orders new trials.
March 27, 1933	Second trials begin.
April 9, 1933	Patterson found guilty and sentenced to death in June.
June 22, 1933	Judge Horton overturns guilty verdict.
November/December 1933	Clarence Norris is tried, found guilty, and sentenced to death. Appeals continue for two years while he remains on death row.
April 1, 1935	U.S. Supreme Court reverses the convictions of Patterson and Norris.
May 1, 1935	Another round of trials begins and Patterson is given a 75-year sentence.
July 26, 1937	Charges against four men are dropped.
1940s	All but one escape or are paroled.

| June 9, 1950 | The last Scottsboro defendant is released from prison. |
| October 25, 1976 | Clarence Norris is pardoned. |

SCOTTSBORO DOCUMENTS

The rest of this chapter presents excerpts from key documents relating to the Scottsboro trials. The document excerpts are described as follows:

April 6, 1931. The testimony of Victoria Price and Dr. R. R. Bridges in the trial of Charley Weems and Clarence Norris for rape on March 25, 1931.

March 27, 1933. Judge James E. Horton's address from the bench before the second trials had gotten under way. This was in response to threats of jury tampering and mob action.

April 4, 1933. Excerpt from a *New York Times* article chiefly about the testimony of the accuser, Victoria Price, and Dr. R. R. Bridges, who examined both women.

April 7, 1933. Excerpt from official court transcript of the testimony of Ruby Bates, one of the original accusers.

April 17, 1933. Excerpts from the official court transcript in the retrial of Charley Weems, of the testimony of Lester Carter, a one-time companion of the two women who brought the charges.

June 22, 1933. Excerpt from the written decision of Judge James E. Horton overturning the jury's guilty verdict and ordering a new trial.

December 2, 1933. Excerpt from the retrial of Clarence Norris before Judge Horton's replacement, Judge William Callahan. This is chiefly the testimony of accuser Victoria Price and a deposition from former accuser Ruby Bates.

April 1, 1935. Excerpts from the United States Supreme Court decision reversing the convictions of Patterson and Norris on the grounds that African-Americans were being excluded from serving on juries.

THE TESTIMONY OF VICTORIA PRICE AND DR. R. R. BRIDGES, APRIL 6, 1931

The nine Scottsboro defendants who were arrested on March 25, 1931, were swiftly tried in April of the same year. They were represented by court-appointed lawyers. (In *To Kill a Mockingbird*, Atticus Finch was also appointed by the court to defend a black man on a charge of raping a white woman.) The presiding judge was A. E. Hawkins; the defense attorneys were Steve Roddy and Milo Moody; and the prosecuting attorneys were Bailey, Thompson, Proctor, and Snodgrass. All these major figures were replaced by others in the next round of trials in 1933.

The following includes an excerpt of the testimony of the chief accuser, Victoria Price, in the first of several sets of trials of the defendants. The manner of her testimony helps establish her character. The reader can also discern whether her later testimony is consistent with what she swears to here in the first trials, and whether other witnesses corroborate her testimony. The defense probes the truth of her marital status, her physical condition just after the rape, her character and past life, and her description of the rape. Some of the cross-examination by prosecuting attorney Bailey concludes her testimony.

The excerpts conclude with the testimony of a physician, Dr. R. R. Bridges, who examined Victoria Price and Ruby Bates shortly after the alleged attack.

Price and Bridges would remain the most important witnesses throughout the five years of trials.

FROM THE TESTIMONY OF VICTORIA PRICE AND DR. R. R.
BRIDGES IN THE SCOTTSBORO TRIAL, SPRING OF 1931

IN THE CIRCUIT COURT, JACKSON COUNTY, ALABAMA.
Spring Term 1931
STATE OF ALABAMA
(287)
vs
CHARLEY WEEMS,
CLARENCE NORRIS.

APPEARANCES:
H. G. Bailey,
J. K. Thompson,   Attorneys for State.
Proctor & Snodgrass

Milo Moody,   Attorneys for Defendants.
Steve Roddy

This cause coming on to be heard was tried on this the 6th day of April 1931, before his honor A. E. Hawkins Judge presiding, and a jury, when the following among other proceedings were had and done, to wit.

. . .

Defendants Charley Weems and Clarence Norris arraigned and plead not guilty.

Indictment read to the jury by Solicitor and the defendants by their counsel plead not guilty there-to.

. . .

Official Stenographic Report of the Oral Proceedings Had in the Case of *State of Alabama vs. Charley Weems, Clarence Norris*, in the Circuit Court, Jackson County, Alabama, Special Session 1931, Case No. 2402, Hamlin Caldwell, Official Reporter Ninth Judicial Circuit, Scottsboro, Alabama. Taken down on April 6, 1931. Case No. 2402.

Examination of Victoria Price by Mr. Roddy

Q   Where did you get on the freight train?

A   Chattanooga, Tennessee.

Q   Who was with you when you boarded that freight train?

A   Ruby Bates.

Q   Is she married or single?

A   Single.

Q   Are you married or single?

A   Single, I have been married.

Q   Are you and your husband divorced?

A   No sir.

Q   Where is he?

A   I don't know.

Q   When did you last see him?

A   I have not seen him in nearly a year.

Q   Where was he when you last saw him?

A   In Huntsville.

Q   Is he there now?

A   I don't know.

Q   Did you leave him at Huntsville?

A   Yes, Sir.

[State Objects to that.]

THE COURT: Yes, I sustain the objections to that.

[Defendant Excepts.]

Q   When were you married?

A   I married the 18th, of last December a year ago.

Q   And you haven't seen your husband in a year?

A   I have seen him once.

Q   Where was that?

A   In Huntsville.

[State Objects to that question.]

THE COURT: Let her answer.

Q   How long ago?

A   I have not been keeping up with the days.

Q   Have you any idea when you saw your husband last?

A   It has been two or three months—about a month I reckon, not hardly
     a month, he was leaving for New Orleans the last time I seen him.

Q   From Huntsville?

A   Yes sir, his home was in New Orleans.

Q   You have not seen him since?

A   No sir.

Q   You don't know where he is now?

A   No sir.

Q   He is not in Huntsville?

A   No sir, I don't reckon he is.

       . . .

Q   You were not hurt, were you?

A   I must was, I wasn't well, I was pretty sick and you would have been
     too.

Q   You were not torn?

A   Oh no, I wasn't torn.

Q   Have you been married?

A   Yes, sir.

Q   How many times?

A   How many times I have been married?

[State Objects to how many times she has been married.]

THE COURT: Let her answer.

A   I have been married twice.

Q   Are both husbands living?

A   What do you think—no.

Q   Either one?

A   No, sir.

Q   Are both dead?

A   No.

Q   Do you know where they are living?

A   I just told both were not living, how could they be living when one
    is dead.

Q   Are you divorced?

[State Objects. Court Sustains. Defendant Excepts.]

    . . .

Q   Did you ever practice prostitution?

[State Objects. Court Sustains. Defendant Excepts.]

A   I don't know what you are talking about.

    . . .

Q   You say you don't know what prostitution means?

A   Why, no.

Q   Haven't you made it a practice to have intercourse with other men?

A   No sir, I absolutely haven't.

Q   Never did?

A   No sir, only with my husband.

[State Objects. Court Sustains.]

Q   And with no other white men?

A   No sir, but with my husband, I want you to understand that, to dis-
    tinctly understand that.

    . . .

Q   Were you struck about the body or head?

A My back was bruised up; I was choked and everything else.

Q Did they have to knock you down?

A He knocked me to my knees.

Q Get you entirely down?

A Sure, he asked me to lay down, he threw me down.

Q He had to throw you down?

A He must have did.

Q Do you know whether he did?

A Sure, do you think I am crazy?

Q Were you beat up about the body?

A My back was beaten up.

Q Which one bruised you up?

A The one that had a knife on me.

. . .

Q Did you say anything to the boys?

A Yes sir, we was begging them to quit and they wouldn't do it.

Q You were begging them to quit?

A Yes sir.

Q And they beat you unconscious?

A No sir, they did not beat me unconscious, I did not say they beat me unconscious; I was unconscious when I got off the train at Paint.

Q Do you remember getting off the train at Paint Rock?

A No sir, when I came to myself I was sitting in a store; I don't know who took me off.

. . .

Q Do you know where you were taken from the grocery store and who took you?

A Yes sir, I was taken to the jail at Mr. Wann's.

Q Here in Scottsboro?

A Yes sir.

Q And have been there ever since?

A Yes sir. I have been there ever since.

Q You don't know who took you off the train?

A Yes sir, I took myself nearly off it and fell the rest of the way.

Q Did the officers come in this gondola and get you?

A No sir, I climbed up on the side of the gondola myself with Ruby's help and when I got to the last step I fell and when I came to myself I was sitting in a store.

. . .

Q Do you know where you were taken from the store?

A Sure, I was taken to the jail; you have repeated that three times.

Q You have been in jail since?

A Yes sir, I have been in jail since.

Q Were you ever in jail before?

[State Objects. Court Sustains. Defendant Excepts.]

Q Do you know any of the police officers in Chattanooga?

A No sir, I don't.

Q Do you know the police matron at Chattanooga?

A No.

Q You are not acquainted with any of the officials among the police in Chattanooga?

A No.

[State Objects.]

THE COURT: I sustain the objection for the present.

MR. RODDY: We will make it competent later if the Court please.

. . .

Q You were beaten up?

A No, I did not say I was beaten, I said I was bruised up right smart.

. . .

Q You had never known the white boys till you got on the train with them?

A That is what I said.

Q You have not been in trouble in Chattanooga?

A No sir, I haven't.

Q Were your clothes bloody?

A No, my clothes wasn't bloody; I wasn't cut up.

Q Were you suffering?

A Well, I wasn't easy, I must have been hurting.

Q Were you torn or lacerated about your privates—did you have a doctor examine you?

A Yes sir.

Q He told you you were all right, didn't he?

Accuser Victoria Price and witness Orville Gilley outside the courtroom in 1931. Photo courtesy of AP/Wide World Photos.

A He did not tell me whether I was or not.

Q He did not tell you anything was wrong?

A I did not ask him.

MR. RODDY: All right.

THE COURT: Is that all?

MR. RODDY: I think that is all.

Re-Direct Examination: Examined by Mr. Bailey

Q Did the doctors make an examination of you after this affair there?

A Yes sir.

Q Where were you when they examined you?

A I was at their office.

Q Here in Scottsboro?

A Yes sir.

Q Do you know how long after this occurrence?

A Just about an hour I reckon; yes, just about an hour and a half after it happened.

Q You came from Paint Rock up here?

A They brought me to the jail.

MR. BAILEY: That is all.

Examination of Dr. R. R. Bridges, witness for the State, by Mr. Bailey

Q Doctor, are you a practicing physician in this county?

A Yes sir.

Q Of what medical institution are you a graduate?

A Vanderbilt.

MR. RODDY: We admit his qualifications.

Q Doctor, do you know this witness just on the stand, Victoria Price?

A Yes sir.

Q Along about the 25th of March last here in Scottsboro, did you make an examination of her person?

A Yes sir.

Q Where was she when you made that examination?

A At my office.

Q About what time of the day was it?

A About four o'clock or a bit after, I don't remember exactly.

Q   Was there any other physician present?

A   The county health doctor, Dr. Lynch.

Q   Now doctor, did you find any bruises on her body anywhere?

A   A few bruises in the lower lumbar region, down about the top of the hips behind, about here (indicating), and there was a few minor scratches on the left arm, I believe, on one of the arms, just short scratches.

Q   Any other bruises anywhere else on the body?

A   No sir.

   . . .

Cross-Examination: Dr. Bridges Is Examined by the Defense

   . . .

Q   These girls had no bruises on them?

A   The Price girl had a few little blue places on the back and lower down in the lumbar region.

Q   Large or small?

A   Small.

Q   She was not lacerated at all?

A   No sir.

Q   Was she bleeding?

A   No sir.

Q   Was the other girl?

A   No sir.

Q   Neither one was bleeding?

A   No sir.

Q   And the discoloration you speak of was very small?

A   Yes sir.

Q   The girls were not hysterical?

A   Not at the office on that examination.

JUDGE JAMES E. HORTON'S ADDRESS

The following document is part of the official court transcript of the second Scottsboro trials of March 1933. The first trials had occurred in the spring of 1931, when the defendants were found guilty and sentenced to death. The executions were delayed as appeals to higher courts were made by the defense attorneys. Notice in the novel the similar expectation that appeals will be made after the jury finds Tom Robinson guilty. Atticus Finch tells his children the morning after the trial, "We're not through yet. There'll be an appeal, you can count on that" (213). After Tom has been shot, Atticus says, "We had such a good chance. . . . I told him what I thought, but I couldn't in truth say that we had more than a good chance" (235).

The Supreme Court of the State of Alabama upheld the convictions of the Scottsboro defendants, but the United States Supreme Court agreed to hear the case and ordered a new trial on the grounds that the accused had not been adequately represented by legal counsel.

The mere fact of the Supreme Court decision was enough to enrage much of the populace as new trials were being planned. A large portion of the community, being only interested in seeing that another guilty verdict be reached as quickly and quietly as possible, were angry about another development: the arrival of a new lawyer for the defense, Samuel Leibowitz, a New Yorker (and therefore an "outsider"). Leibowitz had already demonstrated that he was sharp, tenacious, and at times abrasive; and he was planning to give his clients the best defense he could muster—something that was missing from the first trial in Scottsboro in 1931.

The defense had asked that the trials be moved from Scottsboro, Alabama, to Decatur, Alabama. Even before the prisoners were moved to the new trial site on March 27, 1933, rumors circulated that mob violence was brewing—not only against the defendants but against their attorney, Sam Leibowitz. Other rumors had been circulating that attempts were afoot to intimidate or bribe the jury. On March 24 the sheriff had announced that National Guardsmen would be asked to preserve order at the trials, and the governor of the state had asked that thirty National Guardsmen be ready to go to Decatur to preserve order.

The proceedings began in Decatur, Alabama, on March 27. As rumors and tensions continued to escalate, Judge James Horton responded with a stern address to those in the courtroom. His speech is included here because it invites comparison with Atticus Finch's behavior in the face of a lynch mob and his words, not only to the jury but also to his children.

FROM JUDGE JAMES E. HORTON'S ADDRESS FROM THE BENCH IN THE SCOTTSBORO CASE, MARCH 27, 1933

I have been judge of your court for a number of years and I feel I can say, with a degree of gratification, to the jurors of this county and others on my circuit that so far as I have been able to see, all the jurors who ever sat before me have tried each case as far as they were able according to the law and the evidence, and to render a true verdict in every case.

I never knew a juror in any case to come to me and tell me of influences brought to bear with the purpose of impeding the course of justice. I have every confidence that this venire will do the same. In my experience I have had occasion to preside at trials involving some who were rich and prominent and some who were not so rich or prominent; there were important cases and some that were not so important, but in all I have felt that true justice was meted out.

I have seen jurors with wet eyes and I have heard foremen read verdicts with a voice that quavered, showing the agony experienced in reaching a verdict. Never have I known of a juror who flinched at performing his duty, wherever it might lie.

So far as the law is concerned, it knows neither native nor alien, Jew or Gentile, black or white. This case is not different from any other. We have only our duty to do without fear or favor.

So far, order in the courtroom has been good. Our citizenry has been calm and quiet, but I feel I must tell all our citizens to abide calmly the decisions of the court. In no other way can we enjoy the fruits of liberty. You must follow out the law as it is laid down to you and obey the law as it is.

THE SCOTTSBORO CASE: *NEW YORK TIMES* ACCOUNT

The retrial of Haywood Patterson got under way in early April, shortly after the choosing of the jury and the address of Judge Horton to the courtroom. This document is from a *New York Times* account of the testimony given on April 3. The star witnesses on this day were the chief accuser, Victoria Price, and Dr. R. R. Bridges, who had given her a physical examination within two hours of the alleged rape. Both witnesses had testified in the 1931 trial, but in April 1933 attention is called to Victoria Price's character and the contradictions in her testimony, giving rise to questions about her truthfulness. Furthermore, as this document illustrates, the testimony of Dr. Bridges for the first time is under serious scrutiny, not only from the defense attorney but from the presiding judge.

FROM THE TESTIMONY OF VICTORIA PRICE AND
DR. R. R. BRIDGES, APRIL 3, 1933, AS REPORTED IN
THE *NEW YORK TIMES*

GIRL REPEATS STORY IN SCOTTSBORO CASE

State's Witness at Decatur Trial Screams Denial of "Framing"
Negro Defendants

MORAL ATTACK RULED OUT

Judge Rejects Court Records as Not Affecting the Credibility
of Her Testimony

By RAYMOND F. DANIELL, Special to the *New York Times*.
DECATUR, Ala., April 3.

Victoria Price, whose testimony two years ago at Scottsboro led Jackson County juries to condemn eight of nine negro defendants to death, repeated her charges today before Judge James E. Horton and a jury in the Morgan County Court House at the first of the retrials ordered by the United States Supreme Court.

. . .

At times when Samuel S. Leibowitz, chief of defense counsel, pressed searching questions regarding her past, her lip curled and she snapped her answers in the colloquialisms of the "poor white."

Mrs. Price entered an angry denial when Mr. Leibowitz asked if she had not concocted the whole story of the mass attack by the negroes and forced Ruby Bates, the other victim of the alleged crime, to corroborate her in order to forestall the danger of her own arrest for vagrancy or a more serious offense. . . .

"That's some of that Ruby Bates' dope," she shouted in a voice that shook with anger.

"You can't prove it," she shouted another time when Mr. Leibowitz promised to show the court that the condition in which doctors found her when she was examined at Scottsboro after an armed posse had taken the girls and the negroes off the train on which the attack supposedly took place, was the result of her misconduct the night before in a hobo jungle on the outskirts of Chattanooga.

Certified copies of court records from Huntsville where Mrs. Price lived with her widowed mother were offered by Mr. Leibowitz to show that prior to March 25, 1931, she had been arrested for offenses against the moral code.

. . .

She defended the testimony she had given with as much fire as she defended her reputation, heatedly denying at one moment that she had wrecked the home of a married woman with two babies, and in the next breath thrusting aside seeming inconsistencies in her testimony with apologies for her lack of education and faulty memory.

Although Mrs. Price insisted that she had fought the negroes until her strength gave out, and declared that her head was cut open by a blow from the butt of a pistol wielded by Patterson, Dr. R. R. Bridges, the Scottsboro physician, who testified just before adjournment, said he had found only superficial bruises and scratches when he examined her.

While the doctor was on the stand Judge Horton took a hand in the examination, showing particular interest in the physician's statement that neither Mrs. Price nor her companion, the Bates girl, were hysterical or nervous when they were brought to his office. Not until the next day, he said, did either of them show any signs of nervousness and then, after a night in jail, it manifested itself in tears.

The star witness for the State told the sordid details of the crime before a crowded court with unabashed frankness and plain-speaking. She repeated the lewd remarks she said the negroes made to her without the flutter of an eyelash and in a voice that carried to the furthest corner of the courtroom. The only women in the crowd which heard her story and the very clinical medical testimony which followed were two visitors from

Judge James Horton straining to hear the critical testimony of Dr. R. R. Bridges, who had examined the accusers in April 1933. Photo courtesy of AP/Wide World Photos.

New York. At times they looked as though they wished they had not come.

New York Times, Tuesday, April 4, 1933, p. 10, Vol. LXXXII.

THE TESTIMONY OF RUBY BATES

In 1932, during the time when appeals were being made and the defendants were waiting in jail, a letter from Ruby Bates, one of the accusers, was found in the belongings of a man who was arrested on criminal charges. In the letter Ruby Bates denied to her friend that any rapes had occurred. After much searching and negotiation, Ruby Bates was located and appeared as one of the star witnesses for the defense in the new trials in March 1933 ordered by the United States Supreme Court. What follows is the heart of her testimony.

FROM THE TESTIMONY OF RUBY BATES IN THE TRIAL OF
HAYWOOD PATTERSON, APRIL 7, 1933

Examination of Ruby Bates by the Defense

MR. LEIBOWITZ: Bring out Victoria Price, please.

Q   Is this woman Victoria Price (indicating)?

A   Yes sir.

Q   You are a younger girl than Victoria Price, aren't you?

A   Yes sir.

Q   How long before this ride on the freight train did you meet Victoria?

A   I knew her for some time; we had worked in the mill together.

Q   For how many years?

A   About two and a half years.

Q   When did you first start taking up with Victoria Price—when did you first start to become friendly with her, going out with her?

A   After I went to work at the mill.

Q   Were you a good girl before you met her, good decent girl before you met that girl?

MR. KNIGHT: We object.

THE COURT: You were a worker in the mill before you met her?

A   Yes sir, I was working in the mill when I met her.

Q   Were you a good girl before you met her, good decent girl?

A   Well, yes.

Q   After you started taking up with her did you continue to go around with her in Huntsville?

A   Yes sir.

Q   You were never convicted of any crime?

A   No sir.

Q   You were never in jail?

A   No sir.

Q   Do you know a man by the name of Lester Carter?

A   Yes sir.

MR. LEIBOWITZ: Bring out Lester Carter.

MR. KNIGHT: Wait a minute, I would like for her to describe him.

Q   The attorney asked that you describe him; describe Lester Carter, tell us what kind of looking man is he?

A   Well, he is blond-headed, he has blond hair.

Q   Tall or short?

A   He is not so tall.

Q   Would you recognize him if you saw him?

A   Yes sir.

Q   He was one of the boys in jail with you after the train stopped at Paint Rock?

A   Yes sir.

Q   You knew him before you ever got on the train?

A   Yes sir.

MR. LEIBOWITZ: Bring out Lester Carter.

Q   Who is this boy (indicating)?

A   Lester Carter.

Q   Did you ever have occasion to visit Victoria Price in the Huntsville jail when she was in jail, go to see her?

A   No sir, I never did go to see her.

Q   Where was it you saw Victoria Price shortly before you met Lester Carter?

A   Well, Victoria and myself went down to the chain gang where him and another fellow was.

Q   You met him at the chain gang?

A   Yes sir.

Q   You were with Victoria at that time?

A   Yes sir.

Q   Who was the man on the chain gang with Lester Carter?

A   Jack Tiller.

MR. LEIBOWITZ: Is Jack Tiller in court, in the room there?

MR. KNIGHT: I think he is.

MR. LEIBOWITZ: Bring out Jack Tiller.

Q   Do you know that man that just came in with the blue tie?

A   Yes sir.

Q   Who is he?

A   Jack Tiller.

Q   Some time ago before you went on the freight train did you meet Lester Carter?

A   Yes sir.

Q   Victoria Price, Lester Carter, and Jack Tiller, did you meet them?

A   Yes sir.

Q   After Carter got out of the chain gang and Tiller got out of the chain gang, did you meet with Victoria Price?

A   Yes sir.

Q   Was that a short time before you left Huntsville?

A   Yes sir.

Q   Where was the first place you met up with them when they got out of jail?

A   They came to the mill one afternoon where we were, on Monday afternoon before we left on Tuesday.

Q   What happened?

A   Well, Victoria and Jack and myself and Lester all left and walked up the Pulaski Pike.

Q   Did you go along on the railroad known as the L. & N. Railroad there?

A   When we got back we went down the N. C.

Q   That was at night?

A   Yes sir.

Q   Did you have intercourse with Lester Carter that night?

A   I certainly did.

Q   Did Victoria Price have intercourse with Jack Tiller?

A   She certainly did.

Q   In your presence?

A   Yes sir.

Q   That night it started to rain, didn't it, and you got in a boxcar?

A   Yes sir.

Q   How long did you stay in that boxcar?

A   Stayed there the rest of the night.

Q   With whom?

A   Lester Carter and Jack Tiller and Victoria Price.

Q   The next day did you make an appointment to go out of town?

A   We made the appointment that night.

Q   To go out of town?

A   Yes sir.

Q   You went out of town on Tuesday?

A   Yes sir.

Q   Did Tiller go along with you or did he remain behind?

A   He remained behind.

Q   What was the reason for that?

A   I couldn't say.

Q   Were you, Lester Carter, and Victoria Price on the freight train?

A   Yes sir.

Q   Did you go to Chattanooga?

A   Yes sir.

Q   Where did you spend the night that night at Chattanooga, did you spend the night at Callie Brochie's?

A   No sir.

Q   Where did you hear of the name of Callie Brochie, who told you that name?

A   Victoria Price.

Q   Where did you spend the night that night?

A   Spent the night, I think it is called Hobo Swamp.

Q   Is that near the railroad yards?

A   Yes sir.

Q   Who spent the night with you?

A   Orville Gilley, Victoria Price, and Lester Carter.

Q   Were you there all night?

A   Yes sir.

Q   Was there some fuss about some negroes in the morning?

A   Yes sir.

Q   Tell us about that.

A   Well, there was two negro men passed where Victoria and myself was; Lester Carter and this Gilley had stepped off somewheres.

Q   To get food?

A   Yes sir; these two negroes came by where we were, and we asked them what time did the freight leave out going west and they said about 11:15.

Q   That is your best recollection, isn't it?

A   Yes sir.

Q   Then when Lester came back was there some fuss about you being with some negroes?

A   Victoria told him there had been two negroes came down to where we were and said something to us out of the way and Lester took out after the negroes and had a fuss with some negroes; I couldn't say who it was.

Q   But there was some fuss about it, something that almost led to a fight between Carter and the negro?

A   Yes sir.

Q   That morning did you start coming back to Huntsville on the freight train—that morning after you arrived in Chattanooga did you start to come back?

A   Yes sir.

Q   Who started back with you on that train?

A   Orville Gilley, Lester Carter, and Victoria Price.

Q   Where were you riding, what kind of car on that freight train were you on?

A   I don't remember what kind of car it was.

Q   You got on some freight car?

A   Yes sir.

Q   All of you, Gilley, Lester Carter, and Victoria Price.

A   Yes sir.

Q   When you got to Stevenson did you get off or stay on?

A   We got off and got in a gondola car.

Q   How many gondolas were hooked up together, about how many?

A   There was right around eight of them.

Q   What gondola did you get in?

A   It was either the third or second gondola from a boxcar toward the engine.

Q   The second or third gondola from a boxcar; here is the engine (indicating); that is the car you got in (indicating)?

A   Yes sir.

Q   That is your best judgment?

A   Yes sir.

MR. KNIGHT: Which one?

Q   The second or third car from a boxcar near the engine, is that right?

A   Yes sir.

Q   That is the car you and Victoria and who else got in?

A   Orville Gilley and Lester Carter.

Q   Four of you?

A   Yes sir.

Q   Tell these gentlemen of the jury what happened after that when you got in that car and when the train started out of Stevenson.

A   After the train started out from Stevenson there was some white boys come in the end of the car next to where we were.

Q   In the next gondola?

A   Yes sir.

Q   What happened?

A   And after a while there was a bunch of negroes come over and started fighting; they was all fighting and Lester Carter and this Gilley boy jumped over to help them out.

Q   You mean Lester Carter and Gilley left the gondola in which you were in and went into the next gondola where the fight was between the white boys and the negroes?

A   Yes sir.

Q   Then what happened?

A   The negroes put all the boys off but one, Orville Gilley, and he came back in the car where we were.

Q   Then what happened, when you, Victoria Price, and Gilley were there, did the negroes come in that car where you were?

A   Not that I know of.

Q   Did any negro attack you that day?

A   Not that I know of.

Q Did any negro attack Victoria Price that day?

A I couldn't say.

Q Did you see any negro attack Victoria that day?

A No sir.

COURT: Where was Victoria Price?

A She was in the gondola where I was.

COURT: Same Gondola with you?

A Yes sir.

COURT: Did you stay in the same gondola until you got to Paint Rock?

A Yes sir.

Q When you got to Paint Rock the train stopped, didn't it?

A Yes sir.

Q What happened when the train stopped, what happened to you girls?

A Well, we got off the train, then Victoria was unconscious and they carried her out there to a store.

Q Then what happened?

A They arrested them.

Q Arrested all the negroes?

A Yes sir.

Q They took you to Scottsboro?

A Yes sir.

Q Were you in jail with Victoria at Scottsboro?

A Yes sir.

Q Did you talk with her at Scottsboro?

A Yes sir.

Q You testified on the trial, did you not; each one of those cases in Scottsboro, you took the witness stand?

A Yes sir.

Q You told the story you had seen six negroes rape Victoria Price and six negroes raped you; you told a story like that?

A I told it before, but I was excited.

Q You testified at Scottsboro that six negroes raped you and six negroes raped her, and one had a knife on your throat; what happened to her was exactly the same thing that happened to you. Who coached you to say that?

A She told it and I told it just like she told it.

Q   Who told you to tell that story?

A   I told it like she told it.

Q   Who told you to do that, who coached you to do that?

A   She did.

Q   Did she tell you what would happen to you if you didn't follow her story?

A   She said we might have to lay out a sentence in jail.

THE TESTIMONY OF LESTER CARTER

The retrials continued in April 1933 with the consideration of the defendant Charley Weems. This document is an excerpt from an official court transcript of the testimony of Lester Carter, one of only two of the women's white male companions (in and outside the jail) who testified at trial.

This segment of the transcript shows the characteristic interaction between Defense Attorney Leibowitz, Prosecuting Attorney Knight, and Presiding Judge Horton.

Note here the references to the two women's having known Carter and Tiller intimately before the trial, references to the women crossing state lines, and references to the way in which Carter's testimony contradicts Price's.

FROM THE TESTIMONY OF LESTER CARTER IN THE TRIAL OF
CHARLEY WEEMS, APRIL 17, 1933

Direct Examination of Lester Carter by the Defense

(Carter begins his testimony by identifying himself)

This is Lester Carter. I am 22. That would put me about 19, back in March 1931. My home at that time was in Knoxville, Tennessee. I was born and raised in that part of the country. I know a woman by the name of Victoria Price. I knew her somewhere around fifty or sixty days before March 25, 1931, when this freight train ride took place from Chattanooga towards Huntsville. I met Victoria Price in the jail at Huntsville, Alabama. I was confined in the city jail.

· · ·

Q   Was she confined in the city jail?

MR. KNIGHT: We object to that.

THE COURT: Sustained.

MR. LEIBOWITZ: We except.

A   I knew a man named Jack Tiller, too. I met him in the jail in Huntsville. I later saw her occasionally or frequently. I was very friendly with her. That was fifty or sixty days before this ride. I knew a girl named Ruby Bates. I got acquainted with Ruby Bates through the Price girl during the time I was serving time in jail.

. . .

THE COURT: Never mind about the time you were in jail.

Q   Did you and Victoria Price, Ruby Bates, and Jack Tiller go out together?

A   Yes sir.

MR. KNIGHT: I object to that.

THE COURT: Sustain the objection; that is not evidence. Mr. Witness,
you must not answer so quick. Whenever a question is asked and
objected to, and the Court holds that it is illegal, that puts it out of
the case just as if it never happened.

MR. LEIBOWITZ: We except.

Q   I want to know—now don't answer until the Court says you may—
if the night before you left Huntsville before this train ride, whether
or not you, Victoria Price, Ruby Bates, and Jack Tiller, that is you
with Ruby Bates, and Jack Tiller with Victoria Price, in the presence
of each other, did not have sexual intercourse—

THE COURT: That has been raised so often, Mr. Leibowitz; I have ruled
on that very legal point a half dozen times, and there can't be anything in it except a vicious attempt to get something before the jury
that I have ruled is improper.

MR. LEIBOWITZ: Your Honor, I won't press it further. I want to note an
exception to the Court's ruling, especially in view of the Court's
reference to counsel—

THE COURT: I am ruling according to the law as I understand it.

MR. LEIBOWITZ: I do this in justice to my client; in view of the Court's
characterization that defendant's counsel made a vicious attempt to
force testimony into the record, I want to move for a mistrial.

THE COURT: I decline to do that. If that particular word is offensive to
you, I will withdraw that. Gentlemen (to the jury), you will pay no
attention to the expression "vicious attempt." Don't let that enter
into your consideration or in your minds.

MR. LEIBOWITZ: We respectfully except.

A   I started out at Huntsville, with Victoria Price.

. . .

Q   Where did you go from immediately before you left Huntsville, from
what part of town did you go?

MR. KNIGHT: We object to that.

MR. LEIBOWITZ: I want to show you how they got to the station, what
the arrangements were; that is in rebuttal of Victoria Price's testimony that she never saw this man in her life before the trip.

THE COURT: I will let the question be asked.

Q   Tell us how it was you came to go to the station?

THE COURT: I wouldn't allow you to ask that, "How come them to go."

Q   Did you have a conversation with Victoria Price with reference to leaving Huntsville, you and she and Ruby Bates, giving the details.

MR. KNIGHT: We object to that.

THE COURT: I am not going to allow him to go into details. I will let him show that he had a conversation, but I will not permit him to go into details. I will permit him to ask the witness whether he had any conversation with Victoria Price before they left Huntsville to go to Chattanooga. That covers the point.

MR. LEIBOWITZ: We reserve an exception to the Court's limitation on the question.

A   I had some conversation, without going into the details of it, at Huntsville, with Victoria Price, Ruby Bates, and also Jack Tiller, in company with them, relative to leaving Huntsville and going somewhere. The day and night before we actually left that arrangement was made, around the railroad yards in Huntsville, up near the Lincoln Village.

. . .

Q   Who was to go on that trip?

MR. KNIGHT: We object to that.

THE COURT: Sustain the objection.

MR. LEIBOWITZ: We except.

A   Pursuant to that arrangement, on the following day, we met at the railroad yards in the city of Huntsville. Ruby Bates and Jack Tiller met there besides me and Victoria Price. It was somewhere in the afternoon.

. . .

Q   What happened there; what occurred when you got to the railroad yards in Huntsville?

MR. KNIGHT: We object to that.

THE COURT: I sustain the objection.

MR. LEIBOWITZ: Exception.

Q   May I ask what happened with reference to getting on the train at Huntsville?

A   We decided for three of us to go along—

MR. KNIGHT: We object to that.

THE COURT: Objection sustained.

MR. LEIBOWITZ: Exception.

A   Victoria Price, Ruby Bates, and myself got on the train.

. . .

Q   What happened to Jack Tiller?

MR. KNIGHT: We object to that.

THE COURT: Objection is sustained.

MR. LEIBOWITZ: Exception.

A   Ruby Bates, Victoria Price, and I got on the inside of a boxcar. I talked very little to Victoria Price and Ruby Bates on the way from Huntsville to Chattanooga.

. . .

Q   What was it you said with reference to Jack Tiller?

MR. KNIGHT: We object to that.

THE COURT: I sustain the objection.

Q   Who else was in that boxcar?

MR. KNIGHT: We object to that.

THE COURT: I sustain the objection.

MR. LEIBOWITZ: Exception.

Q   Did you cross the state line of Alabama into Georgia and the state line into Tennessee?

THE COURT: That's unnecessary; we all judicially know they had to do that to get to Chattanooga.

Q   Was anything said about crossing the state line, was any reason given by the prosecutrix, anything specifically said, or directly about that?

A   Yes sir.

Q   About these women crossing the state line, the two state lines with you, as to what the women should do in case you all were caught?

MR. KNIGHT: We object to that.

THE COURT: Overruled—wait a minute, I sustain the objection.

MR. LEIBOWITZ: Exception.

A   Well, whatever talk we had, we finally got to Chattanooga. These women had on overall trousers, ladies' hats, overcoats, ladies' shoes and ladies' hose. We arrived in Chattanooga about eight o'clock, around eight o'clock in the evening. We left the train in the railroad yards there.

I first met Orville Gilley leading away from these railroad yards, on a spur track. Victoria Price and Ruby Bates were with me; the very same girls that were together with me on the train. I was with Gilley then all the rest of the night.

. . .

Q   Where did you next see Victoria Price and Ruby Bates?

A   They was right there on the car then.

Q   Where did you next see them after that?

MR. KNIGHT: We object to that.

THE COURT: The objection is well taken, sustained.

MR. LEIBOWITZ: We except.

A   I was with Gilley all of the time from the time we arrived in Huntsville up until the time when we got back on the train to come to Huntsville. I wasn't with these two girls all the time; me and the fellow Gilley were together all the time.

. . .

Q   Listen, Carter, let me make it plain to you, except for one or two occasions when you left either girl for a short while to go somewhere away from the Chattanooga yards, where you arrived at these railroad yards that night, from then until the following morning, did you—

MR. KNIGHT: We object to that; we don't want that to go before the jury. I think I know what he is after.

THE COURT: Yes, and I imagine this jury will follow the instructions of the Court. I told them not to pay any attention to anything I ruled out.

MR. LEIBOWITZ: Shall I put the question?

THE COURT: Yes, if you want to.

Q   Now, Carter, did you leave these girls at any time?

A   Yes sir.

Q   How many times?

A   A couple of times.

Q   Where was that?

MR. KNIGHT: We object to that.

THE COURT: Sustain the objection.

MR. LEIBOWITZ: Exception.

Q   The couple of times that you went away—

MR. KNIGHT: I object.

THE COURT: Don't interrupt until he puts the question.

Q   Now the couple of times that you left, were you gone for more than a few minutes each time?

A   No sir.

Q   Except for the few minutes that you were gone, were you continuously with Ruby Bates and Victoria Price, all through that night together, with the fellow Gilley right near the railroad yards in the City of Chattanooga and Hobo Swamp there?

MR. KNIGHT: We object to that.

THE COURT: I sustain the objection. Gentlemen, that is excluded and you will pay no attention to the question, or answer—I believe the witness did answer "Yes."

A   Both Gilley and I went and got food that night in the evening and in the morning, for supper and breakfast.

.   .   .

Q   Did you see Victoria Price and Ruby Bates when daylight came the following morning?

MR. KNIGHT: That is objected to.

THE COURT: Sustained.

MR. LEIBOWITZ: Exception.

A   The train started out from Chattanooga back towards Huntsville near about noontime. It was after ten o'clock in the morning. I saw Ruby Bates and Victoria Price just before we boarded the train, the train that we all got on in the railroad yards in Chattanooga, Tennessee. Orville Gilley, myself, Victoria Price, and Ruby Bates were there. There was some other people along, but I didn't know the others; other people sitting on the back watching us board the freight train.

.   .   .

Q   For the purpose of identification, now don't answer this if objected to until ruled on by the Court, did you see any negroes, or did you have any encounter with any negroes during the time that you and Ruby Bates and Victoria Price and Orville Gilley were together at Chattanooga?

A   Yes sir.

MR. KNIGHT: We object to that.

THE COURT: I don't recall any testimony of anybody about any difficulty in Chattanooga.

MR. LEIBOWITZ: I think the jury should be retired so that it may be heard only by the Court; it has reference to a consortium and cohabitation between negroes and whites.

THE COURT: You needn't put that in at all.

MR. LEIBOWITZ: We reserve an exception.

. . .

A   As the train came into Stevenson some of these white boys asked
    myself and Gilley would we help crowd these negro boys off the
    train; they said if we had any man in us we would see that these
    negro boys were put off the train; so after the train left these white
    boys and negro boys got into a fight; they came up closer to the car
    in which we four was riding in. After the train started out of Steven-
    son the scrap started between the whites and the blacks. There were
    some white boys in a gondola near where we were riding; they came
    closer. They got within talking distance. The white boys came to the
    next car. They came from the direction of the caboose. These boys
    were fighting.

. . .

A   If it is testified here that Victoria Price, I, Ruby Bates, and several other
    white men were together in one gondola car leaving Stevenson, I
    wouldn't say that. I would say us four were together. When I left
    that train I walked back to Stevenson, Alabama. I met several of the
    other white boys there at Stevenson. I walked back with some of
    them. None of these white boys had any wounds that I know of that
    were treated in any way in Stevenson. They were not as far as I know
    treated by any doctor in the jail at Scottsboro.

. . .

Q   Did you hear what Victoria Price said to Odell Gladwell at the time
    Gladwell went over to the car after she beckoned to you?

MR. KNIGHT: We object to that because no predicate was laid.

THE COURT: I don't recall any predicate.

MR. LEIBOWITZ: I think I can state positively that I asked Victoria Price
    if she didn't, in the courthouse yard at Scottsboro, motion to one of
    the boys and call him over to talk to her, and she said no, and I then
    asked her if she didn't tell that boy "You are to tell that you are my
    brother." I remember that positively.

Q   Did you hear what she said to the Gladwell boy while at the auto-
    mobile?

A   She asked him—

THE COURT: Was the predicate laid as to this boy?

MR. KNIGHT: Our objection goes to the form of the question.

WITNESS: I am here to tell what happened.

THE COURT: Never mind that. I sustain the objection.

MR. LEIBOWITZ: Exception. You are sustaining the objection as to what
    occurred between Gladwell and Victoria Price; is that because the
    predicate was not laid?

THE COURT: No, because you don't follow it.

A I saw Odell Gladwell, one of the white boys, go over to the car in which Victoria Price was sitting, and I heard Victoria Price say to Odell Gladwell, "One of you boys has got to play like you are my brother; if you don't we will be arrested for hoboing" and Gladwell answered that it was O.K. with him, "I will be your brother."

JUDGE JAMES E. HORTON'S OPINION

On April 9, 1933, Haywood Patterson, the first of the Scottsboro defendants to be tried a second time, was found guilty and sentenced to be executed on June 16, 1933. The execution was stayed on appeal as defense counsel Leibowitz asked that Judge Horton order a new trial. On June 22, 1933, presiding judge Horton responded, stunning the state of Alabama with an unprecedented action. He "put aside" the jury's guilty verdict in the case of Haywood Patterson on the grounds that the evidence did not warrant conviction.

In a lengthy, detailed opinion, Judge Horton combed the evidence presented at trial with great care, analyzing it scrupulously. His opinion is a thorough summary of the evidence up to this point. First, he examines the case for the state, or prosecution, looking for any evidence that would corroborate Victoria Price's charge. Then he turns to arguments for the defense.

As he makes clear, it is his strong opinion that the Scottsboro defendants should not be sentenced to die on the basis of the uncorroborated testimony of one person and other evidence that is only circumstantial in nature. Therefore, he tests the reliability of Price's testimony, trying to discover if there is any hard evidence to corroborate.

FROM THE OPINION OF JUDGE JAMES E. HORTON,
JUNE 22, 1933

The defendant in this case has been tried and convicted for the crime of rape with the death penalty inflicted. He is one of the nine charged with a similar crime at the same time.

. . .

The case is now submitted for hearing on a motion of a new trial. As human life is at stake, not only of this defendant, but of eight others, the Court does and should approach a consideration of this motion with a feeling of deep responsibility, and shall endeavor to give it that thought and study it deserves.

Social order is based on law, and its perpetuity on its fair and impartial administration. Deliberate injustice is more fatal to the one who imposes than to the one on whom it is imposed. The victim may die quickly and his suffering cease, but the teachings of Christianity and the uniform lessons of all history illustrate without exception that its perpetrators not only pay the penalty themselves, but their children through endless generations. To those who deserve punishment who have outraged society and its laws—on such, an impartial justice inflicts the penalties for the violated laws of society, even to the tabling of life itself; but to those who are guiltless the law withholds its heavy hand.

. . .

The court will now proceed to consider this case on the law and evidence, only making such observations and conclusions as may appear necessary to explain and illustrate the same.

. . .

Is there sufficient credible evidence upon which to base a verdict?

. . .

[L]et us now turn to the facts of the case. The Court will of necessity consider in detail the evidence of the chief prosecutrix, Victoria Price, to determine if her evidence is reliable, or whether it is corroborated or contradicted by the other evidence in the case. In order to convict this defendant, Victoria Price must have sworn truly to the fact of her being raped. No matter how reliable the testimony of the defendant and his witnesses, unless the State can make out a case upon the whole evidence, a conviction cannot stand.

. . .

[T]he State relies on the evidence of the prosecutrix, Victoria Price, as to the fact of the crime itself, necessarily claims that her relation is true. The defense insists that her evidence is a fabrication—fabricated for the purpose of saving herself from a prosecution for vagrancy or some other charge.

The Court will therefore first set out the substantial facts testified to by Victoria Price and test it as the law requires as to its reliability or probability, and as to whether it is contradicted by other evidence.

She states that on March 25, 1931, she was on a freight train traveling through Jackson County from Stevenson to Paint Rock; that Ruby Bates was with her on the train. . . . That at Stevenson, she and Ruby Bates walked down the train and got on a gondola car—a car without a top. That the train was filled with chert, lacking about one and one-half or two feet of being full; that the chert was sharp, broken rock with jagged ends.

. . . that in about five or ten minutes twelve colored boys jumped from the boxcar into the gondola, jumping over their heads.

. . .

That one of the negroes picked her up by the legs and held her over the gondola, and said he was going to throw her off; that she was pulled back in the car and one of the negroes hit her on the side of the head with a pistol, causing her head to bleed; that the negroes then pulled off the overalls she was wearing and tore her step-ins apart. That they then threw her down on the chert and with some of the negroes holding her legs and with a knife at her throat, six negroes raped her, one of whom was the defendant; that she lay there for almost an hour on that jagged rock . . . that the last one finished just five minutes before reaching Paint Rock and that her overalls had just been pulled on when the train stopped at Paint Rock with the posse surrounding it.

That she got up and climbed over the side of the gondola and as she alighted she became unconscious for a while, and that she didn't remember anything until she came to herself in a grocery store and she was then taken to Scottsboro, as the evidence shows, in an automobile and that in about an hour or an hour and one-half Dr. Bridges and Dr. Lynch made an examination of her person.

. . .

With seven boys present at the beginning of this trouble, with one seeing the entire affair, with some fifty or sixty persons meeting them at Paint Rock and taking the women, the white boy Gilley, and the nine negroes in charge, with two physicians who examined the women within one to one and one-half hours, according to the tendency of all the evidence, after the occurrence of the alleged rape, and with the acts charged committed in broad daylight, we should expect from all this cloud of witnesses or from the mute but telling physical condition of the women or their clothes some one fact in corroboration of this story.

Let us consider the rich field from which such corroboration may be gleaned.

1. Seven boys on the gondola at the beginning of the fight, and Orville Gilley, the white boy, who remained on the train, and who saw the whole performance.
2. The wound inflicted on the side of Victoria Price's head by the butt end of a pistol from which the blood did flow.
3. The lacerated and bleeding back of the body, a part of which was stripped of clothing and lay on jagged sharp rock, which body two physicians carefully examined for injuries shortly after the occurrence.

. . .

6. Two doctors who could testify to the wretched condition of the women, their wild eyes, dilated pupils, fast breathing, and rapid pulse.

. . .

8. [The presence of] live spermatozoa, the active principle of semen. . . .

The Court will now present the evidence which will show:

that none of the seven white boys, or Orville Gilley, who remained on that train were put on the stand, except Lester Carter;

that neither Dr. Bridges nor Dr. Lynch saw the wound inflicted on the head by the pistol, the lacerated or bleeding back which lay on jagged rocks;

that the semen they found . . . was of small amount [or] dead;

that they saw no [bleeding];

. . .

that these doctors testified that when brought to the office that day neither woman was hysterical or nervous about it at all, and that their respiration and pulse were normal . . . .

Taking up these points in order, what does the record show?

None of the seven white boys were put on the stand, except Lester Carter, and he contradicted her.

. . .

Returning to the pistol butt on the head. The doctor testifies: "I did not sew up any wound on this girl's head; I did not see any blood on her scalp. I don't remember my attention being called to any blood or blow in the scalp." And this was the blow that the woman claimed helped force her into submission.

Next, was she thrown and abused, as she states she was, upon the chert—the sharp jagged rock?

Dr. Bridges states as to physical hurts: "We found some small scratches on the back part of the wrist; she had some blue places in the small of her back, low down in the soft part, three or four bruises about like the joint of your thumb, small as a pecan, and then on the shoulders a blue place about the same size—and we put them on the table, and an examination showed no lacerations [or cuts]."

The evidence of other witnesses as well as the prosecutrix will show that the women had traveled from Huntsville to Chattanooga and were on the way back. There is other evidence tending to show they had spent the night in a hobo dive; that they were having intercourse with men shortly before that time. These few blue spots and this scratch would be the natural consequence of such living; vastly greater physical signs would have been expected from the forcible intercourse of six men under such circumstances.

. . .

Upon the examination under the microscope he [the examining physician] finds that there are spermatozoa [present]. This spermatozoa he ascertains to be nonmotile. He says to the best of his judgment that nonmotile means the spermatozoa were dead.

. . .

While the life of the spermatozoa may be variable, still it appears . . . [that] it would have taken at least several hours for the spermatozoa to have become nonmotile or dead.

When we consider, as the facts hereafter detailed will show, that this woman had slept side by side with a man the night before in Chattanooga, and had intercourse at Huntsville with Tiller on the night before she went to Chattanooga; when we further take into consideration that the semen being emitted, if her testimony were true, was covering the area surrounding the private parts, the conclusion becomes clearer and clearer that this woman was not forced into intercourse with all of these negroes upon that train, but that her condition was clearly due to the intercourse that she had had on the nights previous to this time.

. . .

Was there any evidence . . . on the clothes of any of the negroes?

In the case of *State vs. Cowing*, 99 Minn. 123; 9Am. & En. Ann. cases, 566, the Court said the physicians who testified stated that the semen would have remained on the clothes and could have been found after the expiration of several days. And this is probably a well-known fact. Though these negroes were arrested just after the alleged acts, and though their clothes and pants were examined or looked over by the officers, not a witness testified of seeing any . . . wet or damp spots on the clothes.

[Judge Horton goes on to note that a detailed examination of the women's clothes did not reveal the expected evidence.]

What of the physical appearance of these two women when the doctors saw them?

Dr. Bridges says that when these two women were brought to his office neither was hysterical, or nervous at all. He noticed nothing unusual about their respiration, and their pulse was normal.

Such a normal physical condition is not the natural accompaniment or result of so horrible an experience, especially when the woman testified she fainted from the injuries she had received.

The fact that the women were unchaste might tend to mitigate the marked effect upon their sensibilities, but such hardness would also lessen the probability of either of them fainting. If the faint was feigned, then her credibility must suffer from such feigned actions. And this witness's anger and protest when the doctors insisted on an examination of her person was not compatible with the depression of spirit likely to be caused by the treatment she said she had received.

. . .

Is there any other corroboration? There was a large crowd at Paint Rock when the freight arrived there. While they differed in many details as to the makeup of the train and the exact car from which the different persons were taken, all of which is apparently unimportant, all agreed upon the main fact—that the nine negroes, the two women, and the white boy were all taken from the train. This undisputed fact constitutes about the whole extent of their evidence except a statement by Ruby Bates that she had been raped, which experience the said Ruby Bates now repudiates.

. . .

[Horton then examines the questionable circumstances under which the charge of rape was first made (by Bates): of the three witnesses who testified as to seeing the women at Paint Rock, the first only saw them "standing"; the second saw them only some time after the arrival; the third saw them getting off the car, then starting "to run toward the engine and as they approached a crowd of men they turned and ran back in the opposite direction, and met a part of the posse who stopped them," at which point Mr. Hill, the station agent, coming upon the women, asked them "if they had been bothered."]

Thereupon Ruby Bates stated that they had been raped. The facts appearing that the women instead of seeking the protection of the white men they saw were at first frightened, and the question propounded was in itself suggestive of an answer.

. . .

This is the State's evidence. It corroborates Victoria Price, slightly, if at all, and her evidence is so contradictory to the evidence of the doctors who examined her that it has been impossible for the Court to reconcile their evidence with hers.

. . .

Rape is a crime usually committed in secrecy. A secluded place or a place where one ordinarily would not be observed is the natural selection for the scene of such a crime. The time and place and stage of this alleged act are such to make one wonder and question did such an act occur under such circumstances. The day is a sunshiny day the latter part in March; the time of day is shortly after the noon hour. The place is upon a gondola or car without a top. This gondola, according to the evidence of Mr. Turner, the conductor, was filled to within six inches to twelve or fourteen inches of the top of the chert, and according to Victoria Price up to one and one-half feet or two feet of the top. The whole performance necessarily being in plain view of any one observing the train as it passed. Open gondolas on each side.

On top of this chert twelve negroes rape two white women; they undress them while they are standing on this chert; the prosecuting witness is then thrown down and with one negro continuously kneeling over her with a knife at her throat.

. . .

Her manner [Price's] of testifying and demeanor on the stand militate against her. Her testimony was contradictory, often evasive, and time and

again she refused to answer pertinent questions. The gravity of the offense and the importance of her testimony demanded candor and sin-
cerity. In addition to this the proof tends strongly to show that she
knowingly testified falsely in many material aspects of the case. All this
requires the more careful scrutiny of her evidence.

. . .

Lester Carter was a witness for the defendant; he was one of the white
boys ejected from the train below Stevenson. Whether or not he is entitled to entire credit is certainly a question of great doubt; but where the
facts and circumstances corroborate him, and where the failure of the
State to disprove his testimony with witnesses on hand to disprove it, the
Court sees no reason to capriciously reject all he said.

Victoria Price denied she knew him until she arrived at Scottsboro. It
became a question to be considered as to whether Lester Carter knew
her at Huntsville and saw her commit adultery on several occasions with
one Tiller just before leaving for Chattanooga, and returning on the
freight the next day. The facts he testified to might easily account for the
dead spermatozoa in her vagina. He says he met Victoria Price and Tiller
while in jail at Huntsville; that all three were inmates of the jail at the
same time; that Ruby Bates visited Tiller and Victoria Price while they
were in jail, and he, Carter, met her at the jail; that after all had gotten
out, and he had finished his sentence, he stayed in the home of Tiller
and his wife, and he and Tiller would go out and be with these girls; that
they all planned the Chattanooga trip together; and that just before the
trip, or the night before, all four were engaged in adulterous intercourse.

. . .

Further, there is evidence of trouble between Victoria Price and the
white boys in the jail at Scottsboro because one or more of them refused
to go on the witness stand and testify as she did concerning the rape;
that Victoria Price indicated that by so doing they would all get off lighter.

The defendant and five of the other negroes charged with participating
in this crime at the same time went on the stand and denied any participation in the rape; denied that they knew anything about it; and denied
that they saw any white women on the train. Four of them did state that
they took part in a fight with the white boys which occurred on the train.
Two of them testified that they knew nothing of the fight nor of the girls,
and [were] on an entirely different part of the train. Each of these two
testified as to physical infirmities. One testified he was so diseased he
could hardly walk, and he was examined at Scottsboro according to the
evidence and was found to be diseased. The other testified that one eye
was entirely out and that he could only see sufficiently out of the other
to walk unattended. The physical condition of this prisoner indicates apparently great defect of vision. He testified, and the testimony so shows,
that he was in the same condition at Scottsboro and at the time of the

rape. He further testified that he was on an oil tank near the rear of the train, about the seventh car from the rear; that he stayed on this oil tank all the time and that he was taken from off of this oil tank. The evidence of one of the trainmen tends to show that one of the negroes was taken off an oil tank toward the rear of the train. This near-blind negro was among those whom Victoria Price testified was in the fight and in the party which raped her and Ruby Bates. The facts strongly contradict any such statements.

Conclusion

History, sacred and profane, and the common experience of mankind teach us that women of the character shown in this case are prone for selfish reasons to make false accusations both of rape and insult upon the slightest provocation, or even without provocation for ulterior purposes. These women are shown, by the great weight of the evidence, on this very day before leaving Chattanooga, to have falsely accused two negroes of insulting them, and of almost precipitating a fight between one of the white boys they were in company with and these two negroes. This tendency on the part of the women shows that they are predisposed to make false accusations upon any occasion whereby their selfish ends may be gained.

The Court will not pursue the evidence any further.

As heretofore stated the law declares that a defendant should not be convicted without corroboration where the testimony of the prosecutrix bears on its face indications of unreliability or improbability and particularly when it is contradicted by other evidence.

The testimony of the prosecutrix in this case is not only uncorroborated, but it also bears on its face indications of improbability and is contradicted by other evidence, and in addition thereto the evidence greatly preponderates in favor of the defendant. It therefore becomes the duty of the Court under the law to grant the motion in this case.

It is therefore ordered and adjudged by the Court that the motion be granted; that the verdict of the jury in this case and the judgment of the Court sentencing this defendant to death be, and the same hereby is, set aside and that a new trial be and the same is hereby ordered.

JAMES E. HORTON
Circuit Judge

This June 22nd, 1933.

THE RETRIAL OF CLARENCE NORRIS

To recapitulate: the first Scottsboro trial took place in March 1931; the United States Supreme Court ordered new trials in 1932; the second round of trials took place in the spring of 1933; Judge Horton ordered new trials in the summer of that same year. Thus, in winter of 1933 a third round of trials began. A new judge, William W. Callahan, presided; because in the fall of 1933, shortly after Judge Horton's call for a new trial, Horton was defeated at the polls.

In June Judge Horton had argued that no one should be convicted on the circumstantial evidence and the uncorroborated charge of one witness alone. However, Judge Callahan opened the December trial with a charge to the jury in which he proclaimed a legal interpretation opposite to Judge Horton's:

> The law would authorize conviction on the testimony of Victoria Price alone, if, from that evidence, taken into consideration with all the other evidence in the case, both for the State and for the defendant, convinced you beyond a reasonable doubt that she had been ravished. *The law does not require corroboration.*

Indeed, Judge Callahan was far less receptive than Judge Horton to the case put forward by the defense; he was far less amenable to scrutinizing Victoria Price's character and reliability.

Within a week of the beginning of the third round of trials, Haywood Patterson was found guilty for a third time and Clarence Norris was tried and found guilty. The following document from the third round of trials comes from the court transcript of Norris's trial in December 1933. It includes part of the testimony of Victoria Price and a deposition taken from Ruby Bates. Of interest here are continued inconsistencies in Price's testimony; the continued frustration of the defense attorney (note, for example, early in the testimony in this excerpt that information is presented in an unorthodox way, through questions and not answers); and the attribution of motives to Price by Ruby Bates, who had reversed her testimony in the previous spring of 1933.

FROM THE TESTIMONY OF VICTORIA PRICE AND THE DEPOSITION OF RUBY BATES IN THE RETRIAL OF CLARENCE NORRIS, DECEMBER 2, 1933

Cross-Examination by Mr. Leibowitz

A   My true name is not Mrs. Price. I am not Mrs. Price; my husband's name is not Price. My last husband's name is McClendon. His first name is Enna. I was married to Mr. McClendon in Huntsville, Alabama. I don't know how long it was before this rape that I was married to Mr. McClendon; I had been married to him over a year or two. I did not assume the name of McClendon. I never went by my husband's name. I had another husband, too. His name was Henry Presley. I married him in Fayetteville, Tennessee. I don't know exactly how long before I married my second husband I married my first husband. It was a couple of years. I wouldn't be positive. I was married by a justice. I cannot give you the date of that marriage. I did not have any other husband besides those two. I did not ever use the name of Presley, my first husband's name.

Q   Who did you start out to Chattanooga with the day before—I withdraw that—you ever been convicted of a crime?

MR. KNIGHT: We object to that.

THE COURT: Sustained.

MR. LEIBOWITZ: I haven't finished my question.

THE COURT: It sounded like it to me.

Q   Weren't you convicted of a crime involving moral turpitude—Look this way please, not over that way!

THE COURT: Now Mr. Leibowitz, don't proceed along that line any more.

Q   Were you ever convicted of a crime involving moral turpitude, under the name of Victoria Presley, in the year 1927?

MR. KNIGHT: I object to that.

THE COURT: I doubt whether this witness knows what moral turpitude is; I doubt whether half the lawyers know it or not.

MR. LEIBOWITZ: That is on the question of credibility.

THE COURT: Ask if she has been convicted and I can then determine whether that involves moral turpitude.

Q   What were you convicted of?

MR. KNIGHT: We object to that.

THE COURT: I sustain the objection.

MR. LEIBOWITZ: Your Honor just told me to ask it.

THE COURT: No, not that way—you misunderstood me.

MR. LEIBOWITZ: May I have an answer to my previous question?

THE COURT: I sustained the objection to both of them.

MR. LEIBOWITZ: Exception.

THE COURT: You can ask her if she has ever been convicted of a certain offense, and I can then determine whether you can ask that kind of question.

Q   Were you ever convicted of the crime of adultery?

MR. KNIGHT: We object to that.

THE COURT: I sustain the objection. (To the jury) Gentlemen of the jury, when a question is asked and I sustain an objection to that question, that question and all that involves and all inferences from it, is out of the case, and not evidence in the case, and you must not consider it in arriving at your verdict.

MR. LEIBOWITZ: Exception.

Q   Were you ever convicted of the crime of fornication?

MR. KNIGHT: We object to that.

THE COURT: Sustained.

MR. LEIBOWITZ: Exception.

Q   Were you ever convicted for a violation of the prohibition law?

MR. KNIGHT: We object to that.

THE COURT: Sustained.

MR. LEIBOWITZ: Exception.

Q   Were you ever convicted of vagrancy and drunkenness?

MR. KNIGHT: We object to that.

THE COURT: Sustained.

MR. LEIBOWITZ: Exception.

Q   Were you ever convicted of any crime under the name of Victoria Presley?

MR. KNIGHT: We object to that.

THE COURT: Sustained.

MR. LEIBOWITZ: Exception.

. . .

A   I wasn't working on March 24, 1931; neither was Ruby Bates. I did not leave my home town which is Huntsville, on March 24, 1931, with a man named Lester Carter.

[Lester Carter is brought in.]

. . .

Q   Did you meet a man named Gilley at the trial?

MR. KNIGHT: We object to that.

THE COURT: Sustained.

MR. LEIBOWITZ: Exception.

A   I know Gilley.

Q   Where was the first place you claim that you met Gilley, on the train when you were coming back—had you ever seen Gilley before that time?

A   Not as I remember.

Q   Not that you know of?

A   No sir.

Q   You hadn't spoken to Gilley in Chattanooga, had you?

A   I probably had and didn't know who he was.

Q   Mrs. Price, did you speak to any person in Chattanooga, just "yes" or "no," please?

MR. KNIGHT: We object to that.

THE COURT: Sustained.

MR. LEIBOWITZ: Exception.

Q   Did Gilley bring you some food in Chattanooga?

A   Yes sir.

MR. KNIGHT: We object to that.

THE COURT: I sustain the objection. Gentlemen, she made answer to the question. That is excluded because I had held that the question is illegal.

MR. LEIBOWITZ: Exception.

Q   I will ask you, Mrs. Price, where you spent the night in—

MR. KNIGHT: I object to that.

MR. LEIBOWITZ: I am not going to continue this examination if I am to be interrupted.

THE COURT: You are going on with the examination, and I am not going to allow you to be interrupted. Wait until you are certain that he is through with his question, Mr. Attorney General, before you make any objection.

Q   I am going to ask you, Mrs. Price, if you spent the night in Chattanooga in a wooded section near the railroad yards?

THE COURT: I see that you have gone far enough with it, myself, to make that question illegal, and I sustain the objection to it.

MR. LEIBOWITZ: We except.

Q   I must ask just one more question; don't answer it until objection is made and ruled on by the Court. Did you, there that night, in and about the railroad yards in Chattanooga, have sexual intercourse with one Lester Carter, or one Gilley, in company with Ruby Bates?

MR. KNIGHT: We object to that.

THE COURT: I sustain the objection. Mr. Leibowitz, that question was so palpably illegal that you ought not to have asked a question like that.

MR. LEIBOWITZ: I except to the admonition of the Court and move for a mistrial.

THE COURT: The motion is overruled.

MR. LEIBOWITZ: Your Honor sustained the objection to the question?

THE COURT: Yes, sir.

MR. LEIBOWITZ: Exception.

. . .

Q   May I ask this question: Isn't it a fact that you and Lester Carter were together in the very same jail in Huntsville?

MR. KNIGHT: We object to that.

MR. LEIBOWITZ: On the question of credibility, your Honor.

THE COURT: I sustain the objection.

MR. LEIBOWITZ: Exception.

. . .

A   Before I got down on the chert, I was hit in the head with a gun. They hit me between my eye and the top of my head; hit me along there (indicating). I wouldn't be positive where they hit me. It bled a little bit. It didn't make my head swollen there. Well, it did, a little bit.

I don't know the make of any gun. I don't know what caliber means. I don't know a .38 from a .45. I didn't ever know anything about the caliber of any guns at any time in my life. All I know is that he had the barrel in his hand and hit me with the other end. The barrel is the end the smoke comes from.

Q   Where did you find that out?

THE COURT: I don't see any use in taking up time with that. I would imagine that anyone with common sense would know which was the barrel of a pistol.

MR. LEIBOWITZ: I want to except to the Court's statement in reference to the cross-examination.

A   He hit me with the butt. I don't know which is the butt; I reckon the handle is the butt. The handle is the butt end, I know that. I don't know which way the pistol was when he hit me. I probably might have told you the other day that it was the butt end of the gun; I don't know anything about it. Whichever part he hit me with, he hit me on the head between the eyebrow and the top of the head, right along here (indicating) somewhere. When he hit me, some blood came out, a little bit. I was standing up when he hit me. He didn't hit me; he didn't knock me down. He hit me. They was all shuffling around me there. After the man hit me with the butt end of the pistol, which caused a wound on my head that bled a little, I don't know whether he punched me or not; I don't remember.

Q   Way back in Scottsboro you knew something about the caliber of guns, didn't you, "Yes" or "No," didn't you?

A   I just had been told what they called guns.

Q   You knew all about the caliber of guns in Scottsboro, didn't you?

A   No sir.

Q   Let's see; the very first trial you testified in, in Scottsboro hardly a week or ten days after this supposed rape, do you remember testifying before Judge Hawkins?

A   Yes sir, before Judge Hawkins, I did.

Q   Do you remember being asked these questions and making these answers: "Q. That one yonder, Charley Weems? A. Yes sir. Q. With a gun or pistol? A. A pistol, a .45."

THE COURT: Do you remember whether you said that or not?

A   I probably did, Judge, your Honor.

Q   Now, in the Patterson case, I will ask you if you were not asked this question, and make these answers: "Q. What did you see this defendant do in that fight? A. I seen him knock a boy in the head. Q What with? A. A gun. Q. A pistol? A. A .38." Did you say that?

A   I don't know whether I did or not; I don't remember.

. . .

Q   Were you not asked these questions and made these answers in the Powell, Robertson, Wright, Montgomery, and Williams case: "Q. Did you see the two men who carried the guns? A. Sure. Q. They were both there? A. There was two that had guns absolutely, a .38 and a .45." Did you say that?

A   I don't remember whether I did or not.

Q   If you said it, was it a fact?

A   I don't know the make of a gun.

Q   You don't know a .38 from a .50?

A   To the best of my judgment that is what I called them. I heard them
    called that. I don't know what they was.
        I don't know how many men punched me in the face; I didn't
    count them. I don't know whether there was more than two or not.
    Sure, they punched me in the face; they knocked my head around.
    I wouldn't be positive they punched me in the face; jerked me
    around; they slapped me once kin'ly hard. I didn't say my nose was
    swollen. It did swell up a little bit. My cheeks were swollen a little
    bit. My lips were kin'ly cut. They was bleeding a little bit inside. I
    was cut inside of my lips a little. The place where I was struck my
    lips were bleeding; they was kin'ly busted. I don't remember about
    whether my cheek was also cut on the inside. My whole face was
    swollen up and bruised, black and blue kin'ly. I didn't examine my
    back after I got to the jail at Scottsboro after the trouble. As far as
    my remembrance goes, I didn't find any blood on my back.

Q   On the trial before Judge Horton, did you testify—page 64 of the
    record before Judge Horton—were you asked these questions and
    did you make these answers: "Q. You lay on your back there for
    close to an hour on that jagged rock screaming? A. Yes sir."

                    . . .

Deposition from Ruby Bates

    (Ruby Bates was not present for the trial of Clarence Norris so she
submitted a written, sworn deposition. The testimony shown in brackets
was objected to by the prosecuting attorney.)

A   After we returned from the doctor's office to the jail, there had been
    seven white boys arrested at Stevenson, Alabama, and had been
    transferred to Scottsboro. Lester Carter was also there at Scottsboro
    jail. [Victoria Price told the high sheriff, who was also the jailer, that
    one of these boys, who had been arrested and brought to this jail,
    was her half-brother.] Then she told again that she was attacked and
    raped by these negro boys. She told that to the sheriff. She said that
    there was twelve of these boys. There was not very much said about
    it that afternoon, because it was late and that night Victoria would
    not rest. I didn't know what was wrong. She was scared and we was
    both frightened. The next day we was examined again by the doctors
    and there was a few scratches on our bodies and there was a few
    bruised places. They was caused by the freight train riding [because
    anybody will get sore from riding in a freight train and staying in a
    hobo jungle. This boy, who Victoria claimed is her half-brother, also
    told that Victoria was his half-sister and kept making noise and kept

trying to break out of the jail, until they put him in the same cell with Victoria Price and myself.] Then my mother appeared at the jail. First she asked the jailer why that man was in there with us two girls, and Victoria Price was standing there and she answered ["He is my half-brother." The jailer said he wouldn't be quiet until he was moved into the cell with Victoria.]. My mother tells the jailer that unless he removes that man from the cell she would see what she can do to him for having the man locked up in jail with two girls, when it was against the law. After the boy was removed, Victoria said to me that I must remember to tell the same story as she was telling me. She was at that time telling me what all she had told the sheriff. She had told the sheriff that we had been raped and she made up the story of how we had been raped, and she was telling me the story. . . . We were then removed on Sunday from the small cell to the large cell. There was also a cage in the middle of both cells where the men prisoners was, but there was more men prisoners in the larger cell. The seven white boys that were arrested was in this large cell. Victoria Price would have conversations with different ones of the boys that was arrested and placed in jail for witnesses against the negro boys. I do not know what the conversations was about, only in one conversation she had with one of the boys, the boy with whom she had claimed was her half-brother and with whom she had been making love affairs since she had been in jail, told her that he was going to tell the truth about it at the trial and that he was not going to lie for anybody, her or anyone else. I don't remember what he gave his name, but I remember that Texas was his nickname. I know his name now, Odell Gladwell. I also heard her tell Lester Carter that he must tell that we had been raped by these negro boys. . . . Victoria Price reminded me during all this time that I must tell what she did. She said that unless I did tell what she did, I would get her in trouble. She would have to serve a jail sentence. [She was then expecting to be prosecuted by my mother for carrying me across the state line when I was under 21 years of age and because my mother knew nothing about my going from home.]

THE DECISION OF THE UNITED STATES SUPREME COURT

After both Patterson and Norris were found guilty in December 1933 in another round of trials, the defense again lodged appeals that delayed their executions and postponed the trials of the other men. The case was heard by the Alabama Supreme Court, which denied the motion and refused to reverse the convictions.

The case did not reach the Supreme Court until February 1935, some fourteen months after Norris had been convicted. Then on April 1, 1935, the Supreme Court declared that the state court had erred. The Supreme Court reversed the convictions of Patterson and Norris on the grounds that African-Americans, even those who met the narrow qualifications of the voting board, were systematically being excluded from Alabama juries in general and from the Scottsboro juries in particular. The Court found this situation to be an unconstitutional denial of equal protection under the Fourteenth Amendment to the Constitution of the United States.

Note that the Court determined that in the memory of all witnesses, no African-Americans had ever served on any jury in either county where Norris and Patterson had been tried.

FROM THE SUPREME COURT DECISION RENDERED IN SPRING
OF 1935

NORRIS v. STATE OF ALABAMA
55 s.ct
55 Supreme Court Reporter
294 U.S. 587
No. 534.
Argued Feb. 15–18, 1935.
Decided April 1, 1935.

Action of state through Legislature, courts, or executive or administrative officers in excluding all negroes, solely because of race or color, from serving as grand or petit jurors in criminal prosecutions against negroes, denies equal protection contrary to 14th Amendment (Const. U.S. Amend. 14).

. . .

Evidence adduced by negro defendant in criminal case that for a generation or longer no negro had been called for service in state court on any grand or petit jury within county *held* to make prima facie case of denial of equal protection guaranteed by 14th Amendment, and in connection with evidence that there were negroes qualified for jury service, whose names would normally appear on preliminary list prepared by jury commission, but that no names of negroes were placed on jury roll, and that commission did not properly consider negroes' qualifications, established unconstitutional discrimination, and hence motion to quash indictment should have been granted (Code Ala. 1923/8603; Const. U.S. Amend. 14).

. . .

Evidence adduced by negro defendant in criminal case on motion to quash trial venire *held* to show long-continued, unvarying, and total exclusion of negroes from jury service within county, notwithstanding many negroes were qualified, thereby denying equal protection under 14th Amendment (Acts Ala. 1931, pp. 58, 59/11, 14; Const. U.S. Amend. 14).

. . .

After the remand, a motion for change of venue was granted and the cases were transferred to Morgan County. Norris was brought to trial in November 1933. At the outset, a motion was made on his behalf to quash the indictment upon the grounds of the exclusion of negroes from juries in Jackson County, where the indictment was found. A motion was also made to quash the trial venire in Morgan County upon the grounds of the exclusion of negroes from juries in that county. In relation to each county, the charge was of long-continued, systematic, and arbitrary exclusion of qualified negro citizens from service on juries, solely because of their race and color, in violation of the Constitution of the United States. The state joined issue on this charge and after hearing the evidence, which we shall presently review, the trial judge denied both motions, and exception was taken. The trial then proceeded and resulted in the conviction of Norris, who was sentenced to death. On appeal, the Supreme Court of the state considered and decided the federal question which Norris had raised and affirmed the judgment. 156 So. 556. We granted a writ of certiorari. 293 U.S. 552, 55 S.Ct. 345, 79 L. Ed.—

First. There is no controversy as to the constitutional principle involved. That principle, long since declared, was not challenged, but was expressly recognized, by the Supreme Court of the state. Summing up precisely the effect of earlier decisions, this Court thus stated the principle in *Carter v. Texas*, 177 U.S. 442, 447, 20 S.Ct. 687, 44 L. Ed. 839, in relation to exclusion from service on grand juries: whenever by any action of a state, whether through its Legislature, through its courts, or through its executive or administrative officers, all persons of the African race are excluded, solely because of their race or color, from serving as grand jurors in the criminal prosecution of a person of the African race, the equal protection of the laws is denied to him, contrary to the Fourteenth Amendment of the Constitution of the United States.

. . .

Second. *The evidence on the motion to quash the indictment*. In 1930, the total population of Jackson County, where the indictment was found, was 36,881, of whom 2,688 were negroes. The male population over 21 years of age numbered 8,801, and of these 666 were negroes.

The qualifications of jurors were thus prescribed by the state statute (Alabama Code 1923/8603): "The jury commission shall place on the jury roll and in the jury box the names of all male citizens of the county who are generally reputed to be honest and intelligent men, and are esteemed in the community for their integrity, good character, and sound judgment, but no person must be selected who is under 21 or over 65 years of age, or, who is an habitual drunkard, or who, being afflicted with a permanent disease or physical weakness, is unfit to discharge the duties of a juror, or who cannot read English, or who has ever been convicted of any offense involving moral turpitude. If a person cannot read English and has all the other qualifications prescribed herein and is a freeholder or householder, his name may be placed on the jury roll and in the jury box." See Gen. Acts Alabama 1931, No. 47, p. 59/14.

Defendant adduced evidence to support the charge of unconstitutional discrimination in the actual administration of the statute in Jackson County. The testimony, as the state court said, tended to show that "in a long number of years no negro had been called for jury service in that county." It appeared that no negro had served on any grand or petit jury in that county within the memory of witnesses who had lived there all their lives. Testimony to that effect was given by men whose ages ran from 50 to 76 years. Their testimony was uncontradicted. It was supported by the testimony of officials. The clerk of the jury commission and the clerk of the circuit court had never known of a negro serving on a grand jury in Jackson County. The court reporter, who had not missed a session in that county in twenty-four years, and two jury commissioners testified to the same effect. One of the latter, who was a member of the commission which made up the jury roll for the grand jury which found the indictment, testified that he had "never known of a single instance where any negro sat on any grand or petit jury in the entire history of that county."

That testimony in itself made a prima facie case of the denial of the equal protection which the Constitution guarantees. See *Neal v. Delaware*, supra.

The case thus made was supplemented by direct testimony that specified negroes, thirty or more in number, were qualified for jury service.

Among these were negroes who were members of school boards, or trustees, of colored schools, and property owners and householders.

. . .

We think that the evidence that for a generation or longer no negro had been called for service on any jury in Jackson County, that there were negroes qualified for jury service, that according to the practice of the jury commission their names would normally appear on the preliminary list of male citizens of the requisite age but that no names of negroes were placed on the jury roll, and the testimony with respect to the lack of appropriate consideration of the qualifications of negroes, established the discrimination which the Constitution forbids. The motion to quash the indictment upon that grounds should have been granted.

Third. *The evidence on the motion to quash the trial venire.* The population of Morgan County, where the trial was had, was larger than that of Jackson County, and the proportion of negroes was much greater. The total population of Morgan County in 1930 was 46,176, and of this number 8,311 were negroes.

Within the memory of witnesses, long resident there, no negro had ever served on a jury in that county or had been called for such service. Some of these witnesses were over 50 years of age and had always lived in Morgan County. Their testimony was not contradicted. A clerk of the circuit court, who had resided in the county for thirty years, testified that during his official term approximately 2,500 persons had been called for jury service and that not one of them was a negro; that he did not recall "ever seeing any single person of the colored race serve on any jury in Morgan County."

There was abundant evidence that there were a large number of negroes in the county who were qualified for jury service. Men of intelligence, some of whom were college graduates, testified to long lists (said to contain nearly 200 names) of such qualified negroes, including many businessmen, owners of real property, and householders. When defendant's counsel proposed to call many additional witnesses in order to adduce further proof of qualifications of negroes for jury service, the trial judge limited the testimony, holding that the evidence was cumulative.

We find no warrant for a conclusion that the names of any of the negroes as to whom this testimony was given, or of any other negroes, were placed on the jury rolls. No such names were identified. The evidence that for many years no negro had been called for jury service itself tended to show the absence of the names of negroes from the jury rolls, and the state made no effort to prove their presence. The trial judge limited the defendant's proof "to the present year, the present jury roll." The sheriff of the county, called as a witness for defendants, scanned the jury roll and after "looking over every single name on the jury roll, from A to Z," was unable to point out "any single negro on it."

For this long-continued, unvarying, and wholesale exclusion of negroes from jury service, we find no justification consistent with the constitutional mandate. . . .

CONCLUSION

On May 1, 1935, after the Supreme Court decision reversing the convictions of the winter of 1933 trials, Victoria Price swore out new warrants against all the Scottsboro defendants. New trials began, which continued throughout 1936 and 1937. Token African-Americans served on these juries.

One of the defendants was sentenced to death, but in 1938 his sentence was commuted to life imprisonment by the governor of Alabama; three others received jail sentences ranging from seventy-five to ninety-nine years. Charges of rape were dropped against one, but he received a twenty-year sentence for assaulting a deputy sheriff. Four others were released in 1937 after charges against them were dropped. Several widely read Alabama newspapers and many prominent Alabamians began working for the release of all the Scottsboro defendants in the 1940s. One by one they were paroled throughout the 1940s. The last one to leave prison was released in 1950.

But the Scottsboro case was still not over. In 1970 the National Association for the Advancement of Colored People (NAACP) and others discovered that Clarence Norris, the last of the "Scottsboro boys," was still alive. He had violated his parole by fleeing the state of Alabama in 1946, and he was still subject to arrest should he return to the state where some of his relatives still lived. The last Scottsboro defendant, he had spent the most time on death row and had been a fugitive from justice for thirty years. Finally, on October 25, 1976, Clarence Norris was officially pardoned by Governor George C. Wallace of Alabama. The attorney general of the state of Alabama, Bill Baxley, facilitated the pardon with the written recommendation to the parole and pardons board. Baxley's letter declaring that his research showed Norris to be innocent of the 1931 charges was based largely on the arguments made by Judge James E. Horton in 1933. After much anxiety about returning to Alabama and possibly subjecting himself to arrest, Norris returned in 1976 to accept the pardon.

Strangely enough, the Scottsboro case, which had begun in 1931, was still not entirely over. In 1975 the National Broadcasting Company (NBC) aired a program entitled "Judge Horton and the Scottsboro Boys"; and several weeks later both Ruby Bates and Victoria Price, both now living under different names, filed lawsuits against the network for libel, slander, and invasion of privacy. By 1977, when the suit filed by Victoria Price came to trial, Ruby Bates (who had filed the suit first) had died. In the course of the trial many of the issues, especially those concerning Price's reliability and the physician's examination, were again debated. The lawyer acting for NBC closed his summation with a reading of Judge Horton's 1933 opinion calling for a new trial. Finally, Judge Charles G. Neese dismissed the case before it reached the jury, declaring that there were insufficient grounds for proceeding. And the Scottsboro case drew to a close again.

STUDY QUESTIONS

1. What is your impression of Victoria Price as a result of reading her April 1931 testimony? Explain in some detail.

2. What is the relevance of the questions posed by the defense about Victoria Price's marital status? Explain why you think it is or is not relevant.

3. Victoria Price testified that she had been in the Scottsboro jail since March 25. If you were a juror, what conclusions would you have drawn from this? (Nowhere is this peculiarity explained fully.)

4. Why, do you suppose, Price was asked if she knew "any of the officials among the police in Chattanooga"?

5. Do you find any inconsistencies in Price's testimony during the first trial? Explain.

6. As a member of the jury, how would you have evaluated the physician's testimony in the first trial? Note that he testified for the prosecution, not the defense.

7. In the final paragraph of Judge Horton's address from the bench, the object of his address is no longer the juror. Who is it? Explain your answer.

8. In the *New York Times* article, the issue of Victoria Price's language is raised twice. What does the reporter imply about the importance of her language? Do you find the reporter's assumptions that her language is important a relevant point?

9. The language of the *New York Times* reporter should also be taken into account. Is there evidence that the reporter has an opinion about Victoria Price? Look carefully at his choice of words. Are any of his words "loaded"?

10. Consider why Dr. Bridge's testimony was so important.

11. Compare and contrast the physical state of Mayella Ewell and Victoria Price after the alleged attacks.

12. Identify similarities between Mayella Ewell and Victoria Price. Could their commonly held characteristics account for some of the happenings just after the alleged attacks?

13. In what sense do you suppose a jury member could (and probably did) forgive the inconsistencies between Price's 1931 testimony and her 1933 testimony, to which the *New York Times* reporter draws attention?

14. Compare the character of the accuser in the first trial and the accuser in the trial described in *To Kill a Mockingbird*, including their specious motives.

15. What seems to be the relationship between Victoria Price and Ruby Bates that defense attorney Leibowitz is trying to establish in his first six questions to Bates in her testimony of April 7, 1933?

16. Why do you suppose Mr. Knight, the prosecuting attorney, objects to Leibowitz's question to Ruby Bates that begins, "Were you a good girl . . . ?"

17. Why does Leibowitz want to ask that question? How would it help his case in the eyes of the jury?

18. Why does Leibowitz probe events that occurred *before* the women got on the train?

19. Why does Leibowitz ask Ruby Bates where she met Lester Carter.

20. Since he already knows the answer, why does Leibowitz ask Ruby Bates if she ever visited Victoria Price in jail?

21. Why does Leibowitz ask Ruby Bates in detail about an encounter Bates and Price had with two African-Americans before their train ride?

22. If you were on this jury, how would you evaluate Ruby Bates's testimony? What would you have learned from it? Would you have believed Ruby Bates, based on this brief segment? Why or why not?

23. What appear to be the defense attorney's motives and strategy in examining Lester Carter?

24. Is there a pattern in the prosecutor's objections to the defense attorney's questions of Lester Carter? What specifically does he *not* want the jury to consider?

25. Examine Judge Horton's decisions with regard to the prosecutor's objections to the defense attorney's questions.

26. In what way does Carter's testimony refute previous testimony about the fight between men on the train? Does that testimony throw a different light on Victoria Price's charges? Explain.

27. Do you find Victoria Price's testimony of December 1933 to be believable? Why or why not?

28. Examine carefully the excerpt from Judge Callahan's charge to the jury in the retrial of Clarence Norris in December 1933. Did this necessarily insure a guilty verdict, as Clarence Norris once asserted? Why or why not?

29. In your view, is there evidence in the early part of Victoria Price's December 1933 testimony that Judge Callahan is unbiased? Why or why not?

30. Show in words or pencil sketch what you would expect Victoria Price to look like when she disembarked the train, based on the informa-

tion she gave in December 1933 about what happened in the gondola car.

31. Ruby Bates's mother is mentioned in the December 1933 testimony. What part does her presence play in this drama?

32. The Supreme Court decision rendered in the spring of 1935 highlights the illegality of excluding qualified Negroes from serving on juries. According to Atticus Finch in *To Kill a Mockingbird*, what other jury exclusions are being made in Alabama?

33. Based on the qualifications required for a person to serve on a jury, describe several hypothetical cases in which white citizens might not be tried by a jury "of their peers."

TOPICS FOR WRITTEN OR ORAL EXPLORATION

1. Re-examine the testimony of the chief witnesses for the prosecution, Victoria Price and Dr. Bridges. Remember that after hearing them, the jury found the defendants guilty in just a few hours. Try to envision what occurred in the jury room. Assume that at least one of the twelve men tried to come to grips with this testimony (aloud or silently). How would he have dealt with any doubts about the defendants' guilt based on the testimony presented here? Write an internal dialogue of such a person who eventually voted "guilty."

2. Write a similar agreement based on Tom Robinson's trial. Note again what Atticus Finch has heard about the jury that finds Tom Robinson guilty. Write and/or perform a dialogue between juror Cunningham and a juror who finally convinces Cunningham to vote "guilty."

3. Assuming that rumors are circulating about jury tampering or violence against attorney Leibowitz, rewrite Judge Horton's address to the courtroom as if you were a reporter covering the case.

4. Tell someone who was not present when the speech was delivered what Judge Horton said, interpreting it in plain words and in a more outspoken way.

5. In a written essay, compare the historical situation as the second Scottsboro trial opens with the events prior to Tom Robinson's trial. Consider Atticus Finch's actions and explanations to the children.

6. Write (and perform) a dramatic sketch of a private conversation between two jurors after they have heard Judge Horton's speech to the courtroom in the spring of 1933. It is up to you to create the character of each juror (their points of view, biases, and so on). Remember that no African-Americans and no women served on juries in Alabama at the time.

7. Compare the language of Victoria Price (especially as described in the last paragraph of her testimony reported in the *New York Times*) with the language of accusers Bob and Mayella Ewell in *To Kill a Mockingbird*. What impact, if any, might the language have had on spectators at the trial and readers of the *New York Times* story?

8. Some people have argued (in this case particularly) that events prior to the alleged attack should have no bearing on the guilt or innocence of an accused rapist. Conduct a debate on the issue, using the previous sentence as a proposition.

9. The defense seems to imply that the two women made the accusation of rape in order to divert the attention of the law from other crimes. Explain this in some detail as if you are a defense attorney summing up the situation for a jury.

10. Bob Ewell's charge that his daughter, Mayella, has been raped by Tom Robinson overrides other broken laws and broken codes. Write a comparison of the Ewell situation with the case of the two women on this point.

11. Write a comparison of Victoria Price's attitude as a witness (as it is reported in the *New York Times*) with Mayella Ewell's attitude on the stand in *To Kill a Mockingbird*.

12. Write a newspaper account of Ruby Bates's testimony in light of what you know of earlier events, as if your story were to appear in your local newspaper.

13. The transcript itself does not describe what Ruby Bates looked like, her body language, the way in which she said what she did. Was she believable? Did she appear to be shifty? Self-assured? Naive? Sophisticated? Hard? Nervous? and so on. Prepare a written or actual performance of her testimony, interpreting her appearance from what you know of her language.

14. The physical conditions of both Tom Robinson (in the novel) and two of the Scottsboro defendants were critical issues for the defense and for Judge Horton's opinion. Write an essay comparing the evidence on this point in the two cases.

15. The assumptions in the first paragraph of Judge Horton's June 1933 "Conclusion" are very controversial. Consider whether this weakens or strengthens his argument. Compare that paragraph with his conduct in forbidding certain testimony when Lester Carter was on the stand. Do his actions seem contradictory? Explain why or why not.

16. Assume that Judge Callahan is being investigated at a hearing after the trials in the winter of 1933. The charge, we will assume, is bias and interference with justice in this case. Based on the early testi-

mony of his court during the winter of 1933, construct an argument for finding that he was delinquent in his duty.

17. Examine Victoria Price's testimony of December 1933. Assume that you are one of the defense attorney's team, given the assignment of summarizing her testimony alone for the jury.

18. Allowing yourself a certain amount of artistic license, but at the same time respecting the historical truth of the case as nearly as you can, write detailed stage directions for a television dramatization of Victoria Price's testimony. Consider her dress, her body language, her expressions, her voice—all those things that we cannot derive from an official transcript alone. Read Harper Lee's descriptions of Mayella Ewell for ideas.

19. Make a careful written comparison of comments regarding juries in *To Kill a Mockingbird* and in the Supreme Court decision of April 1, 1935.

20. Convictions in the Scottsboro case were reversed on three separate occasions. Which of the reasons cited in those reversals would have led Atticus Finch to hope for a successful appeal in the case of Tom Robinson? Be specific.

21. As an exercise, discover whether any of your own ancestors would have been unable to serve on juries in Alabama in the 1930s, had they been citizens of that state. The qualifications are listed in the Supreme Court opinion. Explain how you found out about your ancestors and why they might not have been allowed to serve on juries, or might not have been judged by a jury of their peers.

SUGGESTED READINGS

For the definitive history of the Scottsboro trial, see:
Carter, Dan T. *Scottsboro: A Tragedy of the American South*, rev. ed. Baton Rouge: Louisiana State University Press, 1979.

The following are first-hand accounts by the defendants:
Norris, Clarence. *The Last of the Scottsboro Boys.* An autobiography by Clarence Norris and Sybil D. Washington. New York: G. P. Putnam's Sons, 1979.
Patterson, Haywood, as told to Earl Conrad. *Scottsboro Boy.* Garden City, NY: Doubleday, 1950.

Also consult the NAACP papers on the Scottsboro case on microfilm. These are available through interlibrary loan.

There are two other important sources for materials on the Scottsboro case: one is newspaper and magazine files, especially for the 1933 trials.

The *New York Times* covered the case regularly; its issues for that year are readily available on microfilm. Newspapers in your own area, which should be available in the newspaper's own files or in the local library, may also have covered the case. Commentary and accounts of the case also appeared in numerous magazines and other periodicals of the time. Check the *Reader's Guide Index to Periodical Literature* for the year 1933.

Another place to find secondary materials is in the biographies of some of the participants:

Reynolds, Quentin. *Courtroom*. New York: Farrar, Straus and Cudahy, 1950. (This is a biography of defense attorney Samuel Leibowitz.)

3

Historical Context: The Civil Rights Movement

The dramatic impact of the novel *To Kill a Mockingbird* was heightened by the conditions under which African-Americans were living in the deep South, the emerging changes in their legal situation, and the turbulent relationship between the races at the time of its publication. The novel appeared within four years of two of the most dramatic events in civil rights history, both of which occurred in Alabama. The first event was the Montgomery bus boycott, an attempt by African-Americans to force the integration of buses in Montgomery, Alabama. Harper Lee's father had served in the legislature in this town, situated only 102 miles from her hometown of Monroeville, Alabama. The second event was the attempt by Autherine Lucy, an African-American woman, to integrate the University of Alabama, where Harper Lee had been a student six years earlier.

RACIAL SEGREGATION

Racial segregation had always been a way of life in the South. Blacks and whites went to separate schools, separate churches, and separate hospitals; they lived in separate neighborhoods and separate housing complexes. They were treated by separate doctors and separate dentists. They had separate waiting rooms in all offices and bus and train stations, separate rest rooms, and even separate water fountains. White people had access to restaurants, motels, hotels, parks, and other recreational facilities that black people were not allowed to use. It was rare for an African-American to be able to find a place to sit down and eat or sleep away from home. Facilities like the YMCA, YWCA, and public swimming pools were for whites only. African-Americans were usually restricted to one blacks-only car on the train. On buses, they sat in a few designated rows of seats at the back.

The practice in Montgomery, Alabama, was customary everywhere in the South: the African-American stepped into the bus at the front and bought her ticket. Then she stepped back out of the bus and walked around to the rear entrance, where she boarded and then sat in the back. If all the seats were taken in the back half of the bus and seats were available in the white sections near the front, the African-American passenger had to stand. If a white passenger boarded the bus and no seat was available, the African-American passenger nearest the front was expected to rise, give her seat to the white passenger, and stand. If she did not do this voluntarily, the bus driver ordered her to, calling out from his seat at the front. Furthermore, every African-American in that row of seats on both sides of the aisle was expected to get up and stand so that the white passenger would not be sitting in the same row as black passengers.

In movie houses, African-American patrons sat in segregated balconies only. Occasionally black servants in white households attended the weddings or funerals of the families for which they worked, but they always sat in the back of the church. African-Americans did not as a rule shop in clothing stores operated for whites, primarily because they were not allowed to try on clothing that they might expect to buy.

African-American women who worked as maids, cooks, or nurses in the houses of whites were usually provided toilet facilities separate from the rest of the household. When mealtime came, they were expected to eat in the kitchen or on the back porch. If the white employer preferred to take her lunch, say, in the kitchen, the African-American housekeeper ate at a separate table in the kitchen—or she ate standing up, or after the white family's dishes had been cleared away. For the most part, African-American men were not allowed to eat in the houses of whites at all. Food was handed to them out the back door in pans and jars kept for that specific purpose.

When a white person rode in an automobile with a black person, even if there were only two riders in the car, one sat in the front and the other in back.

No African-American was allowed to attend any state institution for higher learning in the South, nor any trade or vocational school run for the education of whites. In the South, very few private schools were integrated, most of them run by the Catholic Church. In the South, no athletic teams of African-Americans played teams made up of white Americans.

Racial discrimination in hiring was open and aboveboard, applications often being stamped "whites only." Jobs for African-Americans were largely restricted to those involving common labor or those servicing the black community only. The only professions open to African-Americans in any significant numbers were the ministry and teaching. In most southern cities and towns, African-Americans were only hired as hard laborers and garbage men; they were specifically barred from supervisory positions and jobs as firemen, policemen, and bus drivers. As one sees in *To Kill a Mockingbird*, the African-American characters are field hands, maids, and garbage collectors. Only two of them have ever been taught to read.

Qualifications laid down for voting were intended to—and effectively did—discourage African-Americans from voting. Because jury lists were derived from registered voters, African-Americans did not serve on juries, like the one called to try Tom Robinson.

In less concrete but possibly more humiliating matters of personal dignity and self-esteem, African-Americans suffered as well. Adults, no matter how old, were always and only addressed by their first names by white adults and children alike. African-Americans, no matter what their age, were expected to address any white person over the age of 12 as "Mr." or "Miss" or "Mrs.," a situation to which Harper Lee draws attention in *To Kill a Mockingbird*. No African-American woman in the South was ever called a "lady," and no African-American man was regarded as a "gentleman"—even though these were the hard and fast descriptors of respect in the South, denoting virtue and decency. In other ways,

African-Americans were regarded by white people as children and as scarcely civilized, an attitude openly expressed by the missionary society in *To Kill a Mockingbird*. Grown African-American males were invariably called "boys."

This was the world of the South in the 1930s, the world of Harper Lee's *To Kill a Mockingbird*.

World War II seems to have been a pivotal event in the lives of African-Americans, because it upset the status quo in race relations. African-Americans who served in the military (although it was still a racially segregated military) performed many jobs that white soldiers performed and, like white soldiers, fought, sustained wounds, and died for their country. Their military service allowed them to see the world outside the South, even outside the United States—a world in which segregation and discrimination were not nearly so pronounced as in the South. The return of African-American servicemen to their homes, after their experiences in a wider world, was a tremendous impetus for change in the status quo.

Most of the struggle in the late 1940s and early 1950s was over the right to vote and the right to serve on juries, an issue that is prominent in both the Scottsboro case and *To Kill a Mockingbird*. Arguments for an end to segregation were rarely and cautiously advanced. In the 1950s, however, agitation to lessen job discrimination grew, and many African-American leaders began to realize that equality of opportunity would never be achieved as long as segregation continued.

The year 1954 was a landmark in the history of civil rights for African-Americans in this country. On May 17, 1954, the United States Supreme Court ruled in *Brown vs. Board of Education of Topeka, Kansas*, that racial segregation of public schools was illegal because it was inherently unequal. The decision inspired more and more African-Americans and many white people to accelerate attacks on segregation. It also provoked those who wanted to maintain segregation to attempt to institute more restrictive laws and to resort, in some cases, to violence.

MONTGOMERY BUS BOYCOTT

One of the most important events in civil rights history began on December 1, 1955, in Montgomery, Alabama. The crisis was put in motion when an African-American seamstress named Rosa Parks, weary from a day of working as a tailor's assistant in a department store, boarded a city bus to go home and sat in an empty seat near the back of the white section of the bus. All the seats for whites having been taken, when a white man boarded the bus, all the African-Americans in the row where Rosa Parks had taken her seat were ordered to give up their seats and stand. All except Mrs. Parks did as they were told. When she refused, she was arrested. Within hours, an African-American boycott of all city buses was being planned.

On December 6, black citizens (who comprised the large majority of bus riders in the city) refused to ride the system's buses until a "first-come, first-served" policy was put into effect. It was the position of the African-American leadership of the city, and included a young Martin Luther King, Jr., that African-Americans would still sit at the back of the bus but that if all seats at the back were filled, they should be allowed to sit in any empty seat. Participation in the boycott was extremely high, and the bus system began to feel the intense economic pressure of losing 90 percent of its passengers. Rates were increased, and white people who were seen giving rides to black people were routinely ticketed. Violence broke out, crosses were burned, jobs were lost, but still the boycott continued.

On February 1, a class action suit was filed in U.S. District Court asking that state laws mandating segregation on public vehicles be judged unconstitutional, in effect calling for an end to segregation on city buses. On February 21 and 22, 1956, warrants were issued for the arrest of 115 leaders of the boycott, yet further peaceful rallies and demonstrations were held. Not until a year after the boycott began was a resolution reached.

AUTHERINE LUCY AND THE UNIVERSITY
OF ALABAMA

During winter of 1956, at the same time that the Montgomery bus boycott was taking place, another ground-breaking series of events in the civil rights struggle was unfolding at the University of Alabama in Tuscaloosa. Ever since 1953, African-American leaders had been trying to arrange for the admission of a black student to Alabama's major state university. Their choice had been between two young women, one of whom was Autherine Lucy. The second prospective student was denied admission at an early stage on the specious grounds of her marital situation. Finally, in the winter of 1956, Autherine Lucy was officially notified that she had been admitted to the university as a graduate student and could enroll for classes beginning in late January 1956.

When she arrived on campus to begin her classwork, her first day seemed to proceed without any ugly incident. However, she was informed that she could neither stay in the university dormitory nor eat in the university cafeteria. Her attorney informed the university that he would be taking legal measures to insure that his client would be afforded the privilege of staying in the dorm and eating in the cafeteria. After all, these rights were accorded to all other university students.

Before the issue could be resolved, on the Saturday after Autherine Lucy's first day in class, violence erupted on the university campus and in the streets of Tuscaloosa. General rioting, including cross burnings, damage to property, and attacks on black citizens, continued for three days. Later, investigators found that very few students had been among the perpetrators. The majority were employees of local manufacturing plants and high school boys from an outlying industrial community. The mob ravaged the campus day and night, on the third day pelting Autherine Lucy with eggs and shattering the window of the car in which she was riding, forcing her to take shelter in Birmingham. At this time, the university's Board of Trustees moved to bar her from campus in an attempt to maintain order. Throughout the spring there were court hearings and appeals for her readmission, and many students at the university argued for her return to campus.

As a response to (1) the Supreme Court ruling that made segregation illegal, and (2) two events in Montgomery and Tuscaloosa, activities of die-hard segregationists increased. These included the outright mob violence and terrorism of the Ku Klux Klan, the more underhanded intimidation by newly formed white supremacist organizations called the White Citizen councils, and the legal maneuvers of legislators.

As Harper Lee was writing *To Kill a Mockingbird* following the Montgomery bus boycott and the brief matriculation of Autherine

Lucy at the University of Alabama, other attempts were made at desegregation. In 1957, African-American leaders in Birmingham were unsuccessful in their attempt to integrate the Birmingham city schools. This was in the same period that federal troops were sent to Little Rock, Arkansas, to enforce court-ordered school integration there. In 1960, the year of publication of *To Kill a Mockingbird*, students in Greensboro, North Carolina, made an attempt to integrate the lunch counters of that city. In the next year, 1961, "Freedom Riders" (both African-Americans and whites) tested the law that made racial segregation on inter-state buses illegal. A *Life* magazine photographer, on his way home to New York City from Monroeville, Alabama—where he had taken pictures for a story on the newly famous author, Harper Lee—was inadvertently caught in the violence when the Freedom Riders were attacked in Montgomery. Before year's end, African-Americans who were committed to nonviolence were attacked with dogs and power hoses by local police while they were marching peacefully in Birmingham. The incident that stands out as the worst terrorism in Alabama as a response to the agitation for civil rights occurred on Sunday, September 15, 1963, when four little girls attending Sunday School were killed by a bomb blast in their church.

This was the atmosphere in which *To Kill a Mockingbird* was completed. Into this complex social and legal climate emerged the novel about a black man wrongfully accused of rape.

The documents presented in this chapter include the 1954 Supreme Court decision in *Brown vs. Board of Education* and articles from the *Birmingham News* and the *Tuscaloosa News* from the winter of 1956. They are presented chronologically to provide a sense of the density of race-related news at the time of the novel's writing and publication.

CHRONOLOGY OF EVENTS

May 17, 1954   United States Supreme Court rules in *Brown vs. Board of Education of Topeka, Kansas*, that racial segregation in the public schools is inherently unequal and, therefore, illegal.

December 1, 1955	Rosa Parks is arrested for refusing to give up her seat on a Montgomery city bus.
December 6, 1955	Boycott of Montgomery city buses begins officially.
January 1956	Autherine Lucy receives a letter granting her permission to enroll for classes at the University of Alabama in Tuscaloosa.
January 30, 1956	The home of Martin Luther King, Jr., is bombed in Montgomery. King is a leader in the boycott and its designated spokesman.
February 1, 1956	Motions are filed in U.S. District Court calling for an end to bus segregation.
February 4, 1956	Violence erupts on the campus of the University of Alabama and in the streets of Tuscaloosa. It continues for three days.
February 11, 1956	Autherine Lucy is forced to flee the campus; the university's Board of Trustees bars her from campus.
February 22, 1956	Warrants are issued for the arrest of 115 leaders of the Montgomery bus boycott.
February 29, 1956	Autherine Lucy is ordered by the courts to be re-admitted to the university, only to be expelled by the Board of Trustees.
November 13, 1956	United States Supreme Court decides in favor of Montgomery bus boycotters, by ruling bus segregation illegal.
December 21, 1956	African-Americans first board buses in Montgomery, Alabama, according to a first-come, first-served basis.
September 1957	Federal troops are sent to Little Rock, Arkansas, to enforce court-ordered desegregation of schools.
Fall 1960	Publication of *To Kill a Mockingbird*. In North Carolina, an attempt is made to integrate lunch counters in Greensboro.

1961	Freedom Riders attempt to test desegregation in the deep South. Violence necessitates the deployment of federal troops.
September 1961	An attempt is made to integrate the University of Mississippi. Lives are lost in the violence that ensues.
September 15, 1963	Four children die when the church they are attending is bombed in Birmingham.
May 9, 1992	Autherine Lucy receives her Masters degree in education from the University of Alabama in Tuscaloosa. A portrait of her is unveiled in Ferguson Center, the busiest building on campus.

DOCUMENTS

May 17, 1954. Excerpt from the United States Supreme Court decision in *Brown vs. Board of Education of Topeka, Kansas* (1954).

Tuesday, January 31, 1956. Three articles from the *Birmingham News*: "Boycott Leader's Home Is Blasted"; "UA Tells Negro She May Enroll"; "Fourth Cross Burned at Tuscaloosa."

Thursday, February 2, 1956. Two articles from the *Birmingham News*: "Negro Student Taking Room Denial to Court"; "Prominent Negro Home Blasted."

Saturday, February 4, 1956. Two articles from the *Birmingham News*: "Negro Says Well-Wishers High Spot of Day at UA"; "1000 in Demonstration at U of A, Witnesses Call It Negro Protest."

Tuesday, February 7, 1956. Three articles from the *Birmingham News*: "Negro Student Barred from UA Campus to Halt Rioting"; "Rioting at the Capstone"; "Negro Determined to Attend Classes."

Saturday, February 11, 1956. One article from the *Birmingham News*: "Carmichael Denies Conspiracy Charges."

Monday, February 20, 1956. One article from the *Tuscaloosa News*: "Return-Lucy Petitions Draw 500 Names at UA."

Wednesday, February 22, 1956. One article from the *Birmingham News*: "Jury Indicts 115 in Capitol Bus Boycott."

Friday, February 24, 1956. Two articles from the *Birmingham News*: "Mass Meeting Speakers Urge Continued Protest"; "U of A Pulls Down Curtain of Secrecy."

Saturday, February 25, 1956. One article from the *Birmingham News*: "UA Faculty Continues Probe of Disorders."

Friday, March 3, 1956. One article from the *Birmingham News*: "Alabama Not Alone in Tradition Fight."

BROWN VS. BOARD OF EDUCATION

The Supreme Court decision toward which the nation's racial turmoil had been building for years was *Brown vs. Board of Education*. The decision rocked Harper Lee's native state of Alabama just
when she was thinking about and beginning to write the story of
unequal justice in a small town there.

The Fourteenth Amendment to the Constitution of the United
States would have seemed to give all citizens of the nation equal
rights. But in 1896, a Supreme Court decision was handed down
in a case entitled *Plessy vs. Ferguson* that lent segregation the sanction of law. As long as public facilities for blacks and whites were
equal, the Court decided, they could be separate.

But inequalities, especially in public education, had long been a
fact of life; and African-American's' struggle for equality of public
facilities, especially public schools, had been escalating since World
War II. Battles were waged in many counties throughout the nation
where the separate schools for African-Americans often lacked
buses, desks, and books, and were housed in leaking, unheated
buildings.

For example, in 1949 in Clarendon County, South Carolina,
African-American citizens began what would become a series of
suits for equality of education for their children. The instigating
circumstance was the decision by the county's all-white board of
education to take away the one school bus for African-American
children in order to add it to the fleet of thirty school buses for
white children. The cases that were brought to court as a result of
agitation in Clarendon County were stepping stones to *Brown vs.
Board of Education*.

In June 1950, civil rights activists won victories for African-
Americans seeking equal treatment in several cases before the Supreme Court, but segregation itself was not seriously challenged.
Still, the question kept arising over whether separate facilities
would or could ever be equal. Limited desegregation had occurred
in postgraduate education around the country: in Texas, at the
University of Maryland, and in the schools at Louisiana State University, the University of Virginia, and the University of North Carolina.

By the time the case for equal education in Clarendon County, South Carolina, reached the federal court in Charleston, South Carolina, Thurgood Marshall, the prosecuting attorney, and his staff decided to attack segregation itself—as well as unequal school facilities—to argue that segregation was an evil that necessarily created inequalities. Separate, they would argue, could not be equal.

Although the court decided in favor of sustaining school segregation in South Carolina in June 1951, another trial challenging school segregation was already under way in Topeka, Kansas, where an African-American—Oliver Brown—lent his name to a suit charging that segregation in the Topeka schools constituted unequal treatment. The suit failed in district court, but it was the expressed legal opinion of the judges that segregation labeled black children as inferior and adversely affected their motivation to learn. One judge explained years later that the court believed a district court could not legally strike down *Plessy vs. Ferguson*, a Supreme Court decision. The highest court in the land, the one that had rendered the decision, would have to be the court to strike the early decision down.

Finally, on May 17, 1954, after hearing several cases that together came to be identified as *Brown vs. Board of Education*, the United States Supreme Court announced that by unanimous decision the "separate but equal" doctrine of *Plessy vs. Ferguson* would no longer be the law of the land.

The decision and the ensuing struggle in the South to negate or ignore it deeply affected all Americans. This history cannot be discounted as we turn to look at the creation of *To Kill a Mockingbird* and the impact it had on the nation.

FROM THE SUPREME COURT DECISIONS KNOWN AS *BROWN VS. BOARD OF EDUCATION OF TOPEKA, KANSAS*

347 U.S. 483

v.

BOARD OF EDUCATION OF TOPEKA,
SHAWNEE COUNTY, KAN., et al.

BRIGGS et al. v. ELLIOTT et al.

DAVIS, et al.

v.

COUNTY SCHOOL BOARD OF PRINCE
EDWARD COUNTY, VA., et al.
Nos. 1, 2, 347 U.S. 483
v.
BOARD OF EDUCATION OF TOPEKA,
SHAWNEE COUNTY, KAN., et al.

BRIGGS et al. v. ELLIOTT et al.
GEBHART et al., v. BELTON et al.
Nos. 1, 2, 4, 10.
Reargued Dec. 7, 8, 9, 1953
Decided May 17, 1954.

Mr. Chief Justice WARREN delivered the opinion of the Court.

These cases come to us from the States of Kansas, South Carolina, Virginia, and Delaware. They are premised on different facts and different local conditions, but a common legal question justifies their consideration together in this consolidated opinion.

In each of the cases, minors of the Negro race, through their legal representatives, seek the aid of the courts in obtaining admission to the public schools of their community on a nonsegregated basis. In each instance, they have been denied admission to schools attended by white children under laws requiring or permitting segregation according to race. This segregation was alleged to deprive the plaintiffs of the equal protection of the laws under the Fourteenth Amendment. In each of the cases other than the Delaware case, a three-judge federal district court denied relief to the plaintiffs on the so-called "separate but equal" doctrine announced by this Court in *Plessy v. Ferguson*, 163 U.S. 537, 16 S.Ct. 1138, 41 L.Ed. 256. Under that doctrine, equality of treatment is accorded when the races are provided substantially equal facilities, even though these facilities be separate. In the Delaware case, the Supreme Court of Delaware adhered to that doctrine, but ordered the plaintiffs be admitted to the white schools because of their superiority to the Negro schools.

The plaintiffs contend that segregated public schools are not "equal" and cannot be made "equal," and that hence they are deprived of the equal protection of the laws. Because of the obvious importance of the question presented, the Court took jurisdiction. Argument was heard in the 1952 Term, and reargument was heard this Term on certain questions propounded by the Court.

Reargument was largely devoted to the circumstances surrounding the adoption of the Fourteenth Amendment in 1868. It covered exhaustively consideration of the Amendment in Congress, ratification by the states, then existing practices in racial segregation, and the views of proponents and opponents of the Amendment. This discussion and our own investigation convince us that, although these sources cast some light, it is not enough to resolve the problem with which we are faced. At best, they are inconclusive. The most avid proponents of the post-War Amendments undoubtedly intended them to remove all legal distinctions among "all persons born or naturalized in the United States." Their opponents, just as certainly, were antagonistic to both the letter and the spirit of the Amendments and wished them to have the most limited effect. What others in Congress and the state legislatures had in mind cannot be determined with any degree of certainty.

An additional reason for the inconclusive nature of the Amendment's history, with respect to segregated schools, is the status of public education at that time. In the South, the movement toward free common schools, supported by general taxation, had not yet taken hold. Education of white children was largely in the hands of private groups. Education of Negroes was almost nonexistent, and practically all of the race were illiterate. In fact, any education of Negroes was forbidden by law in some states. Today, in contrast, many Negroes have achieved outstanding success in the arts and sciences as well as in the business and professional world. It is true that public school education at the time of the Amendment had advanced further in the North, but the effect of the Amendment on Northern States was generally ignored in the congressional debates. Even in the North, the conditions of public education did not approximate those existing today. The curriculum was unusually rudimentary; ungraded schools were common in rural areas; the school term was but three months a year in many states; and compulsory school attendance was virtually unknown. As a consequence, it is not surprising that there should be so little in the history of the Fourteenth Amendment relating to its intended effect on public education.

In the first cases in this Court construing the Fourteenth Amendment, decided shortly after its adoption, the Court interpreted it as proscribing all state-imposed discriminations against the Negro race. The doctrine of "separate but equal" did not make its appearance in this Court until 1896 in the case of *Plessy v. Ferguson*, involving not education but transportation. American courts have since labored with the doctrine for over half a century. In this Court, there have been six cases involving the "separate but equal" doctrine in the field of public education. In *Cumming v. Board of Education of Richmond County*, 175 U.S. 528, 20 S.Ct. 197, 44 L.Ed. 262, and *Gong Lum v. Rice*, 275 U.S. 78, 48 S.Ct. 912, 72 L.Ed. 172, the validity of the doctrine itself was not challenged. In more recent cases, all on the graduate school level, inequality was found in that specific benefits enjoyed by white students were denied to Negro students of the same educational qualifications. *State of Missouri ex rel. Gaines v. Canada*, 305 U.S. 337 59 S.Ct. 232, 83 L.Ed. 208; *Sipuel v. Board of Regents of University of Oklahoma*, 332 U.S. 631, 69 S.Ct. 299, 92 L.Ed. 247;

Sweatt v. Painter, 339 U.S. 629, 70 S.Ct. 848, 94 L.Ed. 1114; *McLaurin v. Oklahoma State Regents*, 339 U.S. 637, 70 S.Ct. 851, 94 L.Ed. 1149. In none of these cases was it necessary to re-examine the doctrine to grant relief to the Negro plaintiff. And in *Sweatt v. Painter*, the Court expressly reserved decision on the question whether *Plessy v. Ferguson* should be held inapplicable to public education.

In the instant cases, that question is directly presented. Here, unlike *Sweatt v. Painter*, there are findings below that the Negro and white schools involved have been equalized, or are being equalized, with respect to buildings, curricula, qualifications and salaries of teachers, and other "tangible" factors. Our decision, therefore, cannot turn on merely a comparison of these tangible factors in the Negro and white schools involved in each of the cases. We must look instead to the effect of segregation itself on public education.

In approaching this problem, we cannot turn the clock back to 1868 when the Amendment was adopted, or even to 1896 when *Plessy v. Ferguson* was written. We must consider public education in the light of its full development and its present place in American life throughout the Nation. Only in this way can it be determined if segregation in public schools deprives these plaintiffs of the equal protection of the laws.

Today, education is perhaps the most important function of state and local governments. Compulsory school attendance laws and the great expeditor for education both demonstrate our recognition of the importance of education to our democratic society. It is required in the performance of our most basic public responsibilities, even service in the armed forces. It is the very foundation of good citizenship. Today it is a principal instrument in awakening the child to cultural values, in preparing him for later professional training, and in helping him to adjust normally to his environment. In these days, it is doubtful that any child may reasonably be expected to succeed in life if he is denied the opportunity of an education. Such an opportunity, where the state has undertaken to provide it, is a right which must be made available to all on equal terms.

We come then to the question presented: Does segregation of children in public schools solely on the basis of race, even though the physical facilities and other "tangible" factors may be equal, deprive the children of the minority group of equal educational opportunities? We believe that it does.

In *Sweatt v. Painter* . . . in finding that a segregated law school for Negroes could not provide them equal educational opportunities, this Court relied in large part on "those qualities which are incapable of objective measurement but which make for greatness in a law school." In *McLaurin v. Oklahoma State Regents* . . . the Court, in requiring that a Negro admitted to a white graduate school be treated like all other students, again resorted to intangible considerations: "... his ability to study, to engage in discussions and exchange views with other students, and, in general, to learn his profession." Such considerations apply with added force to children in grade and high schools. To separate them from others of similar age and qualifications solely because of their race generates a feeling of inferiority as to their status in the community that may affect their hearts and minds in a way unlikely ever to be undone. The effect of this separation on their educational opportunities was well stated by a finding in the Kansas case by a court which nevertheless felt compelled to rule against the Negro plaintiffs:

> Segregation of white and colored children in public schools has a detrimental effect upon the colored children. The impact is greater when it has the sanction of the law; for the policy of separating the races is usually interpreted as denoting the inferiority of the Negro group. A sense of inferiority affects the motivation of a child to learn. Segregation with the sanction of law, therefore, has a tendency to [retard] the educational and mental development of Negro children and to deprive them of some of the benefits they would receive in a racial[ly] integrated school system

Whatever may have been the extent of psychological knowledge at the time of *Plessy v. Ferguson*, this finding is amply supported by modern authority. Any language in *Plessy v. Ferguson* contrary to this finding is rejected.

We conclude that in the field of public education the doctrine of "separate but equal" has no place. Separate educational facilities are inherently unequal. Therefore, we hold that the plaintiffs and others similarly situated for whom the actions have been brought are, by reason of the segregation complained of, deprived of the equal protection of the laws guaranteed by the Fourteenth Amendment. This disposition makes unnecessary any discussion whether such segregation also violates the Due Process Clause of the Fourteenth Amendment.

Because these are class actions, because of the wide applicability of the decision, and because of the great variety of local conditions, the formulation of decrees in these cases presents problems of considerable complexity. On reargument, the consideration of appropriate relief was necessarily subordinated to the primary question—the constitutionality of segregation in public education. We have now announced that such segregation is a denial of the equal protection of the laws. . . .

TUESDAY, JANUARY 31, 1956

Small skirmishes were continually being fought all over the country to end segregation, but little progress was in evidence. Despite the 1954 Supreme Court ruling, in the deep South the schools, as well as other facilities, remained decidedly segregated. The Montgomery, Alabama, bus boycott was a massive leap forward. The boycott had been in the national news ever since December 1, 1955, when Rosa Parks was arrested for refusing to give up her seat on a city bus. Just short of two months after the boycott had begun, it was proving to be an extremely effective way of placing economic pressure on the city: the majority of riders were African-Americans, and the loss of revenue as a result of the boycott was keenly felt. For almost a month, the boycott continued with only minor disturbances. Then, on Monday, January 30, violence erupted with the bombing of the house of one of the boycott's leaders, Dr. Martin Luther King, Jr., a young minister who had been persuaded to serve as the group's spokesman even though he was new to Montgomery. The first article excerpted here, from the Tuesday following the bombing, is a report on the incident.

The second article gives the news of possible integration at the University of Alabama in Tuscaloosa. After several years of legal negotiations and a court ruling in favor of integration by District Judge Hobart Grooms, the University of Alabama notified the African-American woman Autherine Lucy that she could enroll in classes in the School of Education.

Adverse reactions to the admittance of Autherine Lucy had already begun, however, as one of several crosses was burned in Tuscaloosa. This one was burned in the yard of an African-American high school. The story is related in the third article.

BOYCOTT LEADER'S HOME IS BLASTED

BY AL LANIER.
MONTGOMERY Ala., Jan. 31—AP—Standing in front of his bomb-damaged parsonage minutes after the blast, a young Negro minister issued a dramatic appeal last night for calmness despite mounting racial tension here over a prolonged bus boycott.

An explosion which police said was caused either by a hand grenade or dynamite shattered windows at the home of the Rev. M. L. King, the most outspoken leader in the boycott movement.

No one was injured in the blast about 9:15 P.M. (CST).

IT WAS THE FIRST act of violence reported since the initial week of the boycott, which began Dec. 5 in protest to the segregated seating arrangement required on buses by state and city laws. Shots were fired at a few buses during the first week, but they caused no injuries and little damage.

The Montgomery City Commission, whose members recently joined a pro-segregation organization after weeks of unsuccessful negotiations with boycott leaders, offered a reward of $500 for information leading to the arrest and conviction of those responsible for bombing King's home.

Rev. King's wife, their 7-week-old-girl and Mrs. Roscoe Williams, a neighbor, were in the home alone when they heard a thud "like a brick hitting the front porch."

WITH MRS. KING carrying the baby, the two women ducked into a back room just as the explosion shattered windows, ripped a hole in the porch and cracked a porch column.

Arriving home 15 minutes after the explosion from a mass meeting at a church, Rev. King first assured himself of his family's safety and then addressed about 300 Negroes who gathered outside his home.

He began by asking the group to be "peaceful."

"Don't get panicky," he appealed to the crowd. "Don't get your weapons. He who lives by the sword will perish by the sword. Remember that is what God said. . . . "

Then he added: "I want it to be known the length and breadth of this land that if I am stopped this movement (the boycott) will not stop."

AS HE SPOKE, Negroes in the crowd cried "Amen," and "God bless you, Brother King."

Then Police Commissioner Clyde Sellers told the throng: "I will do everything in my power to bring the guilty parties to prison."

Mayor W. A. Gayle, also on the scene, told the Negroes the "entire white community is for law and order and none of us condone or believe in these sort of acts."

Rev. King then addressed the group again: "Go home and don't worry. We are not hurt, and remember, if anything happens to me there will be others to take my place."

. . .

[Mayor Gayle stated] last week that the city commission was through "pussyfooting around" with boycotters. He said there would be no further efforts to reach a compromise because Negro leaders had time and again rejected "all reasonable proposals. . . . "

At the same time, it was revealed that all three members of the City

Commission had joined the Central Alabama Citizens Council, an organization pledged to fight racial integration by all legal means.

**The break-off of negotiations followed the rejection of boycott
leaders of the commission's final compromise plan—a suggestion
that 10 rows of seats in the back of buses be assigned to Negroes
only and an equal number of front seats be allowed to whites.**

With bus company approval the commission also offered to authorize
special buses for Negroes only at peak hours.

BUT BOYCOTT LEADERS, many of them ministers, refused to accept
less than their demand for seats on a "first come, first-served" basis. They
explained that Negroes would continue to sit from the rear toward the
front but would not be required to stand if any seats were vacant.

The protest movement was touched off by the $14 fine given Mrs. Rosa
Parks, a seamstress who refused to move to the rear of a bus.

The pro-white Central Alabama Citizens Council today offered a $500
reward for a solution to the bombing.

State Sen. Sam Engelhardt of nearby Macon County, president of the
council, announced the reward and said, "we deplore this type of demonstration and will do all in our power to preserve segregation in a lawful
manner."

"We must keep our present segregation laws by peaceful and legal
means," the statement said.

Birmingham News, Tuesday, January 31, 1956

UA TELLS NEGRO SHE MAY ENROLL

The University of Alabama today informed a Negro student she will be
permitted to enroll at the institution.

Autherine J. Lucy of 1110 Avenue I, Ensley, received a letter this morning from William F. Adams, dean of admissions of the University, advising
her she may now enroll at the University.

Dean Adams' letter read as follows:

"Dear Miss Lucy:

"In compliance with Judge Grooms [sic] injunctive order, you will be
accorded the right to enroll at the University of Alabama and to pursue
courses of study thereat.

Sincerely yours,

William F. Adams."

Another Birmingham Negro woman, Mrs. Polly Ann Hudson, also is
seeking admissions to the University.

. . .

The University dean's letter to Miss Lucy came after the U.S. Circuit

Court of Appeals in New Orleans upheld a U.S. District Court injunction here directing the University to admit the two Negro women to the school.

The District Court Injunction was issued by Judge Hobart Grooms, who ruled the case is a class action. That means that the court order applies not only to the two women in this case but to all others similarly situated.

Birmingham News, Tuesday, January 31, 1956.

FOURTH CROSS BURNED AT TUSCALOOSA

TUSCALOOSA, Ala., Jan. 31—A fourth cross was burned here last night, this one on the lawn of a Negro high school, and an anonymous caller told the *Tuscaloosa News* the Ku Klux Klan was doing the burning.

The cross last night was at Druid High School, across town from the University of Alabama where two Negro women students expect to register for second semester classes tomorrow or Thursday.

Police were called to the cross-burning scene, but the blaze was nearly finished when they arrived.

A man who would not give his name called the *Tuscaloosa News* to say that the latest cross burnings were the work of the Ku Klux Klan. The caller identified himself as the exalted cyclops, or presiding officer, of the Birmingham Klan.

Two crosses were burned Saturday night and one earlier last week. Another anonymous caller told the *News* after the first cross burning that it was "not a Klan cross."

Birmingham News, Tuesday, January 31, 1956.

THURSDAY, FEBRUARY 2, 1956

When Autherine Lucy arrived on the University of Alabama campus to begin attending classes, it was without the usual student's expectation that she could live in the dormitory and eat in the university cafeteria. Her attorney, Arthur D. Shores, claimed that when the university denied her housing and boarding privileges, it failed to comply with the letter of the law handed down by Judge Grooms. So another legal battle ensued as Autherine Lucy and her attorney filed suit in U.S. District Court.

Violence in Montgomery surrounding the boycott also escalated when the house of E. D. Nixon, the first person to plan the boycott and a prominent NAACP member, was bombed.

Another headlined story on February 2 not included here discussed a political move across the South called "interposition" or "nullification." This was the southern states' response to the desegregation ordered by the Supreme Court. State after southern state began declaring the desegregation order "null and void" because, they argued, states' rights superseded federal edicts. The governor of Alabama, Jim Folsom, although he had called interposition "hogwash," did not veto the bill declaring interposition when it came to his desk from the state legislature.

NEGRO STUDENT TAKING ROOM DENIAL TO COURT

The denial by University of Alabama authorities of dormitory room and board to Artherine [sic] J. Lucy will be carried today into U.S. District Court here.

Atty. Arthur D. Shores, who represents Miss Lucy, said last night "I'll be in court with some motion designed to implement the original order of the court."

THAT ORDER, an injunction against the University prohibiting the barring of any student on a purely racial basis, resulted yesterday in the breaking of the color line for the first time in the school's 124-year history.

While Artherine [sic] Lucy was allowed to register in the School of Education yesterday, she was denied permission to room in the girls' dormitory, and to take meals in the dining room.

School authorities acted under an order by the board of trustees which read:

"The AUTHORITIES of the University are instructed by the Board of Trustees to study each applicant for room and board with respect to welfare, safety and other effects upon the applicant and the other students and other applicants of the dormitory, and to deny such applicant as might endanger the safety or result in sociological disadvantages to the students.

"The authorities are instructed by the board of trustees that if Artherine [sic] Lucy is enrolled, and if she applies for a room in the dormitories and board, that these will be denied her."

THE FIRST WORD that the new student would not be allowed to live in the dormitory came after she had completed registration and went to the office of the dean of women for room assignment.

As she entered the office, newsman were handed typewritten, unsigned copies of the announcement by the board of trustees.

Miss Lucy remained in the dean's office about 15 minutes, and Emory O. Jackson, editor of the Negro newspaper, *Birmingham World*, went in briefly.

Jackson said the dean did not elaborate on the official statement, nor did she offer any suggestion about living arrangements.

The University has a rule of long standing that undergraduate girls entering the school must live on the campus unless they live near enough to return home nightly. . . .

Birmingham News, February 2, 1956.

PROMINENT NEGRO HOME BLASTED

. . . A blast which tore loose boards on a picket fence about 15 feet from the home of E. D. Nixon occurred at about 9:30 last night.

Nixon's wife and a neighbor's child were alone in the house at the time of the explosion. Neither was hurt. Nixon was out of town at the time.

Mrs. Nixon gave this account of the incident:

SHE AND THE neighbor's child whom she explained stays with her while Nixon is away, were watching the fights on television when she heard the noise.

She saw no one and did not know whether the explosive was thrown from an automobile or the sidewalk.

Nixon, who is active in many Negro organizations, was a recent candidate for a place on the Democratic Executive Committee for Montgomery County. He was defeated for that office.

Windows in the home of a Negro minister were shattered in the week's first blasting incident Monday night.

. . .

Earlier yesterday a suit was filed here aimed at ending segregated travel in Alabama. It accused Montgomery city officials with using "violence and intimidation" in an effort to make Negroes ride the boycotted buses.

THE MONTGOMERY City Commission and the police chief are charged in the suit with a "conspiracy to interfere with the civil and constitutional rights" of Negroes.

. . .

The class action attacking city and state bus segregation laws was filed in U.S. District Court in behalf of five Negro women, two of whom have been convicted within the past year of segregation law violations.

The complaint asks that the court declare unconstitutional those sections of the Alabama code and the city code which require separate facilities for whites and Negroes on public vehicles.

Birmingham News, February 2, 1956.

SATURDAY, FEBRUARY 4, 1956

A story by an Associated Press staff writer that appeared at the bottom of page one of the *Birmingham News* on February 4 seemed to be a hopeful sign for race relations at the University of Alabama. Many students seemed to have made Autherine Lucy feel welcome as she attended classes on the previous day.

But this happy picture is belied by a story on the top of page one: "1000 in Demonstration." The violent protest against the admission of Autherine Lucy, which began on Friday night after her classes were over, would continue for three more days. Subsequent investigations identified most of the mob as employees of a local factory and students from a nearby high school.

On the same page as the article presented here is an article about a speech by Senator Eastland of Mississippi, urging southern states to challenge integration laws. He is reported as saying, "There is at stake the preservation of the American system of government with its dual powers, which provide for individual liberty and freedom. There is further at stake the racial integrity, the culture, the creative genius, and the advanced civilization of the white race." Page two of the same edition contained an announcement of a massive White Citizens Council rally in Montgomery.

NEGRO SAYS WELL-WISHERS HIGH SPOT OF DAY AT UA

BY JACK STILLMAN, Associated Press staff writer

Autherine Lucy, only Negro ever to attend the University of Alabama, has discovered that she is not alone.

As she crossed the expansive campus at Tuscaloosa Friday, she was lonely, indeed. There was a University policeman not too far behind. As she went to each class, she found other policemen nearby.

But the policemen were not what broke the lonely spell. It was the students.

LEAVING THE University book store after her first two classes, a young co-ed approached her.

"I wish you luck here on the campus," the girl said.

Another broke in a few minutes later and said: "I hope everything turns out for you here."

For the 26-year-old Birmingham Negro, these remarks were the most outstanding events in her first day at the University.

For her, it was a moment of history. For no Negro had ever before attended the University of Alabama, once a training school for Confederate soldiers. A stronghold of white supremacy had fallen.

DESCRIBING HER FIRST few minutes in Geography I, taught by Asst. Professor Don Hays, Miss Lucy said: "I was just a little expectant. I was looking for whatever happened."

Other student [sic] said an unidentified freshman stalked from the class, exclaiming: "For two cents, I'd drop the course."

Miss Lucy does not recall such an incident. "They were nice. A few of them spoke to me. I was a late arrival, and sat by myself on the front row."

She said this was the only one of three classes she attended Friday where she sat alone. In other classes, she said the students made no distinction between themselves and her.

Since 1952 Miss Lucy had battled to the highest court in the land for the right to attend the University. She does not accept it entirely as a victory for her race, but rather as one of personal significance.

"Right now, everything is so mingled I really don't know what to think," she said.

"Of course, I have been in this fight for so long. It is for me a great personal victory."

AFTER HER 9 A.M. geography class, she went to a class in children's literature in the college of education library.

"I went to the book store to buy some supplies. It was there that some of the other students made me feel that I was a part of the University," she said.

"This was the most stimulating part of the day."

Although the University accepted her as a student, she is barred from the dormitories and dining halls. Her attorney has said he would seek a court order providing her these privileges.

"I will continue to commute from my home in Birmingham to Tuscaloosa," she said. Tuscaloosa is 55 miles from Birmingham.

Birmingham News, Saturday, February 4, 1956.

1000 IN DEMONSTRATION AT U OF A, WITNESSES CALL IT NEGRO PROTEST

TUSCALOOSA, Ala., Feb. 4—An estimated 1000 male University of Alabama students demonstrated from near midnight Friday until 2 A.M. Saturday against the first Negro student to enter the University.

Autherine Lucy registers for classes at the University of Alabama. Photo courtesy of *Birmingham News*.

Two students, one from Birmingham and the other from Decatur, related the story to the *News*.

. . .

According to the students the demonstration started about 11:15 P.M. Friday and ended in downtown Tuscaloosa about 2 A.M. Saturday.

They said the demonstration was definitely a protest against the University's first Negro student, Autherine Lucy, who began classes at the University Friday.

Police at first described the disturbance as a "panty raid" but later confirmed it was directed against the newly admitted Negro woman. There were no arrests.

. . .

University Policy Chief Allen O. Rayfield and Tuscaloosa Night Police Capt. J. P. West made the estimates of the number of students involved.

. . .

The demonstration began in the area of the men's dormitory and the crowd gathered around a cross which was burned in the center of University Ave. After the cross burned, firecrackers and smoke bombs were set off, the two students reported.

. . .

After that, the male students marched toward downtown Tuscaloosa singing "Dixie" and chanting, "Keep 'Bama White. To Hell with Autherine."

Tuscaloosa police made efforts to stop them as they marched into the city proper, the two students said, but no force was attempted.

Some of the students dropped out as the demonstrators went into the city, leaving about 500 in the group. These marched to the flagpole in the center of town, and a student whose name was not learned climbed to the pedestal of the flagpole foundation.

From the pedestal, the student shouted, "The governor will read about this tomorrow. We're in accord with the state of Mississippi and Gov. Talmadge of Georgia. We're setting the example for Auburn."

Then the speaker asked all the students to go home. The demonstration then broke up peacefully.

. . .

Fraternity leaders, student officers and faculty leaders milled through the crowd, speaking to small groups, asking them to break up the demonstration without effect.

Tuscaloosa police told the Associated Press that the demonstration "was nothing more than one of those panty raids."

ANOTHER SOURCE, NOT named, described the cross which burned as a small crude cross, which, in the opinion of some, was burned as a student prank as in the case of several others burned here recently.

Crowds protest in Tuscaloosa, Alabama, as Autherine Lucy tries to attend classes at the University of Alabama. Photo courtesy of *Birmingham News.*

A cross was burned in front of the residence of Dean of Admissions William Adams Thursday night. . . .

Birmingham News, Saturday, February 4, 1956.

TUESDAY, FEBRUARY 7, 1956

Rioting at the University of Alabama escalated as Autherine Lucy tried to attend classes. The first two of the following articles describes in some detail the extent to which the rioting had been allowed to go. Finally, with mobs cruising the campus at all hours of the day and night, and attempted attacks on Autherine Lucy by a mob throwing rocks, eggs, and fireworks, she left the campus, bravely believing that she was embarking on a temporary absence until passions cooled. Buried in the article about her determination to return are veiled references to a Board of Trustees action. It is clear, however, that the Board of Trustees had met officially and issued an edict barring her from classes. Interestingly, all the members of the Board of Trustees at the time (except one) were born during Reconstruction after the Civil War.

NEGRO STUDENT BARRED FROM UA CAMPUS
TO HALT RIOTING

. . . Dean of Men Louis Courson related events of the past several days since Miss Lucy had enrolled at the University.

Then Dr. Carmichael, his mien sorrowful and distressed, told the faculty in a voice barely audible that the present situation could bring disgrace to the school and injure its reputation throughout the nation.

The University president said the "issue" of the moment had affected the sentiments of the southern people for which he said he had the deepest respect.

But, he went on, the "matter has now developed something more basic, more fundamental . . . it involves the question of whether anarchy or law will rule here."

A member of the faculty asked if closing the school had been considered as a means of bringing the agonizing demonstrations on campus to a halt.

"Yes, that is one of the things being considered," Dr. Carmichael replied.

EARLIER, IN HIS TALK to the faculty, Dr. Carmichael had hinted that a continuation of violence on the campus might result in closing of the school.

He said arrangements had been worked out with the mayor of Tuscaloosa to set up a committee which would seek to prevent demonstrations in the future. He said this committee already had assured that more policemen and State Highway Patrolmen would be on the campus last night.

The faculty adopted a resolution expressing strong support of the University administration in its handling of the present situation. The resolution read:

"The faculty of the University of Alabama by unanimous vote expresses sincere regrets over the disturbances that have occurred during the last few days and goes on record as being in complete accord with the actions for the University administration.

"It pledges its complete support of the administration's efforts to preserve law, order and dignity on the University campus."

Later Dr. Carmichael issued a statement through the University News Bureau saying the school would close unless the demonstrations ceased.

University Ave. was blocked off from Hackberry Lane to 10th St. for several hours last night, and motorists had to detour around the south portion of the University.

THREE YOUNG men were arrested yesterday after an egg-throwing incident in front of the Union building on University Ave. during which an Episcopal minister, the Rev. Emmett Gribbin, who conducts the Canterbury chapel on the campus, was struck by an egg.

Those arrested were identified by Tuscaloosa police as Earl Watts, 2603 Sixth St.; Ed Watts, 4410 Vassire Dr., and Kenneth Thompson, whose address was not given, all of Tuscaloosa.

They were charged with disorderly conduct. They made $100 bond each last night, and their trials were set for 9 A.M. Monday in Tuscaloosa Police Court.

The Rev. Mr. Gribbin had pleaded with a group of youngsters not to throw eggs and tomatoes at passing cars and buses, along University Ave.

Trying to reason with the crowd on the corner of the University Union building, the minister said University officials were trying to do everything possible to settle the present difficulty "in a legal and reasonable way." He implored them not to do things which "will embarrass the University and impede the efforts of those trying to bring a peaceful solution to this problem."

"What about that black Supreme Court?" one member of the crowd, with a crew-cut, shouted.

"What about that black governor?" another member of the crowd yelled at the minister. "Why don't you do something about him?"

"Are you in favor of integration?" another member of the group asked the minister.

"No, I'm not," the Rev. Mr. Gribbin replied.

"And as for the governor, there are ways of doing things legally if you have a grievance."

"Don't bother the people going by . . . they haven't done a thing."

The clergyman's words went unheeded.

A BUS AT THAT moment sped by and was spattered with eggs and tomatoes. Shouts went up from the crowd, obviously directed at Negro passengers on the bus.

A few moments later the Rev. Mr. Gribbin was splattered with an egg. The arrest of the three young men followed.

During the day-long demonstration, Miss Lucy was struck by eggs and her clothing "all spattered" although only a handful out of the crowd—which numbered as high as about 3000—ever saw her.

Dean of Women Sarah Healy's car—in which Asst. to the President Jeff Bennett drove her from her first to second period class—was the target of a barrage of eggs 75 of the demonstrators had ready in overcoat pockets.

Most of these were not students. Tuscaloosa Police Chief W. C. Tompkins identified some of them as employees of a Tuscaloosa rubber plant.

They had assembled across the Quadrangle at Smith Hall some 30 minutes before Miss Lucy was due for her 9 A.M. geography class. With her collar turned up, she walked in the front door unnoticed.

The crowd stayed, however. When she left at 10 A.M., she used a back door, which demonstrators were watching, and darted to Dean Healy's waiting car.

Lying on the floorboards, she rode across the campus—leaving behind the dozen officers who had guarded Smith Hall—as the demonstrators foot-raced to the rear of Graves Hall, where she had her next class.

SHE APPARENTLY got into the building before the crowd realized she was nearby, but stones bounced off the car as it sped away. Several windows were smashed.

JUST BEFORE the Rev. Mr. Gribbin was hit with an egg, a staff reporter for the *New York Times*, Peter Kihss, was struck with two eggs while he talked with H. N. Guinn, owner of a Birmingham finance company.

Guinn took Miss Lucy to the University yesterday morning.

The crowd rocked his Cadillac while it was parked on University Ave., near the Union building.

Kihss was talking with Guinn, trying to find out who the latter was, when he (Kihss) was hit by the eggs and jostled by the crowd. Three policemen were only a few steps away at the time, but took no action.

GUINN APPARENTLY was serving as a decoy at the time, to keep the crowd of demonstrators away from the classroom from which Miss Lucy finally emerged to run to a Highway Patrol car for safety.

Another egg-splattering victim of the day was Tuscaloosa Police Chief W. C. Tompkins.

He was spattered with an egg at the flagpole at downtown Tuscaloosa while attempting to turn back the long line of marchers about 10:45 P.M.

An unidentified person was led away by police at the time but apparently was not arrested.

THE REPORT was unconfirmed but an instructor was quoted later as saying he saw two men with rifles, one of them with long-range sights, seated in a car near the Graves Hall parking lot.

When she did not make an immediate exit at the end of the class, word was passed for all to be back today. "We'll get her with rifles," some laughed.

For more than three hours, the crowd kept Graves Hall surrounded, peering frequently into most ground floor windows looking for Miss Lucy and yelling "Kill her," "Hang her" and "Hey Hey Ho Ho, Where'd that Nigger Go."

During this demonstration, a husky Tuscaloosan who identified himself as a Ku Klux Klansman whispered to one of the student organizers that KKK units from Mississippi and Georgia would be at his disposal on Wednesday.

The man said the groups would be "ready to take care of her" in Tuscaloosa or in Birmingham.

WHILE ADMITTING Miss Lucy as a student, the trustees barred her from the women's dormitory and cafeteria. She had been commuting daily from Birmingham.

Miss Lucy and Mrs. Polly Ann Hudson, both Birmingham Negroes, filed suit against the University after being denied enrollment as students.

The women were upheld in U.S. District Court and later in Appellate Court last year following a three-year legal struggle.

While admitting Miss Lucy the board directed school authorities to reject Mrs. Hudson on the basis of her "conduct and marital record." Mrs. Hudson is seeking a divorce.

Mrs. Hudson called the action a "smear" and asked U.S. Dist. Judge Hobart Grooms to hold Dean of Admissions William Adams in contempt of the federal court order. A hearing was set for Thursday on his motion before Judge Grooms in Birmingham.

The National Association for the Advancement of Colored People called on Gov. James E. Folsom to "use full powers" of his office to maintain order at the University and protect Miss Lucy.

Folsom said at Montgomery that he does not plan to call on the National Guard to quell the disorders, but the state "stands ready at all times to meet with any situation properly."

HOWEVER, a National Guard company of 175 men was alerted last night to aid police if necessary.

The men drill regularly on Monday nights and were standing by at Ft. Brandon Armory but were not called on during last night's demonstration.

A special student convocation scheduled for 12:15 P.M. today was called off after the trustees suspended Miss Lucy.

Birmingham News, Tuesday, February 7, 1956.

RIOTING AT THE CAPSTONE

Dr. Carmichael called a special press conference for 3 P.M. He said he would be available then to answer questions for "an abundance of newsmen" on the all-quiet campus.

The scene in the desegregation battle will shift to Birmingham on Thursday when Dean of Admissions William F. Adams must explain to Federal Court why a second Negro applicant, Mrs. Polly Hudson, was not also admitted to the University.

A 'Bama student had earlier forecast a "student protest" in Birmingham at this time.

There were no incidents reported during the morning, with most students remaining indoors, except to go to classes, because of the nippy weather.

In an "open letter" in the *Crimson-White*, student weekly newspaper, Student President Walter Flowers of Tuscaloosa appealed for sensible actions in the situation.

MIMEOGRAPHED petitions were distributed on the campus which read, in part:

"We request that the leaders of the riots . . . and the leaders of such incidents as may take place in the future—those who begin and lead inflammatory chants of dubious taste, those who shout obscene or profane slogans, and especially those who make speeches inciting students to further misconduct, provide leadership for the mob, set time and place for future demonstrations which disrupt schedules and functioning of this university—be apprehended and subjected to severe disciplinary action, up to and including permanent expulsion from this institution, for the safety of the University itself and the well-being of the student body."

FLOWERS HIMSELF led a small group of students holding back the demonstrators last night at the president's mansion. "It's a shame—there are only about 5 percent of them students," one of those in Flowers' group said.

A large portion of the crowd were local high school age youths.

An unidentified boy, who previously had climbed onto the flagpole pedestal in downtown Tuscaloosa to cheer on the crowd, worked his way to the balcony of the mansion where Mrs. Carmichael stood, but she and the University Marshall persuaded him to leave.

Birmingham News, Tuesday, February 7, 1956.

NEGRO DETERMINED TO ATTEND CLASSES

Autherine Lucy, forced to abandon her classes at the University of Alabama yesterday, said today she will spend the next few nights in an undisclosed rural area pending her re-admittance to the University.

Miss Lucy, first Negro student to be admitted to the University, talked to newsmen in the office of her attorney, Arthur Shores, just after he issued an ultimatum to University officials giving them 48 hours to re-admit Miss Lucy.

The 26-year-old Birmingham resident, who attended her second class yesterday with her dress splotched with egg, said the rioting at the Capstone changed her mind about attending her third class.

"With the crowd like it was, I thought it would have been better not to attend classes yesterday afternoon," she said.

She had been advised by University officials not to continue in class and later they asked her to remain away from the University temporarily.

Dressed in a bright pink sweater-suit, Miss Lucy said today she does not believe the majority of the demonstrators yesterday were students. "It was a minority group plus outsiders," she said.

She said she was hit by one egg; on the left shoulder, as she entered a building for her second class. She said nothing unusual went on during the class, and the lecture on children's literature was "very interesting."

Miss Lucy declared she wants to teach in Alabama, and "it would be better for me to finish college in Alabama."

A graduate of Miles College in Birmingham, Miss Lucy taught two years in Carthage, Miss., while her application to the University was pending. Later she worked as a secretary for an insurance company here.

The youngest of nine children, she was born at Shiloh in Marengo County. She alone of her three sisters and five brothers has a college degree.

She closed an interview with reporters by asserting, "I still am determined to attend the University of Alabama."

Word of the action late last night by the board of trustees barring her from the school brought both jubilation and dismay to various members of the student body.

"Well, we won," said one student active in the demonstrations.

"It took her four years and the Supreme Court to get her in and it took us only four days to get rid of her," he said. Actually, Miss Lucy applied only three years ago.

Birmingham News, Tuesday, February 7, 1956.

SATURDAY, FEBRUARY 11, 1956

With Autherine Lucy barred from campus, rioting ceased at the University of Alabama. By this time her lawyer had filed a contempt of court action against the university for barring her from classes. He argued publicly that the mob action and subsequent expulsion of his client were conspiratorial.

Articles other than the one given here include one on the front page of the February 11 *Birmingham News*. It was the report of an appearance by Mississippi Senator James O. Eastland, who had plans to legally maintain segregation. The article mentions that members of the Ku Klux Klan and the White Citizens Council attended the meeting.

Another article on February 11 reports a verbal attack on the KKK and the White Citizens Councils at a major labor union meeting in Miami, Florida. On page two is the report of an effort in Alabama to strengthen segregation in public facilities. The State of Alabama's Public Service Commission, in direct defiance of the national Interstate Commerce Commission, ordered the display of "White" and "Negro" signs on bus station waiting rooms in Alabama.

CARMICHAEL DENIES CONSPIRACY CHARGES

By AL STANTON, News staff writer.

TUSCALOOSA, Ala., Feb. 11—University of Alabama students strolled quietly to their classes Saturday, displaying no outward signs of being the object of an international furor which boiled up after rioting earlier this week.

Peaceful since the last outburst Monday, the students listened calmly as University President Dr. O. C. Carmichael declared Friday that the school is determined to maintain law and order.

THE CENTER of controversy, co-ed Autherine J. Lucy, first Negro student in the 125-year history of the Capstone, is to remain away from the campus at least until Feb. 29, when her petition for contempt action against University officials will be heard.

The 26-year-old Birmingham secretary alleges that the University employed a "cunning stratagem" when it excluded her from the campus at the height of rioting over her admission as a student.

DEMONSTRATIONS CEASED after University officials barred her from attending any more classes. The first outburst erupted late last Saturday, continuing over the weekend.

Birmingham News, Saturday, February 11, 1956.

MONDAY, FEBRUARY 20, 1956

With Autherine Lucy still barred from campus, a number of students petitioned for her return. One interesting aspect of this story involves the backgrounds of some of the students who circulated the petition. Note especially the various pressures that were reportedly brought to bear on students who circulated the petition.

RETURN-LUCY PETITIONS DRAW 500 NAMES AT UA

By BILL McEACHERN, News staff writer.

A petition, started by a small group of students and faculty members at the University last Tuesday asking for the return of Autherine J. Lucy to the campus, had approximately 500 signatures last night, a spokesman for the group said.

Albert Horn, law school senior and honor student whose grandfather fought with the Confederate Army, said the group had been somewhat disappointed that the petition had not met with greater success.

"But," he added, "we are gratified for the response we have received. We feel that considering the tension of the situation, the fact that anyone would sign is promising."

The petition calls for University officials to return Miss Lucy to the campus on their own initiative, as a step toward re-establishing the University's reputation as a law-abiding campus.

Getting signers has not been easy, however. The *News* learned last night that several of the petitioners had received verbal abuse while seeking support. Two University co-eds reported three petitions stolen last Thursday.

Jane Burgess, a senior from Montgomery, said two petitions with 40 names were stolen from her room last Thursday.

Another senior, Martha Soggin, Lawrence, Tenn., whose grandfather helped organize the Ku Klux Klan in Pulaski, Tenn., also had a petition with 20 names on it stolen from her room.

Both girls said they have been subject to "social ostracism" by some of the girls in their dormitory. According to Miss Burgess, one boy, who claimed he had relatives on the Board of Trustees, threatened her with "economic pressure" if she didn't stop circulating the petition.

Her father is a contractor in Montgomery, and Miss Burgess said she thought the boy was referring the "economic pressure" to him.

According to Horn, many persons who agreed with the statements of the petition would not sign because of fear of showing disrespect for Dr. Carmichael, University president. "The petition is in no way meant to be disrespectful to Dr. Carmichael," he said.

The group feels, according to Horn, that many people in the state disapprove of their action. "We feel, however, that it is important for someone to advocate the cause of reasonableness and moderation," he said.

Horn also says that a state senator has expressed disapproval of the group's stand because it runs counter to the recent Interposition Resolution. "Do we understand," said Horn, "that the senator means it is improper for citizens of a democracy to peacefully petition to obtain an objective once the legislative decree is made known?"

The *News* also learned yesterday that an organization is being formed on the campus to help prevent student participation in demonstrations if and when Autherine Lucy returns to the campus.

Tuscaloosa News, Monday, February 20, 1956.

WEDNESDAY, FEBRUARY 22, 1956

On February 22, 1956, with Autherine Lucy barred from campus and her case back in court, attention was fixed on the bus boycott in Montgomery. One hundred fifteen people involved with the boycott were charged with breaking an obscure antilabor union law, making it a crime to organize a boycott.

One of the legal peculiarities at the time involved the spirit of the federal decisions being in conflict with the state segregation laws. Note the similarities in (1) the reasoning of University of Alabama administrators listed in an earlier article for barring Autherine Lucy, and (2) the reasoning apparent here in the verdict handed down by the grand jury in the bus boycott case. Look particularly at what each gives as the causes of violence.

JURY INDICTS 115 IN CAPITOL BUS BOYCOTT

MONTGOMERY, Ala., Feb. 22—(AP)—Montgomery law officers today were to begin rounding up 115 persons indicted for taking active parts in the Negro bus boycott.

Late yesterday a Grand Jury returned 11 true bills against 115 defendants charged with participating in the prolonged protest to racial segregation.

Two Negro Baptist ministers were among the first defendants arrested today for taking part in the mass racial boycott against city buses.

They were the Rev. Ralph D. Abernathy and the Rev. R. James Glasco.

ALONG WITH THE indictments, the Grand Jury report warned that "violence is inevitable" in Montgomery "if we continue on our present course of race relations."

The indictments were returned under a seldom-used state statute which makes conspiracy to boycott a misdemeanor punishable by up to six months in prison and a $1000 fine.

The Grand Jury's written report said the attack on Alabama's segregation laws by the National Assn. for the Advancement of Colored People is primarily responsible for current racial unrest in Montgomery.

"Distrust, dislike and hatred are being taught in a community which for more than a generation has enjoyed exemplary race relations," the jurors declared.

THE GRAND JURY was composed of 17 white men and one Negro, E. T. Sinclair, head waiter at the Montgomery Country Club. There was no way of telling how Sinclair voted on the indictments.

The indictments were returned less than 24 hours after Negro leaders flatly rejected a compromise plan for settling the 11-week-old bus boycott. The proposal had been approved by the Montgomery City Bus Lines and the City Commission.

The great majority of Negroes who once patronized the buses have refused to ride them since Mrs. Rosa Parks, a seamstress, was fined $14 Dec. 5 for not complying with state and city laws requiring separate facilities for whites and Negroes on public carriers.

Mrs. Parks declined to move to the back of a bus when requested to by the driver.

IN A PARTIAL report issued last Friday, a Negro attorney, Fred D. Gray, was indicted for unlawful practice. He is accused of filing an anti-segregation suit in U.S. District Court without the consent of one of the five Negro women whose names appeared on the complaint.

In the final report, the grand jurors said the Montgomery Improvement Assn., led by several Negro ministers, had kept the boycott going by contributing some $18,000.

"Small incidents have been magnified out of their true importance and ugly rumors are being spread among both races," the jurors charged.

The report declared segregation in schools, public transportation and elsewhere would be maintained in Alabama "within these laws which reflect our ways of life."

Thurgood Marshall, chief legal counsel for the NAAPC, has indicated the organization will help defend those indicted for boycotting the buses.

The law under which the indictments were returned was aimed primarily at labor disputes when approved by the Legislature in 1921. It prohibits boycotting by two or more people without "a just or legal excuse."

Birmingham News, Wednesday, February 22, 1956.

FRIDAY, FEBRUARY 24, 1956

On February 23, a massive rally was held by the African-American community in Montgomery, Alabama, to plan a day of "walking and praying." On February 24, three days after the arrest of over one hundred bus boycotters in that city, thousands of African-American citizens in Montgomery protested the arrests and continuation of bus segregation by *walking* wherever they went that day instead of *riding* in private cars or taxis. Also on February 24, Autherine Lucy's case in Tuscaloosa continued to receive front-page coverage. Included here is the story about a university investigation into participants in the mob violence.

As you read the first article presented here, note that the civil rights movement is shown to have been largely born and sustained in the African-American church. In the second article, note Albert Horn's remarks, which imply that the worst element involved in the Lucy case—that is, the lawless rioters—were the ones who controlled the outcome of events.

MASS MEETING SPEAKERS URGE CONTINUED PROTEST

By HUGH SPARROW, News staff writer.
MONTGOMERY, Ala., Feb. 24—Thousands of Montgomery Negroes went afoot to their jobs and to other pursuits today in a demonstration calculated to prove they are standing behind almost 100 Negroes indicted in connection with an 80-day-old bus boycott.

It was the beginning of a day designed by their leaders as "a day of prayer and pilgrimage"—prayer for the indicted and pilgrimage to the courthouse.

The Negroes at a jam-packed church rally last night had been called upon not to use their cars, taxi cabs or buses during the 24-hour day, but to go afoot when they had to leave their homes.

. . .

One speaker in particular, the Rev. Martin Luther King, pastor of the Dexter Avenue Baptist Church, declared in fact that the arrest of a Negro woman for violating the seating law in a Montgomery city bus was largely an incident in connection with the present mass demonstrations.

He said, in fact, that "our trouble is much, much deeper than that."

He appeared to be declaring in but scantily concealed terms that the

Negroes of Montgomery are conducting a boycott not so much against the bus company as against the Negro's lot in general.

. . .

Three songs were sung again and again during the three hours of last night's meeting. They included "Let Jesus Lead You All the Way," "That Old Time Religion" and "Onward Christian Soldiers."

. . .

The Rev. Abernathy declared, in part as follows in formally opening the meeting . . . ."We have kept the struggle Christian and have violated no law. We will continue our protest and none of our actions will be illegal."

. . .

Declared the Rev. King:

"It is true that one of our finest citizens was arrested and fined. That arrest, which occurred on a bus, was just the precipitating cause because the real cause of our struggle is much, much deeper down.

"Our people have been deeply humiliated. Many have been trampled upon. Yet we seek no resort to violence. Our weapon is meekness.

"We realize then and we realize now that with its weaknesses, one of America's glories is the right to justice. Our Constitution talks about life, liberty and the pursuit of happiness. It is a gift, bestowed on all God's children. We started out with the assurance that we were right. And we feel we are still in the right.

"We said in the beginning we did not want the issues distorted. There were some who would not take too great interest in the campaign. But I have said before and I say now that this is a conflict between justice and injustice. It is a fight for the Negro's right to justice, fair play and decency."

. . .

"We started out in the beginning and we are still striving to keep it a movement of passive resistance. It is much more than an economic move. It is a spiritual conflict."

Birmingham News, Friday, February 24, 1956.

U OF A PULLS DOWN CURTAIN OF SECRECY

By AL STANTON, News staff writer.

TUSCALOOSA, Ala., Feb. 24—An intensive investigation, involving questioning of possibly scores of students and faculty members, was under way today at the University of Alabama in connection with the Autherine J. Lucy case.

The inquiry was cloaked in utmost secrecy. University officials refused to discuss any action the school is taking toward placing responsibility for demonstrations which drove the school's first Negro student from the campus Feb. 6.

An unidentified number of students are reported to have been summoned to appear before an investigating committee appointed by University President O. C. Carmichael. Dr. Carmichael told students and faculty members in convocation last week the committee would be named to investigate the demonstrations thoroughly.

. . .

Also yesterday, a petition urging the University to allow Miss Lucy to return to classes was delivered to the office of Dr. Carmichael.

A member of the group which circulated the petition said slightly more than 2000 persons had signed the request, although previously the group said some 500 signatures had been obtained.

. . .

The petition taken to Dr. Carmichael was accompanied by a letter signed by Albert Horn, Tuscaloosa law senior, "for the sponsoring group."

Horn wrote: "We feel that if the only reason for her exclusion was a safety matter and not a further test of the ability to bar Negroes under another guise, then in good faith you should re-admit her."

Despite the stolen petitions, Horn said, the signers represent "the beliefs of a considerably larger number of persons than have actually signed and at any rate our number is larger than the number who actively demonstrated against Miss Lucy's being in school."

Birmingham News, Friday, February 24, 1956.

SATURDAY, FEBRUARY 25, 1956

Four articles on race relations appeared in the *Birmingham News* on February 25: (1) an account of accelerated activity as part of the boycott; (2) an account of Governor Folsom's appointment of a biracial group to study racial problems; (3) a summary of current responses to racial integration issues across the nation; and (4) a report of the continuing investigation of violence at the University in early February, an excerpt of which is presented here.

One article reports that Adam Clayton Powell, a U.S. representative from New York, called for a nationwide work stoppage on the part of African-Americans in support of the Montgomery, Alabama, bus boycott. Another political figure, Governor Jim Folsom, who had always been perceived as a progressive governor in Alabama, had been called to task for failing to take active steps to stop the violence in Tuscaloosa, for failing to make sure that the University followed the court order, and for failing to take more positive measures to fight interposition. The second article from February 25 reports that Folsom was appointing a biracial council to study problems between the races.

There was also news of civil rights activity in Baltimore, where African-Americans were lending their support to the Montgomery boycott; in New Orleans, where Catholic leaders were resisting the state's plan to force desegregation in Catholic schools; in Tampa, where an African-American had hit a bus driver who interfered with him when he sat in a white section of a bus; and in a small town where the White Citizens Council was making plans to retain control of the town in which African-Americans outnumbered whites.

The article presented here indicates the continuing investigation of disorders at the University of Alabama.

In all these stories it becomes increasingly apparent that just as citizens use their own versions of Christianity to support either integration or segregation, they find that the legal system itself sometimes supports segregation and sometimes integration.

UA FACULTY CONTINUES PROBE OF DISORDERS

TUSCALOOSA, Ala., Feb. 25—(AP)—A faculty investigation into the disorders that drove a Negro student from the University of Alabama campus continued Saturday.

The highly secret investigation is headed by Prof. Hubert Emery Mate, assistant to the dean of arts and sciences and a former naval intelligence officer. . . .

Birmingham News, Saturday, February 25, 1956.

FRIDAY, MARCH 3, 1956

An article by an Associated Press writer on March 3 gives a summary of activities throughout the recent months when the civil rights issue was so embattled in Harper Lee's home state of Alabama. Note the description of the legislative and legal actions used by both pro- and anti-segregationists.

ALABAMA NOT ALONE IN TRADITION FIGHT

By BEN RICE, Associated Press writer.

Here in the self-styled "Heart of Dixie," the time of racial crisis is now.

In the past three months subsurface racial tensions repeatedly have broken through the thin crust of apparent peace.

Alabama, of course, is not alone in battle against any shift in the South's racial patterns.

There have been riots at the University of Alabama at Tuscaloosa over the admission of a Negro woman.

In Montgomery, a Negro boycott of the public transportation system is now in its 14th week, though 99 of the movement's leaders were indicted under the old labor law.

COUNCILS GROW

THE NUMBER of strongly pro-segregation Citizens Councils has grown from about 40 to more than 60 in Alabama in the last eight weeks.

The Alabama Legislature now has pending before it a resolution to seek federal funds to transplant Negroes from the state to places outside the region where they are "needed or wanted."

This resolution is indicative of the developing pressures in the Legislature for action against those who would disturb the traditional segregation laws and customs.

The Legislature already has approved a resolution declaring the U.S. Supreme Court decision of May 17, 1954, to be "Null, void and of no effect."

In that now-historic decision the Supreme Court held that segregation in public schools on the basis of race was unconstitutional.

VOICES OF MODERATION

THE VOICES of moderation in Alabama have been few. Gov. James E. Folsom called the nullification "hogwash."

. . .

Another Alabama House resolution asked for an investigation to determine whether the National Assn. for the Advancement of Colored People
is Communist controlled.

The NAACP has been the guiding hand behind the fight against segregation throughout the South.

The running fight to maintain racial barriers was not confined to Alabama during the past week.

MISSISSIPPI PROTESTS

FOR EXAMPLE, in neighboring Mississippi last week the state Legislature adopted an "interposition" resolution protesting the ruling.

The Mississippi legislators also called on Congress to submit a constitutional amendment to the 48 states, declaring that the states alone had
the right to regulate public schools.

In addition, the Mississippi House set up a $5000 library fund to ac-
quire books on the races of mankind. The floor debate specified they
should be books indicating the white man's superiority over the Negro.

Before the measure was sent to the Senate, however, Rep. Walter Phil-
lips from Hancock County warned that such a measure would border on
"thought control." He said Hitler had advocated a master race "and paid
the consequences."

Virginia is another state which has protested the Court decision in a
legislative resolution. Georgia has declared it to be "null, void and of no
effect."

ASKS NAACP BAN

In LOUISIANA the state brought action to dissolve the National Assn.
for the Advancement of Colored People under an old anti–Ku Klux Klan
law.

The suit, filed by Atty. General Fed [sic] LeBlanc, asked the state court's
[sic] to ban NAACP meetings.

The law under which the suit was filed requires every type of organization to file annual membership lists with the secretary of state. This,
the state charged, the NAACP has failed to do for the past three years.

LeBlanc's action came after the NAACP twice had shaken Louisiana in
a matter of days. Actions brought by the NAACP ended with a federal
court ruling knocking out the state's 1954 laws designed to get around
the U.S. Supreme Court ban on school segregation.

The NAACP followed this decision with a suit last Wednesday asking
for integration in New Orleans public schools.

THE TWO ALABAMA CASES which have attracted worldwide attention, of course, are those of Autherine J. Lucy, a 26-year-old Negro secretary and ex-school teacher, and the Montgomery bus boycott.

For 29 months Miss Lucy sought the right to enroll at the University of Alabama through the federal courts. She won and became the first Negro ever admitted to the 125-year-old school.

It was a short-lived victory. Riots broke out on the school's campus. The board of trustees suspended the Negro woman. She sought a contempt of court motion against 13 trustees and University officials. Federal Dist. Judge H. Hobart Grooms rejected the contempt motion, but ordered Miss Lucy returned to school by Monday.

LUCY EXPELLED

WITHIN HOURS after that court action, the trustees met again in secret session and ordered Miss Lucy "permanently expelled" on disciplinary grounds.

The tensions developed over the Lucy case were indicated by the fact that three University officials and an Alabama Circuit Court judge testified in federal court she might be killed if she tried to return to the campus.

Further complicating the Lucy case was a damage suit by three construction workers and a truck driver for $4 million.

The four civil damage suits, filed in a State Circuit Court Friday, stemmed directly from charges made by Miss Lucy and her attorneys in the federal court action which were dropped on the day of the hearing, last Wednesday.

MONTGOMERY BOYCOTT

THE MONTGOMERY BOYCOTT began immediately after the arrest Dec. 1 of a Negro woman for refusing to take a seat in the section of a bus reserved for Negroes upon orders of a bus driver.

Car pools were organized with donations from church funds. Negro taxi drivers set up regular routes. Many Negroes walked to work.

FINALLY, a Grand Jury in Montgomery, a town of 125,000 with a Negro population of 46,000 indicted 99 boycott leaders for violation of a 1921 law making it illegal for two or more people to conspire to hinder a business operation. Originally, the law was adopted as the result of a labor union dispute. Hearings on these boycott cases will be held March 19.

Birmingham News, Friday, March 3, 1956.

CONCLUSION

Autherine Lucy now has an honored place in the history of the University of Alabama. But she was not ever to have a place in a University of Alabama classroom. Shortly after she was barred from campus indefinitely as a result of campus violence, her attorney accused the university Board of Trustees and administration of being in collusion with the Ku Klux Klan and the White Citizens Councils to permanently keep her from the campus. He argued that they had allowed the violence to proceed by failing to close the campus expediently and effectively, and by refusing to consider alternatives other than barring her from campus as a way of avoiding further outbreaks of violence. The courts ruled that the University was in violation of the law in refusing to allow her re-admission, so the Board of Trustees did re-admit her; but hours later they expelled her for slandering them by claiming they were in a conspiracy with the Klan. At a time when students as a group had few civil rights, including no rights to free speech, it was within the board's power to do this. Autherine Lucy would eventually receive her graduate education outside Alabama, and the University of Alabama would go through other tumultuous days before African-Americans began regularly attending classes there.

If we consider the matriculation of Autherine Lucy and the Montgomery boycott as two of the many battles in the war for equal rights, we would have to say that the battle waged by Autherine Lucy was lost. The other battle, the boycott, was more immediately successful. The case, which had been filed with the courts shortly after the boycott began, eventually came before a three-judge panel in federal court. Two of the judges found the bus segregation ordinance to be unconstitutional, and the third judge insisted that the case be heard by a higher court. The case eventually reached the Supreme Court, which decided in December 1956 that the segregation ordinance was unconstitutional.

STUDY QUESTIONS

1. Contrast the actions perpetrated at the King home on January 30 with the message he used in responding.

2. Dr. King's statement on February 23 seems to imbue the bus boycott with greater meaning than a simple action to allow African-Americans to sit down on Montgomery city buses. Examine this and explain why King needs to do this now.

3. Consider the Montgomery City Commission's compromise plan on the bus boycott. Was it acceptable? Why or why not?

4. Would the plan demanded by the boycotters allow segregation to continue? Explain.

5. History has not dealt kindly with the University of Alabama Board of Trustees and President Carmichael's handling of the Autherine Lucy case. Were you in Carmichael's shoes, what would you have done differently?

6. What grounds do you suppose Autherine Lucy's attorney had for accusing the University of conspiracy? From what you have read, was the charge justified?

7. On the matter of race, numerous splits are evident among educators, students, politicians, and laborers. Discuss what has unfolded about these splits in the stories you have read here.

TOPICS FOR WRITTEN OR ORAL EXPLORATION

1. On January 31, the opposing sides in the integration battle are shown appealing to Christian doctrine and using Christian emblems in opposite ways. Discuss.

2. Write an essay, using supplementary materials, on the place of the United States Supreme court in effecting civil rights changes during the 1950s.

3. The Montgomery bus boycott was ultimately a successful experiment in applying steady economic pressure in an effective way. Write or conduct a debate on the hypothetical advantages and disadvantages of this form of social protest.

4. As a student leader, construct an argument for the University of Alabama Board of Trustees asking that Autherine Lucy be admitted to the dormitory facilities.

5. In his speech reported on February 4, Senator Eastland said that the "higher civilization" of the South depends on continued segregation

of the races. Using your own definition and scale for determining levels of civilization, how would you rank those who oppose integration based on their actions as reported here?

6. How might Atticus Finch define a "higher civilization"?

7. Stage a debate between someone representing President Carmichael after Autherine Lucy has been barred from campus and someone representing Autherine Lucy herself.

8. Much in *To Kill a Mockingbird* is a tension between "past" and "present." Discuss this statement. Then scrutinize the newspaper articles for the same tension. Write an essay on the subject.

9. Write an essay on how you might have reacted to the Board of Trustees' dictate to bar Lucy, had you been president of the University. Then write about your reactions if you had been a student.

10. Assuming that you are sympathetic with Autherine Lucy, would it have been morally acceptable *not* to get involved with the rioters? Or was it incumbent on a morally correct person to become active on her behalf? From what we know of Atticus Finch, what would have been his course of action? Remember, he did not volunteer to defend Tom. Explore this issue in the form of a paper or a debate.

11. Throughout *To Kill a Mockingbird* reason and lawfulness are represented as admirable qualities over passion and lawlessness. The same forces seem to be opposed in the winter of 1956 when Harper Lee was beginning to formulate her novel. In an essay, discuss the opposition of these forces in terms of both the novel and the history of 1956.

12. In the civil rights struggle, emblems and rituals have a central place in the strategy of both segregationists and integrationists. In an essay, examine such things as the U.S. Constitution, the Confederate flag, the cross, prayer vigils, burning of documents, and so on.

13. Having read *To Kill a Mockingbird*, and now having learned something of the social and political atmosphere—particularly throughout the South—at the time of its publication, why do you suppose many people (both Northerners and Southerners) who experienced that era claim that it has made a difference in their lives? Write an essay on the subject.

SUGGESTED READINGS

Some of the most interesting sources of history of the period are firsthand accounts from the people who were there. These include:

Durr, Virginia Foster. *Outside the Magic Circle: The Autobiography of*

Virginia Foster Durr, ed. Hollinger F. Barnard. Tuscaloosa: University of Alabama Press, 1985.

Hampton, Henry, and Steve Fayer. *Voices of Freedom: An Oral History of the Civil Rights Movement from the 1950s through the 1980s.* New York: Bantam Books, 1990.

Raines, Howell. *My Soul Is Rested.* New York: G. P. Putnam's Sons, 1977.

The most comprehensive histories of integration in education, including the history of Autherine Lucy, are the following two works:

Clark, Culpepper. *The School House Door.* Oxford: Oxford University Press, 1993.

Kluger, Richard. *Simple Justice.* New York: Alfred A. Knopf, 1976.

A more general history of civil rights written at the time of the agitation would include the following works:

Clarke, Jacqueline Johnson. *These Rights They Seek.* Washington, DC: Public Affairs Press, 1962.

Gaston, A. G. *Green Power.* Birmingham, Alabama: Birmingham Publishing, 1968. (This book gives the perspective of a highly successful African-American businessman.)

Manchester, William. *The Glory and the Dream.* New York: Bantam Books, 1975.

An excellent background on politics in Alabama, leading up to the civil rights action of the 1950s, is the following:

Barnard, William, *Dixiecrats and Democrats: Alabama Politics, 1942– 1950.* Tuscaloosa: University of Alabama Press, 1974.

Several biographies of those involved in civil rights action in Alabama just before and just after the publication of *To Kill a Mockingbird* include:

Bass, Jack. *Taming the Storm: The Life and Times of Judge Johnson and the South's Fight over Civil Rights.* Garden City, NJ: Doubleday, 1993.

Bennett, Lerone, *What Manner of Man—Martin Luther King, Jr.* Chicago: Johnson Publishing, 1968.

Bishop, Jim. *The Days of Martin Luther King, Jr.* New York: G. P. Putnam's Sons, 1971.

Davis, Michael D. *Thurgood Marshall: Warrior at the Bar, Rebel on the Bench.* New York: Carol Publishing Group, 1992.

Goldman, Roger L. *Thurgood Marshall: Justice for All.* New York: Carroll and Graf, 1992.

Kennedy, Robert, Jr. *Judge Frank M. Johnson.* New York: G. P. Putnam's Sons, 1978.

Lewis, David L. *King: A Critical Biography.* New York: Praeger Publishers, 1970.

Sikora, Frank. *The Judge.* Montgomery, AL: Black Belt Press, 1992.

Studies that focus on particular participants in the civil rights struggle, both those working to end segregation and those working to preserve it, include the following:

Chalmers, David. *Hooded Americans*. Garden City, NJ: Doubleday, 1965.

Cleghorn, Reese. *Radicalism: Southern Style*. Atlanta: Southern Regional Council, 1968.

Frazier, Franklin. *The Negro Church in America*. New York: Shocken Books, 1974.

McMillen, Neil R. *The Citizens' Council*. Urbana: University of Illinois Press, 1971.

An excellent source of information comprises the newspaper and magazine accounts of the events of the time. Consult the newspaper "morgue" for issues during the 1950s and 1960s.

View the television series made for the Public Broadcasting System, "Eyes on the Prize," 1992.

4

Realities and Stereotypes

At the time of its publication, reviewers of *To Kill a Mockingbird* praised the novel for its accurate portrayal of life in a small southern town in the 1930s—the everyday lives of ordinary and extraordinary people, the social and racial discord and harmony, the economic hardship, and the cultural richness. Through a realistic delineation of her characters, Harper Lee succeeded in challenging certain stereotypes, especially the image of the upper-class Southerner, the African-American, the community outsider, and the ideal "little lady."

A central development in the novel's theme is the children's growing ability to see members of their community in a new light: Boo Radley, Dolphus Raymond, the African-Americans, and Mayella Ewell. Atticus's constant challenge to stereotype is undoubtedly his most persistent message. Don't view people as types, he says; instead, walk in their shoes and see them as individuals. Even the mob is made up of individuals. Readers of the novel relive the same awakening that Atticus encourages in his children, as they are challenged to discard old, stock notions about certain character "types."

The challenge to stereotype in the novel is extraordinarily com-

plex in its effect on its readers. The northern reader found old
notions about the South and Southeners replaced by Lee's realistic
portraits. But southern readers also had their eyes opened. Many
of them for the first time saw the African-Americans who had been
living in their midst all their lives as complex characters. In a South
where for generations integration meant chaos and disloyalty,
many Southerners encountered in Atticus a kind of man who, although living and working among them for generations, had remained unseen and unknown.

Furthermore, Lee's other characters were at variance with what
her readers—north and south—had been taught and conditioned
to accept: for example, the proper little girl, the prospective southern belle.

The documents included in this chapter provide the reader with
materials that can be used to evaluate portraits in the novel. They
include both (1) the testimonies of people like those in the novel
who are frequently "typed," and (2) the culture's stereotype of
these groups. As background for studying the character of Atticus
Finch and other Southerners in the novel and the extent to which
the novel provides the reader with a corrective lens for thinking
about Southerners, two portraits are included: one a fictional view
of the upper-class Southerner during the Civil War, and the other
a letter in which an elderly Southerner during the civil rights era
reveals his own exaggerated and outmoded notions that tended to
lead to stereotypes.

The "belle" is also an important member of the white upper
class in the South. In *To Kill a Mockingbird*, one of the chief conflicts is over Scout's failure to show much promise as a proper
little southern lady. She plays rough boys' games with boys; she
curses and fights like a boy; and she dresses in overalls. The documents in this chapter help to evaluate the gender struggle in the
novel. There is an interview with three daughters of prominent
southern parents who provide some sense of what it was really
like to be a little girl in the deep South when Scout was growing
up. Also included is a statement of the expectations that "typed"
little girls. The image of the perfect little girl emerges in *The Charm
of Fine Manners*, written by Helen Starrett.

The class of poor whites is both portrayed and discussed at
length in *To Kill a Mockingbird*. At least one historian writing on
poor whites in Alabama has concluded that *To Kill a Mockingbird*

perpetuates the stereotype of the poor white. To evaluate these characterizations, documents in the section on the poor white Southerner include a memoir by the son of a sharecropper. The section also incorporates literary portraits of poor whites, including an assessment by Shields McIlwaine and excerpts from fiction written by two Southerners, Erskine Caldwell and William Faulkner. These two, more than any other writers, gave the world a portrait of the poor white Southerner. The section also offers historical views of poor whites by Dan Carter, a historian, and Virginia Durr, a civil rights activist.

The African-American was frequently typed, as an excerpt from a scholarly article tells us, as either a lovable, shuffling child or as the incarnation of evil. *To Kill a Mockingbird* showed to both Northerner and Southerner more rounded, realistic African-American characters. The primary document in this section is an interview with an African-American woman who grew up in Alabama during the 1920s and 1930s. In addition to the scholarly excerpt on African-American types, and in contrast to the portraits in *To Kill a Mockingbird*, a typical portrayal of an African-American by a prolific and popular novelist in the early part of the twentieth century is included here.

One of the two central themes of *To Kill a Mockingbird* concerns how the children come to discard the community-held stereotype of the eccentric, Boo Radley: that is, how they begin to see him sympathetically as another human being rather than as the witch or monster they at first thought him to be. To help the reader understand the pattern of demonization of the eccentric by communities like Maycomb, this section offers an excerpt from a sociological discussion of the outsider and a historical commentary on those all-American eccentrics, the Salem witches.

In summary, the documents presented in this chapter reveal the realities as well as the stereotypes of people and life in America. We can use them to study, evaluate, and appreciate Harper Lee's portrayal of Southern life.

THE SOUTHERN GENTLEMAN

Perhaps no two single things shaped the world's view of the southern gentleman as much as Margaret Mitchell's novel, *Gone With the Wind* (and the movie based on the novel), and the image of upper-class Southerners that frequently emerged in the press during the civil rights era.

The first was an image of a gallant, romantic gentleman who, like the landed gentry of England, loved high adventure, had impeccable manners, and was addicted to gracious living, tradition, fox hunting, gambling, and mint juleps. He was a man of action with an exaggerated sense of chivalry, not far removed from his forebears who fought duels at the slightest insult. This view of the southern gentleman had been formulated by many post–Civil War novelists, including Thomas Dixon and Thomas Nelson Page, excerpts from whose works are presented here.

The second view of the upper-class Southerner, almost a self-parody, is the less flattering one that emerged during the 1950s. This is an image of a man who resists change and progress with all his might, who holds fiercely to values and ideals that are dead and gone. His blindness and backwardness, as he clings to the "good ole days," make him a figure of ridicule. This image is conveyed in a letter written by a former state senator from Alabama who objects to the integration of the university.

Harper Lee's portrayal of Atticus Finch exploded those stereotypes. Atticus is not a man of fox-hunting type action. He is not a dyed-in-the-wool Confederate who reveres the past above all else. And he is certainly not a bigot who would fight to the death to keep the South segregated.

FROM THOMAS NELSON PAGE, *GORDON KEITH*
(New York: Charles Scribner's Sons, 1903)

Gordon Keith was the son of a gentleman. And this fact, like the cat the honest miller left to his youngest son, was his only patrimony. As in that case also, it stood to the possessor in the place of a good many other things. It helped him over many rough places. He carried it with him as a devoted Romanist wears a sacred scapulary next to the heart.

His father, General McDowell Keith of "Elphinstone," was a gentleman of the old kind, a type so old-fashioned that it is hardly accepted these days as having existed. He knew the Past and lived in it; the Present he did not understand, and the Future he did not know. In his latter days, when his son was growing up, after war had swept like a vast inundation over the land, burying almost everything it had not borne away, General Keith still survived, unchanged, unmoved, unmarred, an antique memorial of the life of which he was a relic. His one standard was that of a gentleman.

. . .

Gordon, like some older men, hoped for war with all his soul. . . . He would be Julius Caesar or Alexander the Great at least.

. . .

One day Gordon was sent for to come home. When he came downstairs next morning his father was standing in the drawing-room, dressed in full uniform, though it was not near as showy as Gordon had expected it to be, or as dozens of uniforms the boy had seen the day before about the railway stations on his journey home, gorgeous with gold lace. He was conscious, however, that some change had taken place, and a resemblance to the man-in-armor in the picture over the library mantel suddenly struck the boy. There was the high look, the same light in the eyes, the same gravity about the mouth; and when his father, after taking leave of the servants, rode away in his gray uniform, on his bay horse "Chevalier," with his sword by his side, to join his men at the county-seat, and let Gordon accompany him for the first few miles, the boy felt as though he had suddenly been transported to a world of which he had read, and were riding behind a knight of old. Ah! if there were only a few Roundheads formed at the big-gate, how they would scatter them!

About the third year of the war, Mr. Keith, now a brigadier-general, having been so badly wounded that it was supposed he could never again be fit for service in the field, was sent abroad by his government to represent it in England in a semi-confidential, semi-diplomatic position.

. . .

Thus, it was that, while Gordon Keith was still a boy of about twelve or thirteen, instead of being on the old plantation rimmed by the great woods, where his life had hitherto been spent, except during the brief period when he had been at Dr. Grammer's school, he found himself one summer in a little watering-place on the shores of an English lake . . . surrounded by gardens and parks.

. . .

[Young Gordon rows out on the lake with another boy.] In the bow was a flag, and Gordon was staring at it, when it came to him with a rush that it was a "Yankee" flag. He was conscious for half a moment that he took some pride in the superiority of the oarsman over the boys in the other boats. His next thought was that he had a little Confederate flag in his trunk. He had brought it from home among his other treasures. He would show his colors and not let the Yankee boys have all of the honors.

MR. BONNER'S RESPONSE TO INTEGRATION

EX-ALUMNI HEAD ASKS MOVE TO "KEEP UA WHITE"

A former state senator and past president of the University of Alabama Alumni Association today proposed petitions urging the Capstone's Board of Trustees to bar Autherine Lucy from the campus permanently and "keep the University a white man's university."

The petition was proposed by J. M. Bonner of Wilcox County in a letter to the *News*.

Mr. Bonner's letter, addressed to "All friends of the University of Alabama," is quoted in full.

"Our University today faces the greatest crisis of its 125 year existence. It must answer NOW the most momentous question of its history: Will it continue to live, a great White Man's University?

"My answer is: It must live. It shall not die.

"But it cannot so live without a fight. I call now on every Southern White man to join in this fight.

"I proudly take my stand with those students who resisted, and who will continue to resist the admission of a negress named Lucy. Their enthusiasm may have carried them a wee bit far; but their actions were prompted by loyalty to and love for our University, and the conviction that ours is a White Man's College. I do not find it in my heart to condemn them.

"I take up the cudgel and gladly join with them in the fight they have fearlessly begun.

"To this end, I suggest to them, and to friends of the University in every part of Alabama, that petitions be circulated on the Campus, in Tuscaloosa, and in various parts of the state, worded substantially as follows:

" 'We, the undersigned students, former students and friends of the University of Alabama, hereby petition the Board of Trustees of the University of Alabama as follows:

" '1. That the admission of Lucy to our University never be tolerated.

" '2. That no student of the University be punished for any action heretofore taken in resisting her admission.

" '3. That every member of the faculty, from TOP to bottom, be given to understand that the University of Alabama will continue to be operated for WHITE students only.'

'Respectfully submitted.' "

"As a former student, and as a former President of the U. of A. Alumni Society, I would like for my name to be the first name signed to that petition."

Tuscaloosa News, Tuesday, February 21, 1956.

THE IDEAL LITTLE GIRL

In *To Kill a Mockingbird* Scout is constantly bedeviled by members of her family and the community for not being a proper little girl. Her chief tormenter is her Aunt Alexandra, who has argued heatedly with Atticus over Scout's dress as well as her tomboyish behavior. But she is also castigated by Mrs. Dubose and even by her brother, Jem, who at first scorns her for acting like a girl and later for not acting like a girl.

The two documents in this section suggest that there was, indeed, an ideal little girl, but that as often as not, it was an ideal that was rarely translated into reality.

The ideal little girl, not only in the 1930s South but in the 1950s South and other places when *To Kill a Mockingbird* came out, was an image of pure femininity. Great stress was placed on her training to be a lady—in the South, one might even say, her training to be a "belle." As the interview that opens this section suggests, such training meant careful attention to dress and language, as well as manners and play. The ideal little girl never wore jeans or slacks. She wore skirts and dresses, often with appropriate hat and gloves. Such attire seems foreign to our Scout. As recently as the late 1950s, little girls in boarding schools and somewhat older girls in colleges were subject to disciplinary action if they wore jeans outside their dormitories, except on picnics or outings for which they received special permission to vary their attire. This was true of many parts of the country, but especially in the South.

It was expected of little girls that they be soft-spoken, demure, and refined in their speech. No proper little girl would dream of using coarse language or improper grammar, as Scout often does. Older women gave private lessons in elocution—how to speak properly.

Femininity even guided the play of ideal little girls. Requirements in demure posture meant that she did not participate in rough physical play. Instead, hers was girl's play: she had baby dolls and bridal dolls; she played house; she had tea parties and dress-up parties. She learned to dance demurely in her white gloves and long dress, and to arrange flowers at the junior garden club.

The documents presented here include an interview with three women from prominent southern families and an excerpt from a book of manners directed especially to little girls. Helen Starrett refers to the speech of little girls, their companions, their reading habits, and their quiet comportment—all of which have direct reference to Scout!

The section indicates, as does *To Kill a Mockingbird*, that the expectations and realities of little girls were often two entirely different things.

INTERVIEW: A PERSPECTIVE ON THE 1930s

Like Scout in *To Kill a Mockingbird*, the three women in this interview grew up in the deep South of the 1930s. All three were members of what could be described as prominent southern families. Mary Anne Norton Meredith's mother was a large landholder, her father a successful merchant in Tuscaloosa, Alabama. Camille Maxwell Elebash, also of Tuscaloosa, was reared by a grandmother and mother, both of whom were landowners, and by a father who was a professor of engineering and a pioneering aeronautical engineer at the University of Alabama, a businessman, and World War I navy pilot. Cecil Butler Williams grew up in Jacksonville, Florida. Her father, a practicing attorney, was one of Florida's most prominent state senators. The three women discuss many of the issues raised in *To Kill a Mockingbird*: how they defined a "good family" (the topic that was so dear to Aunt Alexandra's heart and so baffling to Scout and Jem); the poor whites in Alabama and Florida (very like the Cunninghams in *To Kill a Mockingbird*); their relationship with African-Americans; and the expectations and realities of those who would grow up to be proper southern "belles." The interview took place in 1993.

Interviewer: In historical and fictional stories about the South in the time
    in which we're interested—the 1930s—one hears frequent reference
    to what were called "good families" or "old families." What is your
    understanding of that term?

Mary Ann: Gee, I never really thought about it.

Camille: Nobody had very much money. In the Depression years. If your
    father had a job, you had a good family.

Mary Ann: Yes, if your father was gainfully employed.

Cecil: Yes, if your mother stayed at home and everyone had a maid or two.

Camille: And a cook.

Mary Ann: And a nurse *and* a yard man.

Cecil: But that did not mean you were a wealthy family.

Mary Ann: Good families were all good church members.

Camille: We considered ourselves a "good" family, but we were land poor. We owned a great deal of land but it wasn't bringing in any income in the thirties. There was just no cash flow. On the other hand, there was not much tax on land.

Mary Ann: That describes our situation as well at that time.

Cecil: I guess I was a city child. Land ownership didn't enter the picture much, though I suppose ours was considered a good family. My father was a lawyer. We had some land in the county that my father went hunting on. But I never thought about land. It just wasn't part of my life.

Camille: I think "good" families were differentiated by a certain accent, too.

Mary Ann: It was the way people talked.

Camille: It was the pronunciation of "I." Didn't say "niiice" and "whii-ite," dragging the "I" sound out.

Cecil: I think yours and Mary Ann's background are different from mine, growing up in a larger town.

Interviewer: In that your father was a lawyer, perhaps your experience is much closer to Scout's in *To Kill a Mockingbird*.

Cecil: That's true. Yes, I think so. My father was of the old school. Integrity was the byword. They looked down very much on those who cheated and stole, especially from the poor. And I remember him talking about one well-off family who did just that and became very prominent later. It was an attitude. You never cheated anybody, and especially anybody lesser than you. And you never said a cross word or spoke badly to someone who couldn't speak back to you.

Camille: Yes, I think "good" families had a strong sense of responsibility to the people whose lives they could affect. I know when the Depression came and my family's bank failed, their main concern was to see that other people got their money back even if they lost out themselves.

Mary Ann: This is interesting, I think. I had a grandfather who was on the board of that bank. And they all felt the responsibility to pay back that money.

Cecil: I think among people like ours in the South, there was the idea of *noblesse oblige*.

Interviewer: Did you know people in the 1930s who were like the really poor whites of Old Sarum in Harper Lee's novel?

Cecil: Oh yes, in north Florida where I grew up there were extremely poor people out in the country. My aunt and uncle had an orange grove which we visited occasionally, and there were some really, really poor people in part of the woods. They were so thin and so pale. You never see anybody that looks like that any more.

Camille: In my case, I had a lot of contact with both black and white sharecroppers. My grandmother lost all her cash money when the family bank crashed. She had a place where she farmed. The one north of here had white sharecroppers and the one south of town had black sharecroppers. And the white sharecroppers were just as pitiful as the black sharecroppers.

Mary Ann: Oh yes, they were terribly malnourished and diseased. Many had hookworms.

Camille: And what a friend of mine used to call turnip green arms—extremely long, very thin arms.

Cecil: Have you ever read Marjorie Kinnan Rawlings's stuff about Florida? The poor whites I knew were just like that. But they were very proud. They wouldn't take handouts. And I'd also see these same poor people from the hill when we visited up in North Carolina. They were just as bad off and fiercely proud.

Camille: There was a difference between genteel poverty and dirt road poverty.

Interviewer: By which you mean a kind of *Tobacco Road* type of poverty?

Mary Ann: Camille and I went to school with people like that in the thirties.

Camille: When I went to Stafford School, I always took two lunches, one for myself and one for someone else.

Mary Ann: Of course. They were HUNGRY.

Camille: This is what's funny. I still feel a moral responsibility to those sharecroppers who worked for my grandmother. They still call me when they need me. I still send checks to them.

Cecil: Yes, because your family was responsible.

Camille: Not many years ago we got a job for one woman whose family farmed on our land. She couldn't read. And do you know that her great-grandfather was headmaster of an academy before the Civil War?

Cecil: Good gracious!

Mary Ann: Then she came from educated people.

Camille: Yet by the thirties her family was sharecropping on my grand-mother's farm.

Interviewer: What happened? Was it the war?

Camille: My husband always said it was the Civil War. They just went back to the dirt. And they had fought in the Civil War even though they never owned slaves. Many of these men died in the Civil War. There were lots of widows left with absolutely nothing except a houseful of children to rear. And do you know it was the blacks who took care of these poor white families. They cut wood for them and shared with them and looked in on them. I had experience with another class of poor white people in the thirties in that we lived so close to the railroad station. I remember seeing the bums coming up the street from the railroad station. And I remember seeing our backyard filled with these poor men, eating what my grandmother had given them. They never asked for a handout. They would only ask for work—if they could chop wood, for example.

Mary Ann: Our mothers belonged to an organization called the Junior Welfare, a precursor of the Junior League. They helped take care of children whose mothers had to work and helped get food and clothes to the needy. And there was such need.

Cecil: Yes, I always thought it was funny that my mother went to help take care of children whose mothers had to work and left her own child to be taken care of by a nurse!

Interviewer: Were you allowed to play with the children of poor whites?

Cecil: I don't remember any prohibitions about it. It just didn't come up.

Camille: I brought a lot of little children home with me from Stafford School, but I was never allowed to go to their homes. Maybe I was never invited. I did spend one night with the little girl whose father was on the police force. I remember his collection of weapons, in-cluding some bloody knives, put a scare into me.

Mary Ann: I don't remember playing with what you call poor white chil-dren. I do remember two little girls who lived in town whose family had a very tough time. They lived just behind my father's business and I think they resented my better situation. They threatened to beat me up. I was terrified of them.

Interviewer: As members of prominent families, what was your relationship with black people when you were little girls of Scout Finch's age?

Mary Ann: Your first experience with a black person was with your nurse. And the black people that took care of these little white children instilled in us the most wonderful traits. They stood for everything that was honest and Christian.

Cecil: I remember complaining to my nurse Lessie that a little boy had hit me. And she said, "Well, go hit him back." Part of your character came from your nurses.

Mary Ann: And they were really religious.

Cecil: And you minded your nurse.

Camille: I remember the black sharecroppers who worked for my grandmother. She supported them all year long and paid all their medical bills. Then when the farming was done, they split the proceeds. She got half and they got half, with the understanding that their medical costs would come out of their half. And they trusted her implicitly. I loved to go down to Hale County on settlin'-up day when they were paid because I could spend the day with the little black children. And that's where I learned to love to dance.

Mary Ann: We were incredibly attached to the black people we knew well.

Cecil: But I read somewhere in a book on the South that while the white people felt very attached to the black people back then, the black people didn't feel that way about us.

Mary Ann: Still, we were taught to be respectful of black people.

Camille: Heavens yes. I would have had my mouth washed out with soap so fast if I had ever referred to a black person with any word other than colored!

Cecil: My parents always used the respectful term "colored."

Camille: My main playmates for most of my childhood were black boys. Black families lived on the street behind us and my two best friends came over from there to play football with me. Their names were Josie and Jessie and they were part black, part Indian, and part white. We played football every day. We thought their mother was mean as a snake and we never knew who their father was. Jessie is now president of a black college and Josie owns a highly successful catering business. And I used to pick cotton with a black man and his children.

Cecil: I played with black children, too, but in my own house. I remember when I was a little girl, I begged Mama to let our cook's little girl come play with me. And Mama invited her over and told me not to let her out of the yard because, you know, someone might hurt her feelings.

Mary Ann: I had black playmates, too. I remember a wonderful black girl who played with my sister and me. She was so much fun.

Camille: Still, you never went to the houses of black people as a guest.

Interviewer: Were you proper, dainty little southern girls?

Mary Ann: I was very fond of dolls. I was kind of a girl-girl. But I also climbed trees. I remember mother saying one day, "Don't you think you're getting too big to be doing tumble-saults on the floor?" But obviously Camille was the real tomboy.

Camille: I only played with boys. I played tackle football with boys until I was about twelve or thirteen. One day when I was tackled, I got the wind knocked out of me, and I went home and put on a dress and never played football again.

Cecil: I played boys' games too, and my best friend was a boy. We had a club and we initiated new members by feeding them leaves of the elephant-ear plant. We'd give them nose drops with mustard in it. It's a wonder we didn't kill somebody with our initiations.

Camille: I remember hating getting dolls and things for Christmas. I wanted trains and trucks and things that the boys got. We ended up using my dolls to re-enact kidnapping. We'd just throw them out the window.

Cecil: I also played jump-rope and jacks, and I skated.

Camille: I remember stopping everywhere on my way home from school. And mother never had to worry about me.

Interviewer: In *To Kill a Mockingbird*, Atticus is reprimanded by Aunt Alexandra and Mrs. Dubose for not dressing Scout properly. Do you remember a special dress code for little girls?

Cecil: I don't remember any taboo against little girls wearing trousers, but we were usually dressed in dresses because I remember my mother saying that little girls should always wear pretty panties because they spent so much time on their heads.

Mary Ann: We definitely weren't allowed to wear pants to school. It was unladylike to be sunburned. But nobody ever bugged me about it.

Camille: Oh, no.

Mary Ann: Never.

Cecil: In those days, blue jeans were really tacky.

Mary Ann: As my husband says, he struggled very hard so as not to have to work in bluejeans.

Mary Ann Norton and her mother and baby sister provide a perfect picture of the proper little girl and the ideal family in the South in the 1930s. It is in marked contrast to Scout and her family. Photo courtesy of Mary Ann Norton Meredith.

Cecil: Little girls got dressed up in the afternoons and you went to the park. We usually wore little dresses, except in the summer when you wore sunsuits.

Mary Ann: We were dressed up in the afternoon and taken to town, or we would ride to the end of the trolley line and back.

Camille: You remember our Sunday School dresses? What I hated was when they got a little too small or a little too shabby, they were converted into everyday dresses.

Mary Ann: Most of our dresses were handmade, smocked. We all wanted to look like Shirley Temple.

Cecil: One exception to handmade dresses were what were called Natalie dresses brought down by these people from New York. They would have special showings, and Mama would buy me one or two Natalie dresses, which you would only wear on very special occasions.

Mary Ann: You never went anywhere barefoot.

Cecil: That's quite true. If you saw someone at school barefoot, that was pitiful. The family never appeared around the house half-dressed. And you were always dressed up for dinner. Of course, it was easy when you had someone else serving you dinner.

Interviewer: Was there a special code of behavior for little girls who were expected to grow up to be southern ladies?

Camille: Well, it was alright for boys to fight, but girls weren't supposed to. It was perfectly alright for my brother to fight, but I was not allowed to. Of course, I did it anyway.

Cecil: Yes, we weren't supposed to, but I did beat up a little boy once. I remember his mother called to complain to Mama, and for once Mama stood up for me. I remember her saying, "Well, he started it and he's two years older than she is and she is a girl."

Mary Ann: Normally, little girls didn't resort to violence. I only had one fight.

Cecil: Speech was a biggie, really. There were just certain things you didn't say. You were corrected a lot.

Mary Ann: Correct grammar was extremely important.

Camille: We weren't to talk like the black children we played with.

Mary Ann: I can tell you, cuss words were certainly not prevalent. I never heard them.

Camille: I don't remember Mamma and Daddy ever saying a bad word.

Cecil: There were certain coarse words you hear today that I never heard until I was an adult. You were brought up to be a lady, which meant you were not allowed to be coarse.

Cecil Butler at Christmas: A ladylike little girl in a Southern home in the 1940s. Unlike Scout, Cecil probably never dreamed of getting an air rifle for Christmas. Photo courtesy of Cecil Butler Williams.

Camille: Little girls were never allowed to raise their voices.

Mary Ann: That's an important point. Ladies and gentlemen never raised their voices.

Camille: I was never allowed to say "shut up."

Mary Ann: Mainly what you were taught was good manners.

Cecil: And you were never allowed to brag or be sarcastic One word we could never say was "pregnant."

Mary Ann: I knew the word, of course, but I believe I was grown before I ever heard that word spoken aloud. You always said "expecting."

Cecil: There was a certain code of behavior expected on Sundays. We could go down to the beach and get snacks and a coke, but we couldn't drink cokes on Sunday. Many years afterwards I asked my mother why we couldn't drink cokes on Sunday, and she couldn't remember why.

Mary Ann: Of course, we didn't play cards or go to the movies on Sunday.

Interviewer: Movie theaters back then weren't even open on Sundays, were they?

Camille: I think that changed with air-conditioning. People would go to the movies on Sunday to get out of the heat.

Cecil: I don't know that we can say that the three of us were typical of little southern girls.

Mary Ann: It was a carefree time for us. We certainly seemed to live in a kinder, gentler world.

FROM HELEN EKIN STARRETT, *THE CHARM OF FINE MANNERS*
(Philadelphia: J. B. Lippincott, 1920)

We must persistently strive against selfishness, ill-temper, irritability, indolence. It is impossible for the self-centered or ill-tempered girl to win love and friends.

. . .

One of the greatest blemishes in the character of any young person, especially of any young girl or woman, is forwardness, boldness, pertness. The young girl who acts in such a manner as to attract attention in public; who speaks loudly, and jokes and laughs and tells *stories* in order to be heard by others than her immediate companions, . . . who expresses opinions on all subjects with forward self-confidence, is rightly regarded by all thoughtful and cultivated people as one of the most disagreeable and obnoxious characters to be met with in society.

. . .

What are the characteristics of the agreeable and beautiful manners that are the ornament of charm of the well-behaved girl? First, we should place gentleness, quietness, and serenity or self-possession.

. . .

Self-control should extend to our speech, temper, and pleasures. To be able to control the tongue is rightly esteemed one of the greatest of moral achievements. . . . There is a dignity about silence under provocation that is impressive and effective.

. . .

We may without harm divert the mind for a little each day by light miscellaneous reading, but young people especially need to be warned against indiscriminate novel or story reading. . . . If you discover that your taste is more for the improbable, highly wrought pages of fiction . . . you should summon your self-control and compel yourself to a different sort of reading.

. . .

Of course, the main source of knowledge of the more important events that are going on in the world is the daily or weekly newspapers; and yet there is scarcely any reading so utterly demoralizing to good mental habits as the ordinary daily paper.

. . .

I should rejoice to see you form friendships with good, high-minded, intelligent, gentle-mannered girls of your own age.

. . .

I cannot imagine a really refined young lady chewing gum even in the privacy of her own room, so offensive is it to good taste. . . . She will not rush noisily up and down stairs or through the house . . . startling everyone with unpleasant noises.

THE POOR WHITE SOUTHERNER

The poor white Southerner is a classic character in *To Kill a Mockingbird*. There are the shiftless, down-and-out poor like the Ewells, whose children never complete school and whose father is constantly drunk and lawless. And there are the more respectable poor like the Cunninghams, who pay their debts and work hard but are nonetheless bigoted. The issue of class is brought forward in the novel repeatedly, and Jem and Scout have frequent discussions about it. Their father is willing to give them his wisdom on the subject, and Aunt Alexandra, who forbids Scout to associate with poor whites, inflicts her opinion of all the citizens of Old Sarum, where most of the poor whites live. Wayne Flynt, in his study entitled *Poor But Proud: Alabama Poor Whites* (1989), believed that Harper Lee had not dispelled the stereotype of the southern poor white. Has she? The point of the following selections is to test the genuineness of her portraits.

Fictional representations by southern novelists gave the world its primary view of poor whites. The novelists most famous for their portraits are Erskine Caldwell, author of *Tobacco Road* (which was the basis of one of the longest-running plays in Broadway history and in its day considered the most scandalous book on the library shelf), and William Faulkner, who represented much of the decay of the South through characters such as the Snopeses in "The Long Hot Summer" and "Barn Burning," a family whose very name has become synonymous with unprincipled poor whites, and in the character of Wash Jones.

The first excerpt is the memoir of the son of a southern sharecropper. Here we have the reality of being poor and white from the perspective of a man who lived through it during the 1920s and 1930s. In the second excerpt Shields McIlwaine outlines the literary portraits that perpetuated the view of the poor whites. He summarizes the image of the poor white portrayed by writers like Caldwell and Faulkner. Another excerpt, from Erskine Caldwell's *God's Little Acre*, reveals the utter poverty reflected in the living conditions of Jeeter Lester and his family. It is also a comment on the shiftlessness to which their poverty has led.

From William Faulkner we receive a sympathetic treatment of

the poor white Southerner. "Wash," in the short story of the same name, is despised by blacks and whites alike. Wash, a man both whites and blacks refer to as "poor white trash," deludes himself that the southern aristocrat on whose land he lives considers him a friend; in fact, the old landowner considers Wash and his kind as chattel to be used and discarded.

There are also two brief nonfictional portraits of poor whites, one by historian Dan T. Carter and one by social activist Virginia Durr. Carter describes Victoria Price, the mill worker who accused the "Scottsboro boys." Durr describes poor whites from the vantage point of an upper-class Southerner.

FROM VERNON JOHNSON, "A MEMOIR: GROWING UP POOR
AND WHITE IN THE SOUTH"
(Unpublished Memoir, 1993)

Vernon Johnson, the author of the memoir that follows, was the child of a white sharecropper in Louisiana. After the death of his father, his family moved to Nashville, Tennessee, where he graduated from high school and enlisted in military service during World War II. He received his Ph.D. in English from Vanderbilt University and had a career as both a university teacher of English and a theater director. His memoir was written in 1993.

I was born in 1921 in rural Louisiana, the youngest of four children of Lola and James Franklin Johnson. There were six in our family: my father, my mother, and four children—two girls and two boys. My father and mother were peripatetic farmers, renting or working on shares—on small bits of land that we did not own and that we generally left after a season or two.

There were three phases to our life together as a family: (1) We were tenant farmers—as long as my father lived, and then for a while beyond, living with our grandparents; (2) then we lived in a small one-man town, a mill village where my mother worked as a school janitor; (3) and at last, when my mother was fired (for a whim—because she was a woman), and when necessity demanded, we moved to the city: we joined the great flood tide of farmers and ex-farmers to the Big City—to Nashville; and there we remained.

The life of a sharecropper was a hard one. The land my father farmed was never much; whatever you could handle with a mule, a plow, basic farm equipment, and your own labor. And it was generally poor land because the landlords would not or could not spend the money necessary to keep it rich and eternally productive—as all that land had been once. We never made any permanent roots because we did not stay in one place long enough to do so, although my mother and father always made fine friends, in the short time that various places, and farms, endured.

If there was a logo for our family, I think it would be a wagon wheel— a wagon wheel and dust, rising up over a dirt road; or maybe a wagon, loaded with all the small belongings of a family, and six people sitting on top somewhere, seeing everything that was past disappear, and seeing the future, unknown but hopeful, somewhere around the next curve. And you never carried much, of course; only what you could take with you, in one small wagon bed. And loaded in there somewhere, in my family, would be song books, along with a family Bible.

My father could not read or write—he went to school for less than a year and could barely print out his name. His mother died in childbirth, his father a few months later—and then in that same year a great fire destroyed a large part of the city of Newton, along with all the old records, so the only things left of the old days, for the most part, were old memories. My father in fact never knew when he was born; he did not even know the year, so he guessed at 1880, and he picked December 6 as a birthday. Taken in by a maternal uncle, for a few years, he was treated harshly, with a cold kind of neglect, while others around him were treated well, and so one day, when he was big enough to run, he ran. Thus my father, in effect, grew up on his own, in the logging camps and the cotton fields, where he worked all his life.

Because he was illiterate, did not own property, and moved around from place to place, laws which were enacted to keep blacks and poor whites disenfranchised kept him from voting or serving on juries, which were made from voting lists. In short, he would not have been able to participate in government in any way.

My mother was 18 when she married my father and he was probably around 32. She was a tall woman with a sharp, strong face and blue-gray eyes. She had had to quit school in the eighth grade to work fulltime, but she was extremely quick and an excellent student. She also learned to play the piano and the organ, and sometimes played, as a substitute, in the churches that we attended. Her favorite subject was mathematics. (Once after my father died, when she was working at the only job available to her—janitress in a country school—as she remembered, a seventh-grade teacher wrote on the board a problem which neither she nor the class could figure out. At the end of the class, my mother pointed out that they had read the problem wrong, and she solved it for them, instantly. The children got a big kick out of that: the janitor solving a problem that had stumped the teacher.) Because of her superior education, in our family, and despite her youth and the fact that she was a woman, she handled all the business and monetary affairs of our family, such as they were; all the contracts. And the landlords often resented this, sometimes with open insults. On more than one occasion my mother and father angered the landowners for whom they worked by insisting that my mother scrutinize the contracts and other legal documents presented for my father's "mark." She was, in all, imbued with boundless energy, curiosity, good humor, determination, and physical strength, as well as strength of character.

The other important adult in our group was my grandmother. She had known a life of hard necessity. The fourth of twelve children born to Marcus and Mary Ann Myers, her childhood was the Civil War, her youth the years of defeat and Reconstruction. Objectively, she was a bag of bones with a floor-length dress, a serrated face (marked by deep brown eyes), and long white hair—her hair, when she let it down, came down to her waist, her one sensual moment in a life devoted to work and to duty; she loved the combing of her hair. That was in fact the way she had been since Eden; and it seemed to me there was still about her something of the dew of creation.

I knew my grandmother only as a frail, stooped woman with wizened arms about the size of match sticks and with no muscles at all—who could, nevertheless, lift a great, double-bladed axe high above her head (by will alone, it seemed, obviously not from strength) and somehow bring it thunderously down on huge chunks of wood, to cut up kindling: she could even chop and split logs, an act of absolute awe for me, for I always expected, at any moment, to see the axe fall from those arms and split her skull open; in which case, I would run into the house telling about that horrible tale. And somehow she managed to crawl or creep, or move as if by magic, across the floor or the yard—to clean it, or move it, or hammer it, or cut it up or cook it, whatever was demanded. She did all this regularly and without complaint; and she came up barely to my mother's shoulders. There was, however, as I eventually learned, another side to my grandmother.

When young, she was 5'8"—athletically built and agile. Like my mother after her, she could and did cook, sew, plow, clean house, handle mules, skin and cook farm animals or wild game, handle a hammer and saw, and do anything else required on a farm of the day. If she had been a man, she would probably have been a carpenter, or maybe a cowboy. She loved working with wood; and she used to make furniture. When young, in the old days, she used to break horses—for the genteel ladies who were more inclined to faint than work, or to palpitate when faced with decisions, or maybe get neurasthenia.

The farming system by which my father made his living worked in two ways. You could rent a farm and plant both a vegetable garden, for the family to live on, and a cash crop (always cotton) to sell; or you could farm on shares (sharecropping), a system in which you would concentrate on cash crops and split the profit down the middle with the owner. We did both, always managing to have the vegetable garden. The entire family, including the children, helped in this. My earliest memory in fact is of picking cotton (all together, in open fields, under an autumn sun). You picked it, stored it, then hauled it away to be processed and baled. It was a hard life but for us it was always special.

By the 1930s the land was worn out and poor in the South. But even in the good days it was already diminished. Landlords spent nothing, expenses rose, and prices fell; sometimes you spent more than you ever made. (And in the great boom days of the 1920s, the farmer was forgotten; and ignored.) You could expect to produce about half a bale of cotton an acre in Scott County, Mississippi, where my father and mother first started out; on the land of the Delta, as my father's brother once wrote from Natchez, you could expect two bales an acre.

There was also a continuous problem of diet. My mother remembered buying a cow, on credit, to provide milk for the family.

With the farm we rented or worked for a season on shares, there came a tiny, four-room house made of wood, with a tin roof.

At times, like other sharecroppers, my father had to supplement the family income with other jobs. In the late fall or in between farms he would work as a logger for the sawmills. And as the land became poorer and poorer, he anticipated selling his farm equipment and working full-time as a sawmill laborer.

We lived a happy if hard life. We played in the dirt yard, often made up our own games. In the house in bad weather or in the evenings, we amused ourselves with songs and reading and word games.

My sister remembers most pleasantly that in good weather, especially in the fall after crops were harvested, my grandfather would gather the older girls and their friends and take them on hayrides—a horse and a wagon, filled with kids, out across the fields and along small dirt lanes, sometimes under a golden autumn moon. "That," she remembered, "was the greatest."

The constant moving meant that there was always the horror of a new school for the children, and the unfailing challenge from a sea of hostile faces. My sister, remembering these constant new challenges, noted, "I felt like a chicken in a bunch of wolves."

The poor people we knew were very much like us. They were devout church-goers and devoted family members. Most were intelligent and believed in working hard, living upright lives, and keeping meticulously clean, even if their clothes were made of flour sacks (which was often the case), and even if they owned no property, and spoke "ungrammatically" and with an accent that grated on upper-class ears.

We knew even then though that not all poor people were like us. Some had never received a modicum of education, were totally ignorant even of the world around them, dirty, diseased, immoral, destitute. My mother remembered one family that only had one plate and who anticipated with some joy the death of any of its numerous family members so that the little food they had would go farther. She remembered another family so ignorant they thought that their daughter who had moved across the Mississippi River had actually moved across the Atlantic Ocean.

My sister always remembered a small boy of six who used to walk for a long distance, across fields, to get water from our well, because his family had none of their own. So every day he would drag huge containers that he could hardly carry, back across the stubbled fields. It was well known that the boy's father beat him, especially if he saw anyone helping the child. The laws were different in those days. You could stop a lynching, or punish a robber; but you could not stop a man from beating his son.

All these were the exceptions, however, not the rule among the people they knew.

My father died one day in December after an illness contracted while working outdoors, in the rain. He was obviously ill that morning, my mother remembered, and perhaps feverish; but he insisted that he was all right. He had worked many times when feeling worse than that, he said. And so he went. He was working as a laborer, in a lumber yard, to earn extra money, with Christmas coming on. They brought him back some time in mid-afternoon, after he had collapsed on the job.

He lay there ill for several days, getting worse instead of better, it seemed; but he would not permit my mother to call a doctor: that would eat up every cent that they had saved, and he knew that he could push it through, as he always had, in the logging camps and in the fields, so many times before. One day, to prove his strength, he told her to prepare supper, and he would come to the table, and they would sit there and talk, like before. He collapsed half-way across the room, and my mother carried him back to the bed. Over his protests, then, my mother at last called the doctor. But it was too late. On the morning of December 6, on the day that he had picked for his birthday, my father died. He thought that he could survive, on sheer will and determination alone, as he had so many times before. But he could not. He died of double pneumonia.

They rang the church bell to indicate death, and friends and neighbors came over, to prepare the body and dig the grave; and then they sat all night, in the room lit by candles and lamps. They buried him in Coax Church cemetery. Then when it was over, my mother walked back to the graveyard alone, to place some shells over his grave. She could not afford a stone.

A few days after my father died, while my mother was still half crazy with grief, the landowner appeared, trying to force her to move. Noting that "business is business" and speaking in terms of vague legalese, he threatened to throw her out, onto the road, immediately, if she did not move. Because she was a sharecropper's wife, he assumed that she was, of course, stupid, illiterate, and incapable of rational protest; and she could not understand such arcane things as contracts. But she did. By this time, grief had changed to fury. She told him that she knew what the contract said, and so did he, because he had made it out and she had signed it; and she read portions of it to him. Then she told him to get out of her house; and she said that she intended to stay there until spring if she wanted to. And she told him once more: "Get out!"

The death of my father, and shortly afterwards of my grandfather, was the end of a poor but curiously Edenic way of life for us. After that, as my mother tried to support her four children and a widowed mother, we not only became more keenly aware of hardships, we became more aware of the limitations and humiliations of being poor.

We moved to another tiny lumber mill town in Louisiana where my mother's relatives worked and where she got a job as a school janitor. This was in a town literally owned by one man, the mill owner, and run by one or two of his henchmen. The store was a company store into which everyone in town immediately plowed back the money they had just been paid by the company. Many people borrowed heavily from the owner in order to meet basic needs in time of stress and were, thus, virtually trapped there forever, trying to pay off their debts; and they were paid in company scrip good only at the company store. The residents of the little town also lived in the mill owner's houses and so were doubly at his mercy.

This was not what mattered to us, though. We deeply loved the little town. We had stability, peace, security; we had a fine house and many friends, and space, and we looked across the street to the school that we would all attend.

We only worried about rich and middle-class people when they impinged on our lives in a direct way—to evict a widow from land, for example. They were there, and we just kept a wary eye and ignored them. We never worried much about rich people or about the privileges they had that we didn't have. This was not any conscious noble decision; it was just that it never occurred to us to do so. This was where we were, and this was what we were. And it seemed to us that we had something they did not.

Even though we lived in the deep South, we had absolutely no dealings with black people. No black people lived in the town where my mother worked. A sign posted just outside the town actually forbade black people from entering. Once in Urania, when I was about five years old, there occurred one of the most astonishing things of my life. I was on the front porch one morning, very early, when an old man with a short white beard appeared, just up the street, heading our way. It was obvious even from a distance that something was terribly wrong. He had been in some dreadful accident, and you could tell that he still suffered because he never moved his head, either to the left or the right: perhaps something was wrong with his neck. I looked at this for a moment then rushed back into the house to burst out to my mother: *There's a man in the street, and he's been burned all over!* It was obvious what had happened, for my mother just that morning had burned some toast and had scraped off the edges to make it edible. She walked, with some consternation, to the front door with me and looked out. The old man was directly in front of our house. Never moving, staring straight ahead. If he moved his neck, quite obviously his face would crack.

My mother, after an impulsive laugh, restrained herself admirably, then explained about Negroes. They were black. Black all over. All the time. They had been brought over as slaves, before the Civil War. And slavery was wrong. Yes, they had slaves in the Bible. But you found perfection only in heaven, and in this world you just did the best you could. God made several races in fact: Black, White, Yellow, and Red; and to God, they were all equal. This was the first time I had ever become aware that not all people were white, like me.

My brother remembered a time when my grandfather, Sim Rasberry, had saved a young black man from a lynch mob. A girl, it seemed, had been molested by somebody, and this man was blamed. A violent mob was on his trail. When the man appeared, frightened beyond reason and panting, Grandpa permitted him to hide. Then he directed the man off in one direction, and, when the mob appeared, directed them off in another. My brother watched all this from the front yard; Grandpa was quite calm, he said, and never twitched a muscle.

My grandmother and mother believed that all people are equal before God. They may not be on this earth—no sharecropper ever failed to perceive that—but they were all the same before God: and when you got to Judgment Day, God would not ask what color you were, or what clothes you wore, or what your grandfather possessed. He would ask: What did you *do*? For my grandmother—and mother—all relationships, and all real human values, had to stem from this. This is not to say that my family were advanced political thinkers or social reformers, for they were not: Negroes lived in one world and we in another (and both virtually at the very bottom). It was rather a basic human fact.

Nor were my family southern chauvinists. When I got old enough to understand the Civil War, I received a rather mild shock. The South *should* have lost, Grandma said. They deserved to lose, for they stood for slavery, and slavery was wrong. This from an old woman whose idolized father had fought in the war (in a long, dreadful retreat through Georgia) and who had seen three invading armies plus Confederate scroungers and marauding bummers burn, ravage, and destroy the land and kill—and sometimes torture—the people. And as a child, she had seen Union troops, bivouacked in her front yard, shoot and kill (perhaps by accident, perhaps not) a neighbor woman, standing in her own doorway. No man should ever *own* anybody else, Grandma said, not in any way in any form. And nobody should ever have to *bow* to anybody else—to nobody except God.

The Enemy that we knew wore a white face, not a black one; and he drove a fine buggy, or as the years passed, a fine late car, and he wore a white shirt and a tie. He was the "Preacher" who cheated my grandfather; the confidence man who bilked his "congregation" out of money; the landlord who tried illegally to kick my mother and her family out onto the road at Christmas time; the man who owned the little lumber town; the Principal, the "educator," who fired her—for a whim, because she was a woman; the rich farmer's wife who tried to get my mother to forge the farmer's signature; the traveling salesman, to whom she had to take a shotgun, threatening to shoot him through the screen, to get him to leave.

A day came in this little town in Louisiana when my mother lost her job. The mill manager decided that a man should do the job she had, and she was fired. This meant we lost both income and the rooms we lived in, which were attached to the school where she worked. He was a plump little man with fat white hands. In desperation and hope, all five of us, along with my aunt and her family, moved to the city, to Nashville, Tennessee—along with great hordes of people forced off the land, to find a new life in the city. We changed rural poverty for urban poverty.

Our economic poverty was often far more intense in the city than it had been on the land. My mother and grandmother worked at backbreaking labor in cotton mills and other factories. Many times, during the Depression there in Nashville, we almost literally starved or froze to death. As we attended the city schools and churches, we felt more keenly economic and class differences. My brother and sisters could never complete high school because they had to go to work, and I was not able to attend college until the G.I. bill paid for it after World War II. I remember that my cousin, who had an excellent high school record and the money to pay for her education, was told after an interview with a Vanderbilt University dean that she was not "Vanderbilt material." Later my sister, who had gone with her, believed that she was rejected because her clothes and her speech gave her away as "working class."

The city was cold and cruel, its harsh realities keenly suffered, but it also brought opportunity and a wider world. There were libraries, the YMCA, and church and community organizations designed to support the poor. And eventually there were more opportunities for work. For my mother's children, at least, the city would finally be the way out of the grinding poverty of the poor, rural South.

FROM SHIELDS McILWAINE, *THE SOUTHERN POOR-WHITE FROM LUBBERLAND TO TOBACCO ROAD*
(Norman: University of Oklahoma Press, 1939)

Creating in the naturalistic manner, William Faulkner and Erskine Caldwell have brought about five culminations in the history of fiction about the poor-white: (1) the frank and full representation of the sordid elements in these people, (2) the emphasis upon sex, especially in comedy, (3) the exploration of stupid poor-white minds, (4) the tragic concept of the poor-white, and (5) the complete studies of poor-white men to match those of women. . . .

To some critics, [Faulkner's] characters were "the dregs of human-kind," "bad dream of reality," and "creatures almost too sick or too depraved to be called human." And one reviewer thought that readers of Caldwell's *Tobacco Road* (1932) would "probably finish it—with disgust and a slight retching." But these southern naturalists are merely emphasizing a side of poor-white life that has existed both in fact and in literature for two hundred years.

. . .

[I]t remained for Faulkner to study fully the slow, dull wits of poor-whites in a series of inner-monologues which make up his novel, *As I Lay Dying.* . . . In Faulkner's book, for the first time, we follow the twilight minds of an entire family: Mrs. Addie Bundren, the dying woman, who had been decent before marrying a poor-white; Anse, her lazy, stupid husband; and five children: Cash, simple but capable with tools; Darl, an idiot; Dewey Dell, a slow-witted, sensuous girl; Vardaman, a normal child; and Jewell, the result of Addie's illicit relation with a preacher, and, therefore, a brighter person than the other children. . . . Faulkner has made an attempt to convey a sense of the callousness, limitation, and, at times, the strange acuteness of poor-white minds.

. . .

Certainly, the Lesters [from Caldwell's novels] were a simple, if not weak-minded lot. Jeeter had few brains, and his wife Ada had fewer. Indeed, during most of her married life of forty years, she had been silent. Dude, Ellie May—perhaps all of the seventeen Lester children were hare-brained. And not one of them could read or write.

With so little of brain to provide either will or foresight, Jeeter, along with his family, in the struggle to eat, became a beast, driven by hunger to live and then by sex to "pleasure himself." In such a dog-eat-dog existence, he had lost all morality and family sense. He sold Pearl, his twelve-year-old daughter, to Lov for a wife; the price was seven dollars, a gallon of cylinder oil, and some quilts. Jeeter hates his mother, a pellagra-ridden sack of bones, for living so long. To him she was "nothing more than a door-jamb," and whenever he could keep her from eating he did so. Nor did Jeeter have a mite of fatherly kindness.

FROM ERSKINE CALDWELL, *GOD'S LITTLE ACRE*
(New York: Grossett and Dunlap, 1932)

The Lesters stood around in the yard and on the front porch waiting to see what Lov was going to do next: There had been very little in the house again that day to eat; some salty soup that Ada had made by boiling several fatback rinds in a pan of water, and corn bread, was all there was when they had sat down to eat.

. . .

The three-room house sat precariously on stacks of thin lime-rock chips. . . . The centre of the building sagged between the sills; the front porch had sagged loose from the house, and was now a foot lower than it originally was. . . . Most of the shingles had rotted, and after every windstorm pieces of them were scattered in all directions about the yard. When the roof leaked, the Lesters moved from one corner of the room to another.

FROM WILLIAM FAULKNER, "WASH," IN *THE PORTABLE FAULKNER*
(New York: Viking Press, 1946)

[Wash's] sole connection with Sutpen plantation lay in the fact that for years now Colonel Sutpen had allowed him to squat in a crazy shack on a slough in the river bottom on the Sutpen place, which Sutpen had built for a fishing lodge in his bachelor days and which had since fallen in dilapidation from disuse, so that now it looked like an aged or sick wild beast crawled terrifically there to drink in the act of dying.

[Wash's claim to one and all that he can't fight in the Civil War because he has to stay behind to look after the plantation owner's affairs causes even the slaves to deride him, because everyone looks down on Wash.]

The Sutpen slaves themselves heard of his statement. They laughed. It was not the first time they had laughed at him, calling him white trash behind his back. They began to ask him themselves in groups, meeting him in the faint road which led up from the slough and the old fish camp, "Why ain't you at de war, white man?"

. . .

[The slaves, who are allowed in the Colonel's house, stop Wash when he tries to enter it in the Colonel's absence.] This time it was a house servant, one of the few Negroes who remained; this time the Negress had to retreat up the kitchen steps, where she turned. "Stop right dar, white man. Stop right whar you is. You ain't never crossed dese steps whilst Cunnel here, and you ain't ghy' do hit now."

[After the old Colonel returns, he gets Wash's fifteen-year-old granddaughter pregnant, giving Wash to understand that he will "do right" by her. Instead, the Colonel says to Wash's granddaughter after the birth of his son that if she was a mare she could have a decent stall in the stable. Wash, realizing the Colonel's callousness and betrayal, kills him. And as he waits for the Colonel's friends to come and get him, he contemplates his revelation about this man whom he had always idolized.]

What need has a fellow like Wash Jones to question or doubt the man that General Lee himself says in a handwrote ticket that he was brave? "Brave," he thought. "Better if nara one of them had never rid back home in '65"; thinking *Better if his kind and mine too had never drawn the breath of life on this earth. Better that all who remain of us be blasted from the face of earth than that another Wash Jones should see his whole life shredded from him and shrivel away like a dried shuck thrown onto the fire.*

DESCRIPTION OF VICTORIA PRICE FROM DAN T. CARTER, *SCOTTSBORO*
(Baton Rouge: Louisiana State University Press, 1979)

Under the glow of such attention, the hitherto reticent Victoria Price began to expound at length on her plight. Victoria, slender and "pert"— a handsome woman who spoke vigorously in the accents of up-country mill workers—told newsmen how she had "grown up hard" in Huntsville cotton mill villages. She recalled that she had quit school at nine and gone to work in the mills and since 1927 had been the only support of her widowed mother. The work was regular and the pay adequate until the Depression, but after 1929, cutbacks grew longer and salaries lower. She desperately looked for work, but she emphasized to reporters that she did not think of doing what a lot of other girls do. . . . "I guess you heard the rest. Mister, I never had a 'break' in my life."

. . .

[Dan Carter writes about seeing Victoria Price Street in her old age.]
As I watched her hobble from the courtroom, however, I was struck by my ambivalence toward this woman. During the 1930s she had struggled to survive on two to three dollars a week as a cotton mill worker. In the midst of this collapsing economy she had lived by her wits and

(according to her accusers) the use of the only collateral she possessed, her body.

FROM VIRGINIA FOSTER DURR, *OUTSIDE THE MAGIC CIRCLE*
(Tuscaloosa: University of Alabama Press, 1985)

On Saturday mornings, mining families would come walking down our street on their way into Birmingham. There was no paved road and none of these people had a car. These great large families were miserable looking, pale and stunted and almost deformed. Pellagra and worms and malaria were common among the poor whites in the South at that time. Pellagra was a dietary disease, and those who had it would break out in white splotches. Late in the afternoon on Saturday the same families would come home; the children would be hollering, and the adults, both men and women, would be drunk and falling down.

· · ·

I was told by my mother and father and everybody whom I respected and loved that these people were just that way. They were just poor white trash. If they had pellagra and worms and malaria and if they were thin and hungry and immoral, it was just because that was the way they were. It was in their blood. They were born to be poor white trash. They dipped snuff and drooled tobacco juice. If they smelt bad and were dirty, well, they liked being that way.

· · ·

We were brought up, or at least I was brought up, to believe that the distribution of wealth was ordained by God. It was "in the blood." You were born to be either wealthy and wise and rich and powerful and beautiful and healthy, or you were born to be poor and downtrodden and sick and miserable and drunken and immoral. There was very little you could do to change your fate because it was "in the blood." It was a very comforting thought, you see, because when you saw people starving and poor and miserable, you thought, "Well, it isn't my fault. I didn't do anything to cause it. God just ordained it this way."

THE AFRICAN-AMERICAN

Harper Lee presented to both Northerner and Southerner a portrait of the African-American as a human being: a black man who could feel pity for a poor white woman, and a black woman who had learned to read from books of legal commentary. Lee's portrait of the African-American and the situation faced by many African-Americans opened the eyes of her readers, many of whom had thought of black people only in terms of stereotypes. The documents presented here include both the reality and the myth that Lee's novel addresses.

The primary document is an interview with an African-American woman who grew up in a small town near Birmingham, Alabama, during the 1930s, when Scout Finch was also a child in Maycomb, Alabama. The second document is an excerpt from a scholarly study in the field of popular culture by Donald Bogle. He establishes categories of racial stereotypes: "toms, coons, mulattoes, mammies, and bucks." The "tom" (actually referring to "Uncle Tom," a character created in 1952 by Harriet Beecher Stowe in *Uncle Tom's Cabin*), was understood to be a willingly subservient tool of white people. These stereotypes were perpetuated not only in novels and dramas but, as Bogle discovers, in American film. And it was just such stereotypes that *To Kill a Mockingbird* challenged. Calpurnia does not fit any "mammy" stereotype of the African-American woman. And Tom Robinson is neither shuffling, comical, nor evil, in the tradition of male stereotypes outlined by Bogle.

They were stereotypes long in the making, as the excerpt from Thomas Dixon's *The Flaming Sword* illustrates. Dixon, a prolific and popular novelist at the turn of the century, wrote sympathetically of the Ku Klux Klan and the superiority of the white race. Dixon uses sensationalism and hysteria to create a situation very like the one created by Bob Ewell in the courtroom of *To Kill a Mockingbird*.

A final excerpt from the autobiography of Virginia Durr, a southern lady turned social activist, shows the upper-class attitude that found the poor to be forever poor and somehow responsible for their miserable condition.

INTERVIEW: GROWING UP BLACK IN THE 1930s IN McCULLEY'S
QUARTERS, ALABAMA

Mrs. Peacolia Barge, born in 1923, lived as a small child in an area called McCulley's Quarters and grew up in Bessemer just outside Birmingham, Alabama. Mrs. Barge completed her college degree after her marriage and then began a long career in teaching. Her grandparents were slaves in Alabama, and her three children are college-educated, professional men and women. She defies all stereotypes, just as Calpurnia does in *To Kill a Mockingbird*. The interview that follows was conducted in 1993.

Interviewer: Tell me what you know of your background and ancestry, Mrs. Barge.

Mrs. Barge: My mother and father came from two different areas of Alabama. My mother grew up on the Morrisette Plantation in Alabama. We know that my grandmother was a servant there in 1880. My grandmother had more privileges than other servants because she worked in the house rather than in the fields. And she never lived in the slave quarters. When the overseer left the plantation, she and her family were allowed to move into his house. Her father was owned by one Alexander Bryant from Kentucky, and he willed his slaves to his children. From his will, we found that my family that found its way to Alabama was worth $385. All of my great-grandfather's and great-grandmother's children were born in slavery. The curious thing is that even though their children were born in slavery, they weren't married until 1867, after the Civil War. And researching the records, we found that there were a surge of marriages after the War, as if only then were they allowed to be married. Anyway, the Morrisette Plantation was where my grandmother met my grandfather. They were married in 1884 at a time when we were led to believe few blacks ever married. When I was growing up, I knew nothing about all this. Anything related to slavery, we didn't want to hear it. I don't think any blacks wanted to hear anything about slavery. My mother grew up on the Morrisette Plantation and came to Birmingham when she was 21 years old. My father's people came from the area near Panola, Alabama. This may shock you, but the plantation owner had seven or eight children by two of his slaves. One of those offspring, Lorenzo Dancy, was my father's father. We assume my father was illegitimate since there are no records of any marriages there.

Interviewer: How was town life near Birmingham different from rural life when you were young?

Mrs. Barge: My father seemed to think living near Birmingham was a great improvement over the country. He said he left the country because he hated to be told what to do and he could be more independent in the city. He always said that he would refuse to be treated like a boy. I've been trying to understand my father's rebelliousness. There were times when he would rebuke people who said certain things to him, because he thought everything had something to do with race. Nobody could ever tell him he couldn't have a thing or do a thing. He carried the Bessemer Housing Authority to court in 1954 to keep them from taking his property for a housing project. No black person had ever challenged the Authority. He didn't win, of course—he knew he wouldn't win. But my father would challenge anybody. I think it went back to his early environment. He felt he and other young men were being dealt a raw deal from the overseers of the land. The workers were being cheated out of their profits. Mother moved to the Birmingham area to get away from a bad personal situation. But lots of people moved off the land because of crop failures. The land was just worn out and the South was suffering from terrible droughts. People got deep into debt—debts that were kept on the books, even when they had actually been paid off. It was hard to challenge the records kept by the landowners. Through the twenties and thirties, many black people hoboed away from the South because they realized that on the farms the more you worked the more you owed. For myself, I was never taken to the country until I was quite a big girl.

Interviewer: So, you would describe yourself as a small-town girl, growing up just outside Birmingham?

Mrs. Barge: Yes.

Interviewer: And you are writing a history of that area?

Mrs. Barge: Yes, McCulley's Quarters was a place where poor, working-class black people, like my mother and father, lived until they could afford to move to a bigger house or could afford to buy their own house. Someone I have contacted wrote me that the area was once part of a plantation—a slave quarters. Even when we were there, three white families lived in McCulley's Quarters in large houses on the edge of the neighborhood and owned all the other houses. I remember that one white woman in particular, Mrs. Kate, kind of kept up with what was going on in the neighborhood and came around to help when there was sickness or a death in the black families.

Interviewer: What were the houses like? the living conditions?

Mrs. Barge: They were all shotgun houses, mostly two-room places. No electricity, of course. Even after TVA [Tennessee Valley Authority] came to the Birmingham area, we had no electricity until my father, who could be very stubborn and hot-tempered, fought and fought until he managed to get electricity run to our house. The thing we hated most about not having electricity was that we couldn't use a radio. It wasn't until about 1940 that we got a radio.

Interviewer: About how large was McCulley's Quarters?

Mrs. Barge: It was only about a one-block area, but it had everything we needed—a grocery store and a barber shop and a blacksmith shop.

Interviewer: How did a typical little girl spend the day when you were about six years old?

Mrs. Barge: Oh, I led a sheltered life. Mother always kept me dressed in the dresses she made and I was kept close around the house. I visited neighbors and played house and read. I never wore slacks or jeans. And I never took part in the boys' rough games. Boys picked berries in the summer and sold scrap iron.

Interviewer: As a child, did you have contacts with white people? That is, did you have a sense of yourself as black and without certain opportunities?

Mrs. Barge: Except for the few white people who lived in the Quarters, as a child I didn't know many white people or have a sense of being discriminated against. My friends were right there in the Quarters. There were very, very few children there, so I remember primarily being with the adults. It wasn't until after I started to school that I became aware that we couldn't go to certain parks, couldn't swim in certain places. During the thirties my mother had to begin taking in washing and ironing for white people, so I began to see the white people she worked for. Then later I came to realize other differences. For example, there were no hospitals for black people. The one or two hospitals that would take black people put them in the basement. And of course the black doctor, who had been taking care of you, would not be allowed to practice—to attend you in the white hospital.

Interviewer: Did your family have any contact with white people who were in an economic situation similar to yours—people whom we would call "poor whites"?

Mrs. Barge: My mother and I didn't, but my father did at his work. I remember him talking particularly about the woman who worked as a nurse at the factory who always abused any black workers she had to treat who were injured on the job. Many workers would just try to treat their own wounds rather than go to her to help them. Some would pull their own bad teeth for the same reason, rather than be badly treated by some white dentist. A few of the men my father worked with were white and poor. Many years later I learned that he had once gotten into an argument with a white worker, hit him over the head with his lunch bucket, and knocked him out. I never knew what the argument was about, but my father thought he had killed the man so he left and went back to Aliceville, Alabama. He stayed for a few days until the foreman sent a message to him by my mother telling him that the man wasn't really hurt and that they wanted him to come back to work. Actually, I think my father was more highly regarded by the factory management than white workers were.

Interviewer: Were conditions rougher in the 1930s during the Depression, or was it more or less more of the same?

Mrs. Barge: We were always poor, but the Depression was definitely worse. People who had had jobs lost them or, like my father, were laid off for periods of time. And if you worked, the pay was often something like 3 or 4 dollars a week. What my mother always said was that people used the old plantation skills to survive: growing gardens, canning, making absolutely everything and buying almost nothing.

Interviewer: What was education like for African-Americans in Alabama at that time?

Mrs. Barge: My mother, growing up on what had been the Morrisette Plantation, was well educated. Churches maintained schools in the country, and children who showed promise as good students were sought out and sent to these schools, if their parents would pay. My mother was sent for a time to Snow Hill Institute. Her parents scraped and picked cotton so that she could attend, but she didn't finish. The last year the crops were too bad, and she couldn't go. Most, of course, were not educated. My father attended school through the third grade only. In my generation, most children I knew attended school, though many left at an early age to go to work. I believe that compulsory schooling to the age of 16 did not come about until about 1941.

Interviewer: What occupations were open to African-Americans as you were growing up?

Mrs. Barge: For women, aside from domestic work and labor like laundering, the only professions or trades were nursing and teaching. Of course, you only nursed or taught black people. Many women worked as cooks in private homes or restaurants, as maids in private homes or businesses. There were no black sales clerks in stores. Men worked in the mines, in factories, as delivery boys, carpenters, and bricklayers. They could operate elevators, but they couldn't become firemen or policemen or salesmen. Some black men worked as tailors. Those who went into professions became doctors or dentists or principals or preachers within the black community.

Interviewer: What about your father?

Mrs. Barge: My father worked first in the mines, then in the mills in the area making pipes. It was extremely hard work. The heat was so intense that few people could endure pouring the hot metal to shape the pipes. There were, of course, no black foremen. My father said that the white owners and managers assumed that all black men had inexhaustible physical strength. They were ordered to do physically back-breaking jobs over and over and over again. Work in the mills broke the health of many men long before they could retire. My father finally quit because he said that the foremen couldn't get it through their heads that black men didn't have endless strength.

Interviewer: What were the legal barriers that African-Americans faced?

Mrs. Barge: Well, of course, we weren't allowed to register to vote. Even though I was a schoolteacher for twenty years, I didn't register to vote until the late sixties. There were a few black attorneys who would take on cases, but at least in Birmingham in the thirties and forties, black attorneys couldn't practice in the courthouse. Their very presence in the courtroom was bitterly resented by many people.

Interviewer: What was the feeling in the black community about Autherine Lucy's attempt to enter the University of Alabama?

Mrs. Barge: They didn't know exactly what to think. But it was horrifying for us. Terrifying. I thought I would have just given up. Everyone was very scared for her life. The older people were especially scared for her. They thought that the people would kill Autherine. There were other cases of black people trying to enter the state universities, in Tuscaloosa and Birmingham, at the time. Nobody thought they had much of a chance because every excuse in the world would be brought up. I knew one young woman who was told that she would be accepted, but when her mortgage company heard about it, they threatened to cancel her mortgage. They said if their white customers found out that their company was providing a mortgage for a black person who was trying to go to white schools, they would take their business elsewhere. So they couldn't afford to continue mortgaging her home if she kept trying to go to the university.

Interviewer: What about the Montgomery bus boycott?

Mrs. Barge: We were always given the same treatment on buses throughout the South that Rosa Parks received. Most of us had to ride the
buses. We bought our tickets at the front of the bus and then went
around to the back door to get in. A sign marked where the white
section ended and the black section began. If the white section was
filled and more white people got on, you were ordered out of your
seats and the driver would move the sign back to make the white
section bigger. It was a terrible humiliation as well as being terribly
uncomfortable. We would be jammed together in the back like sar-
dines. Even worse was when some of the whites would get off and
some drivers would refuse to move the sign back up so that we could
have more room and a few black people could sit down.

Interviewer: Mrs. Barge, despite the difficulties and humiliations you have
lived with in the South, you don't seem to put all white people into
the same category.

Mrs. Barge: No, you shouldn't put people into categories. Many of those
bus drivers treated us badly. We disliked them and made fun of them
behind their backs. But some of them were good men who were
polite and considerate and would even hold the bus for us when
they knew we were late. No, not all black people are the same and
not all white people are the same.

FROM DONALD BOGLE, *TOMS, COONS, MULATTOES, MAMMIES
AND BUCKS: AN INTERPRETIVE HISTORY OF BLACKS IN
AMERICAN FILMS*
(New York: Continuum, 1989)

After the Tom's debut, there appeared a variety of black presences bearing the fanciful names of the coon, the tragic mulatto, the mammy, and
the brutal black buck. All were character types used for the same effect:
to entertain by stressing Negro inferiority. Fun was poked at the American
Negro by presenting him as either a nitwit or a childlike lackey.

Always as Toms are chased, harassed, hounded, flogged, enslaved, and
insulted, they keep the faith, n'er turn against their white massas, and
remain hearty, submissive, stoic, generous, selfless, and oh-so-very kind.
... Although Tom was to outdistance every other type and dominate
American hearth and home, he had serious competition from a group of
coons. They appeared in a series of black films presenting the Negro as
amusement object and black buffoon. ... The pure coons emerged as ...
those unreliable, crazy, lazy, subhuman creatures, good for nothing more

Stereotype of the African-American man from Thomas Dixon's *The Flaming Sword* (1937).

than eating watermelons, stealing chickens, shooting craps, or butchering the English language.

. . .

Mammy is distinguished . . . by her sex and her fierce independence. She is usually big, fat, and cantankerous. . . . Mammy's offshoot is the Aunt Jemima. . . . Generally they are sweet, jolly and good-tempered—a bit more polite than Mammy and certainly never as headstrong.

. . .

Bucks are always big, baaaddd, over-sexed and savage, violent and frenzied.

FROM THOMAS DIXON, *THE FLAMING SWORD*
(Atlanta: Monarch Publishing, 1939)

When the twilight deepened into the full shadow of night, a huge black figure came out of the woods, stood for a minute in the bushes on the edge and looked in every direction. . . . The dark form moved carefully in a wide circle around the house and approached the dog run from the back. . . . The thing stood still in his tracks for a long time, listening for approaching footsteps. . . . The thing moved directly toward the house now with the soft sure tread of a leopard. It stopped at the porch and looked through a window of the living room from which poured a flame of light. . . . She saw for the first time in the light of the lamp his thick bulging lips from the corners of which saliva was trickling, and a wave of horror swept over her.

FROM VIRGINIA FOSTER DURR, *OUTSIDE THE MAGIC CIRCLE*
(Tuscaloosa: University of Alabama Press, 1985)

The poor black children always looked ashen. They wore flour sacks as clothes, with nothing under them. And they often had two great streams of snot hanging down from their nose. They were very unattractive looking. I would feel sorry for them and ask my family about them, and they would say, "This is just the way they are. They are born this way. They don't have any pride or ambition. If you gave them anything, they would just get drunk or spend it on something foolish. They are immoral and spend their money unwisely." And here they were living on five or six dollars a week, if they were employed.

" ' Yassam, but dat ain't all, m'am.' "

Stereotype of the African-American from Thomas Dixon's *Sins of the Fathers* (1913).

THE COMMUNITY OUTCAST

In *To Kill a Mockingbird*, the character Boo Radley can be labeled with many names: outcast, eccentric, witch, vampire. One of the main plot lines of the novel involves the children's coming to terms with the terror of the unknown, which is exemplified by Boo Radley. Although he first appears in their minds in stereotype, Boo gradually achieves human proportions. From a devil, he becomes a savior. Boo is part of an old tradition of "the different one," the "recluse." In surveying that tradition, we learn something of Boo and much more of the community that sees Boo as a horror.

Even though the presence of a mysterious and devilish outcast in communities is as old as civilization, the outcast or eccentric has one striking historical American manifestation—the Salem witch.

The first excerpt included in this section is from a historical study of witchcraft in Salem, Massachusetts, in the seventeenth century. At that time, hundreds of citizens were arrested as witches and some were actually hanged on "gallows hill." As you read the excerpt, note the similarity between how the community viewed the Salem witches and how the Maycomb community viewed Boo.

Although the hysteria over witches in Salem was extreme, the situation in different forms exists in most communities—and certainly in the fictional community of Maycomb, Alabama. In most social units there exists one or more individuals who don't "fit in" with the rest. They live isolated from community life, typically as hermits or recluses; and their antisocial behavior often fails to follow community norms. In fact, the community may blame them for various troubles and ill fortune. At times such outcasts are in open conflict with the community, for example, in legal disputes. Thus, they become scapegoats. Such was the case with Boo Radley.

For these reasons alone—because such outcasts are unknown and superficially different—the community projects onto them all things mysterious, magical, even insidious and evil.

Christina Larner writes in *Witchcraft and Religion* (1984) that witches were "the disturbers of social order; they were those who could not easily cooperate with others; they were aggressive. Witches, like male bullies, were not 'nice people' " (87). Larner also indicates those things that the community blamed on witches:

"These were sudden illness, certain accidents, lingering illnesses for which no cause was clear, strokes, unexpected deaths, the failure of crops, especially if other people's were doing well, the drying up of milk, human or animal, strange behaviour in animals and in fishing villages, disasters at sea" (74).

In another perspective, Terence Morris includes in the introduction to his book *Deviance and Control* (1976) a statement that sheds light on the modern "witch": "People tend to define the 'normal' in terms of what they expect, what they are used to, and what they believe to be morally acceptable" (15).

The third excerpt in this section addresses the nature of any outcast, not just the witch. Psychologist Thomas Szasz, who shocked the mental health community with his views of the deviant, argues that any person who is somewhat eccentric or difficult is locked away in a prison or institution in our society.

FROM PAUL BOYER AND STEPHEN NUSSBAUM,
SALEM POSSESSED
(Cambridge, MA: Harvard University Press, 1974)

The first three women to be accused could be seen as "deviants" or "outcasts" in the community—the kinds of people who anthropologists have suggested are particularly susceptible to such accusations [of witchcraft]. Tituba . . . was a West Indian slave; Sarah Good was a pauper who went around the Village begging aggressively for food and lodging; "Gammer" Osborne, while somewhat better off, was a bedridden old woman.

. . .

In the most literal sense, of course, a large majority of the total group of accused witches would fall into the category "outsider," since 82 percent of them lived beyond the bounds of Salem Village. . . . There was more than one kind of "outsider" in Salem Village. Particularly vulnerable on this score were those Villagers who had been living in the community for only a short time, or whose arrival had had a disruptive social impact.

. . .

[For example, Bridget Oliver Bishop of Salem Town] "did entertain people in her house at unseasonable hours in the night to keep drinking and playing at shuffle-board, whereby discord did arise in other families, and young people were in danger to be corrupted." . . . Though she had lived within the Village for seven years, Bridget Bishop remained, in the most literal sense, an outsider—and one whose arrival had brought discord and family conflict in its wake.

FROM THOMAS S. SZASZ, "POWER AND PSYCHIATRY," IN
DEVIANCE IN AMERICAN LIFE
(New Brunswick, NJ: Transaction Publishers, 1989)

Typically, the person who is committed to a mental hospital has not broken the law. He is locked up because he has what is called a "major mental illness"—such as depression or schizophrenia—and because he is said to be "dangerous to himself or others." . . . The belief that such persons are crazy and do not know what is in their own best interests makes it seem legitimate to incarcerate them. This is a socially useful arrangement: it allows some people to dispose of some other people who annoy or upset them. . . . The poor, the old, and the young are committed to mental hospitals—not because they have more schizophrenia and depression than others, nor because they are more dangerous than others, but because they have less power than others.

. . .

Thus, in Anglo-American law, people have a right to be depressed or to talk crazy. At the same time, however, the so-called normal people in society do not want to put up with such behavior. Since they cannot control it one way, they will try to control it another way. That is how psychiatric sanctions have come into being and why they have become so popular; they satisfy a popular need for controlling certain behaviors that are not illegal but which "normal" people want controlled.

. . .

The very essence of the mental hygiene laws is thus to serve a purpose quite different from, indeed diametrically opposed to, the preservation of individual liberty. What is that purpose? It is to preserve and promote a common ideology or world view—that is, a shared sense of what is "normal"; it is also to preserve and protect the family from its excessively disruptive members—that is, from parents, children, or aged relatives who interfere with the well-being of the dominant members; and finally, it is to do so under medical and therapeutic, rather than penological or punitive, auspices—thus muting rather than polarizing conflicts in the family, on the job, in society as a whole. In short, just as individuals need "tranquilizers," so society, too, needs to have its conflicts defused and pacified.

STUDY QUESTIONS

1. Compare and contrast the Keith family, as it is represented in the excerpt from Thomas Nelson Page's book, with the Finch family in *To Kill a Mockingbird*.

2. Are Gordon Keith's heroes ones that Atticus would likely choose? Explain.

3. Is Mr. Bonner (his letter appeared in the *Tuscaloosa News*), who was also a senator and a Southerner, more like or unlike General Keith and his son? Is there anything in the two portraits that you would call typically southern?

4. To what extent does "the past" figure as a major element in both portraits of the southern gentleman?

5. Contrast the dress, speech, and behavior expected of little girls with the realities presented in the interview and the portrait in *To Kill a Mockingbird*.

6. In what ways does Atticus appear to train Scout to violate the community code for little girls?

7. Scout decides to spend time with two women who seem to become her models of womanhood. These are Miss Maudie and Calpurnia, rather than Aunt Alexandra. Analyze and speculate about why she chooses these two women rather than the models of "proper" womanhood, Aunt Alexandra and the missionary ladies.

8. There seem to be class divisions even among the very poor. Explain, basing your analysis on the novel and the recollections presented here.

9. What effect did the Civil War have on the lives of black and white Southerners, as that issue is raised in these recollections and in *To Kill a Mockingbird*?

10. Compare the description of the setting of the Lesters' household in Erskine Caldwell's *God's Little Acre* with that of the Ewells in *To Kill a Mockingbird*.

11. Discuss the attitudes and characteristics that poverty has created as described by Vernon Johnson, Shields McIlwain, William Faulkner, Erskine Caldwell, and Harper Lee.

12. Using the various documents, including *To Kill a Mockingbird*, discuss the link between poverty and morality as it was popularly regarded at the time.

13. Compare Victoria Price and Mayella Ewell with particular reference to their economic situations. To what extent might one argue that

economics produced both the tragedy of Tom Robinson and the Scottsboro tragedy?

14. Consider Donald Bogle's categories of stereotype. In this light, discuss the stereotypes created by the citizens of Maycomb in *To Kill a Mockingbird*.

15. Compare the emotion that Thomas Dixon attempts to evoke and his means of evoking it in *The Flaming Sword* with Bob Ewell's description of the alleged rape in *To Kill a Mockingbird*. Keep in mind that Dixon was a minister, financially well-to-do, a highly educated and successful writer who was actively involved in politics at the national level.

16. Consider Donald Bogle's categories and then examine the various African-American characters in *To Kill a Mockingbird*. Discuss how Harper Lee's African-American characters dispel the stereotypes of the mammy and the buck, in particular.

17. Using excerpts from Thomas Szasz's essay, consider this question: Is Boo Radley the only one who fits the pattern of outcast in *To Kill a Mockingbird*? Explain.

TOPICS FOR WRITTEN OR ORAL EXPLORATION

1. Write an essay on "the good family." What are the spoken or implied characteristics of "the good family" in your own culture or community? What part do tradition, social standing, and material possessions play, if any? Compare and contrast your community's view of the good family with that of Aunt Alexandra, Scout, and Jem, and the people whose impressions are documented in this chapter.

2. Note the place of "bearing arms," the Civil War, and the honor of battle in young Gordon Keith's memory of his father. Paint a verbal or graphic picture of the elder Keith in his typical mode and in his finest hour. Contrast it with Atticus in his typical mode and in his finest hour.

3. What material things does the young Gordon Keith associate with his father? What material things do the Finch children associate with Atticus? Write a contrast, noting how Atticus departs from the image of the usual southern gentleman.

4. With no (or only slight) revision, deliver Mr. Bonner's letter as a parodic speech.

5. Write a contrast of Atticus's view of his southern past with that in the two selections by and about southern "gentlemen."

6. One historian of poor people in the South sees most fictional por-

trayals as reinforcing a stereotype. Compare the fictional portrayals of the poor white with the historical ones. Do the fictional portrayals, including Harper Lee's, seem more stereotype than real? Explain.

7. Many middle-class or upper-class people seemed to have much more contact with and sympathy for African-Americans than for poor whites. Explain, using the novel as part of your source material.

8. Write an essay on Boo Radley as a typical creation of a "witch" by the community.

9. Expectations of little girls have changed since the 1930s. From your own experience and observation, what gender-based dress and manners remain? Would Scout be more or less typical of the little girl of the 1990s?

10. Debate this proposition: that social class makes a difference in the behavior expected of little girls.

11. Collect one bit of oral history from some older person you know. Let your focus be on one of the subjects presented in this collection of documents. For example, does your interviewee remember the Scottsboro trials or the civil rights era? Can you infer something from your interview about the realities and stereotypes discussed in this section?

12. What is the effect of *To Kill a Mockingbird* on your thinking? Has it challenged any images you had of Southerners, African-Americans, or little girls? Discuss.

SUGGESTED READINGS

See the full text of works excerpted in this section. Also examine novels by Thomas Nelson Page, Thomas Dixon, William Faulkner, Margaret Mitchell, Eudora Welty, and Erskine Caldwell for characterizations of Southerners.

For an excellent historical study of the poor white, see:

Flynt, Wayne. *Poor But Proud: Alabama's Poor Whites*. Tuscaloosa: University of Alabama Press, 1989.

For a depiction of life in the 1930s, see the Public Broadcasting System's film "The Great Depression."

Other historical sources include the following works:

Cash, W. J. *The Mind of the South*. New York: Vintage Books, 1969.

Grafton, Carl, and Anne Permaloff. *Big Mules and Branchheads: James E. Folsom and Political Power in Alabama*. Athens: University of Georgia Press, 1985.

Hackney, Sheldon. *Populism to Progressivism in Alabama*. Princeton: Princeton University Press, 1969.

Hamilton, Virginia Van der Veer. *Alabama: A Bicentennial History*. New York: W. W. Norton, 1977.

Tindall, George Brown. *The Emergence of the New South 1913–1945*. Baton Rouge: Louisiana State University Press, 1967.

Wiener, Jonathan M. *Social Origins of the New South: Alabama 1860– 1885*. Baton Rouge: Louisiana State University Press, 1978.

5

The Issue of Heroism

Over thirty years after the publication of *To Kill a Mockingbird*, the question of heroism, especially the heroism of the civilian (as opposed to that of the professional soldier), has become an issue. Although in earlier times there might have been little debate over Atticus's heroism, in the late 1980s and the 1990s history has been "revised" and law and literature have been "deconstructed." Previously accepted ideas about moral behavior and ultimate meaning have been re-examined and overturned, often in light of more recent interpretations of moral behavior. At times, heroes are suddenly damned because they are found wanting when they are measured against the social and moral views of an age not their own.

The question of what constitutes a hero like Atticus Finch arises in a time when Americans can look back on civilian citizens of the 1950s, both black and white, who performed heroic actions (e.g., in the civil rights struggle) and those who suffered as a result of their heroism (e.g., in refusing to cooperate with the "witch hunts" of Senator Joe McCarthy). Many of the courageous people, especially during the civil rights era, were lawyers and judges like Atticus Finch. And, coming into print at the height of the civil rights struggle was *To Kill a Mockingbird*, a novel that first gave the world the image of the courageous southern attorney, an image that subsequently became popular in literature and film.

One reason why the controversy over the Atticus Finch image arose in the 1990s is because overt public resentment against lawyers (expressed in the popularity of lawyer jokes, for example) promoted re-examination of lawyers and ethical behavior. Particular controversies in the legal profession also provoked another look at Atticus, who is cited by many lawyers as a professional model. On one hand, some have argued that the great lawyer, of which Atticus is an exemplar, is a "gentleman" of character who has a sense of ethics built in by the religious society he or she has embraced from childhood. On the other hand, some believe that this point of view is largely nonsense and that all lawyers—gentlemen or not—need a written code of ethics to keep them in line.

Monroe Freedman, who fired the first shot in the following skirmish, represents the latter school of thought. His column from the *Legal Times* is largely a refutation of Professor Thomas Shaffer, who in numerous books and articles has upheld Atticus Finch as the gentleman/lawyer who instinctively acts admirably because through the years proper ethics have become a part of his character. Shaffer's implication is that such men need no code of ethics as Freedman defines them. But Freedman also argues that Atticus Finch is revealed in the novel to be less than admirable: as a legislator, he makes no move to change the system of racial injustice and even seems to condone the actions of his bigoted fellow Southerners.

Freedman's critics, including R. Mason Barge, believe that he is demanding perfection of Atticus and applying the values of the 1990s to a character who inhabits the 1930s. Barge turns the tables on Freedman, asking him to be responsible for conditions in New York City in the 1990s.

One might even say that Atticus Finch, a character in a novel that exploded stereotypes, himself ironically has become a stereotype. As the following documents show, Atticus, whose fame comes from his actions as a defense attorney, was himself on trial in 1992.

MONROE FREEDMAN: "ATTICUS FINCH, ESQ., R.I.P.:
A GENTLEMAN BUT NO MODEL FOR LAWYERS"

A new ethical role model for lawyers is being promoted in scholarly books, law reviews, and bar journals. His name is Atticus Finch. He looks a lot like Gregory Peck. He is a gentleman. He has character.

"For me," writes a California trial lawyer in the October 1991 issue of the *ABA Journal*, "there is no more compelling role model than Atticus Finch. . . . Fine citizen, parent and lawyer, Finch . . . would remind us that this burden [of meeting a higher standard of behavior and trust] is never too much to bear."

Another commentator, in a November 1990 essay in the *Stanford Law Review*, eulogizes Atticus Finch in a different fashion, but with much the same sense of admiration: "[T]here is no longer a place in America for a lawyer like Atticus Finch. There is nothing for him to do here—nothing he can do. He is a moral character in a world where the role of moral thought has become at best highly ambivalent."

And so on. Atticus Finch, the hero of Harper Lee's novel *To Kill a Mockingbird*, has become the ethical exemplar in articles on topics ranging from military justice to moral theology. If we don't do something fast, lawyers are going to start taking him seriously as someone to emulate. And that would be a bad mistake.

The whole business begins with the idea that understanding and abiding by the rules of ethical conduct is not enough. Rather, it is said, a crucial element that is too often overlooked is "character." The notion of character traces back to what Aristotle called "virtue." The quality of virtue or character is not directly concerned with *doing* the right thing, but rather with *being* the right type of person. That is, the person of character will "naturally" act upon the right principles.

THE APPOINTED MODEL

Atticus Finch is a lawyer in the small town of Macomb [sic], Ala., in the 1930s. As most readers will remember, in the course of the novel a black man, Tom Robinson, is falsely accused of raping a white woman, who, in fact, had been trying to seduce him. Finch is appointed to defend Robinson.

Finch would prefer not to have been appointed but, recognizing his duty as a member of the bar, he carries out the representation zealously. He even risks his own life to protect Robinson from a lynch mob. As we are told in the book, as well as in recent commentaries on lawyers' ethics, Finch acts as he does because he is a gentleman.

Is Atticus Finch, then, a role model for lawyers? I think not.

In risking his life to save Robinson, Finch is undeniably admirable. But am I really expected to tell my students that they should emulate Finch by putting themselves between a lynch mob and a client? I may be a staunch proponent of zealous representation, but I can't sell what I won't buy.

It's true that Finch, having been appointed by the court to defend an unpopular client, gives him effective representation. That's an important ethical point, but it is also a relatively small one. And a refusal to accept a court's appointment is punishable by imprisonment for contempt.

What looms much larger for me is Atticus Finch's entire life as a lawyer in Macomb [sic] (which, ironically, is what "character" is all about).

DOWN WITH GENTLEMEN?

Let's go back to the idea of the gentleman. Part of my problem with it is that too many people who have carried that title have given it a bad name. Gentlemen tend to congregate together to exclude others from their company and from their privileges on grounds of race, gender, and religion. In short, the gentleman has too often been part of the problem of social injustice and too seldom part of the solution. Aristotle himself was an elitist who taught that there is a natural aristocracy and that some people are naturally fit to be their slaves.

Consider Finch. He knows that the administration of justice in Macomb [sic], Ala., is racist. He knows that there is a segregated "colored balcony" in the courthouse. He knows, too, that the restrooms in the courthouse are segregated—if, indeed, there is a restroom at all for blacks inside the courthouse.

Finch also goes to segregated restaurants, drinks from segregated water fountains, rides on segregated buses, and sits in a park that may well have a sign announcing "No Dogs or Colored Allowed." Finch is not surprised when Robinson, having been convicted by a bigoted jury, is later shot to death with no less than 17 bullets while making a hopeless attempt to escape from prison to avoid execution.

Even more telling, Atticus Finch instructs his children that the Ku Klux Klan is "a political organization more than anything." (David Duke, can you use a campaign manager who looks like Gregory Peck?) Finch also teaches his children that the leader of the lynch mob is "basically a good man" who "just has his blind spots."

In this respect, Finch is reminiscent of Henry Drinker, author of the first book on the American Bar Association's Canons of Professional Ethics, which governed from 1908 until 1970. In his 1953 book, *Legal Ethics*, Drinker wrestled with what he considered a particularly difficult ethical conundrum: If a lawyer has been convicted of lynching a black man, is the lawyer guilty of a crime involving moral turpitude and therefore subject to disbarment?

Finch also is capable of referring to Eleanor Roosevelt not as a great humanitarian or even as the First Lady but, mockingly, as "the distaff side of the Executive branch in Washington" who is "fond of hurling" the concept of human equality. Finch's daughter, Scout, is at least as intelligent as Jem, but it is Jem who is brought up to understand that, following his father, he will be a lawyer. Scout understands that she will be some gentleman's lady. Toward that end, she is made to put on her pink Sunday dress, shoes, and petticoat and go to tea with the ladies—where she is taunted with the absurd proposition (which she promptly denies) that she might want to become a lawyer.

BEYOND NOBLESSE OBLIGE

Atticus Finch does, indeed, act heroically in his representation of Robinson. But he does so from an elitist sense of noblesse oblige. Except under compulsion of a court appointment, Finch never attempts to change the racism and sexism that permeate the life of Macomb [sic], Ala. On the contrary, he lives his own life as the passive participant in that pervasive injustice. And that is not my idea of a role model for young lawyers.

Let me put it this way. I would have more respect for Atticus Finch if he had never been compelled by the court to represent Robinson, but if, instead, he had undertaken voluntarily to establish the right of the black citizens of Macomb [sic] to sit freely in their county courthouse. That Atticus Finch would, indeed, have been a model for young lawyers to emulate.

Don't misunderstand. I'm not saying that I would present as role models those truly admirable lawyers who, at great personal sacrifice, have dedicated their entire professional lives to fighting for social injustice. That's too easy to preach and too hard to practice.

Rather, the lawyers we should hold up as role models are those who earn their living in the kinds of practices that most lawyers pursue—corporate, trusts and estates, litigation, even teaching—but who also volunteer a small but significant amount of their time and skills to advance social justice. That is the cause that Atticus Finch, a gentleman of character, chose to ignore throughout his legal career.

Legal Times, February 24, 1992.

R. MASON BARGE: "FICTIONAL CHARACTERS, FICTIONAL ETHICS"

In Rebuttal

In his article, "Atticus Finch, Esq., R.I.P." (Feb. 24, 1992, page 20), Monroe Freedman reached the right conclusion for the wrong reason.

To say that Atticus Finch is an improper ethical role model for attorneys is like saying that Mother Teresa is an improper ethical role model for the Khmer Rouge.

. . .

Sitting on this lofty perch of "legal ethics," Mr. Freedman attacks a fictional character for not attempting to change the "racism and sexism" of a fictional town. Of course, the principal action of this rather short novel is that of a southern lawyer placing his career and life on the line for a wrongfully accused black man. How can we explain this contradiction?

Mr. Freedman wants to extol corporate lawyers. Let me propose as an example a person who makes $200,000 a year beating the hell out of Mexican farm workers, but devotes a "small but significant" amount of time advancing "social justice," which I read to mean Mr. Freedman's political views.

Now, why is that not exactly what Atticus Finch did? Apparently, it is because Freedman would hold Atticus Finch responsible for the entirety of the sins of the society in which he lived, while holding actual lawyers responsible for only a "small but significant" amount of *pro bono* work.

My point is that there is no logical consistency to Mr. Freedman's article. He derides the fictional account of an extraordinarily brave and morally driven man, while sounding the drum for a less fictional but even more conventional "corporate lawyer" who does some *pro bono* work. One must conclude that Mr. Freedman is simply more comfortable criticizing Alabama in 1930 than New York in 1990.

. . .

In my book, any lawyer who takes on the establishment *pro bono publico* is a hero. I hope Mr. Freedman would agree, and if so, I'll make a deal with him. We'll worry about racism down here, and you just go on living in the good old days, when New York was marginally less racist than Alabama and its inhabitants could arrogate moral superiority to themselves. And when you get around to cleaning up some of those sewers you call cities, give me a call, and we can talk about what a bad guy Atticus Finch was.

CHEAP SHOT

Let's see now, what other sins does Mr. Finch commit? Mr. Freedman isolates Finch's statement that the Ku Klux Klan is basically a "political organization," apparently attempting to discredit Finch by tying him to the KKK and David Duke. A cheap shot, certainly. Even worse, an ignorant criticism. The KKK *is* basically a political organization, both functionally and historically. In fact, from the point of view of dialectical materialism, the KKK is *entirely* a political organization.

Finch also dares to criticize Eleanor Roosevelt. Why does Mr. Freedman love Eleanor Roosevelt more than Atticus Finch? Is it because Finch's forebears were not as successful as the Roosevelts in exploiting the sweat of the lower classes, and he was thus forced to make a living in a corrupt society, while Mrs. Roosevelt was free to do good deeds in white gloves without threat of poverty and ostracism? Does he find somebody else's dirty linen, i.e., pernicious racism, smellier than the Irish and Italian women who died in Manhattan shirt factories?

Well, Finch says that the leader of the lynch mob is basically a good man. This is a fundamental concept of Christianity and certainly a defensible and good-faith moral position.

. . .

Let's see. Finch knows that there is a "colored balcony" in the courthouse and fails to protest. One must grant the point. Atticus Finch only risked his life and career for the sake of one black man. He did not dedicate himself to ceaseless toil with absolute sacrifice to forcing 1930 Alabama into racial and sexual equality, unlike Gandhi or your average legal ethics professor, who would have if he could have. So we judge Mr. Finch by his imperfections, do we?

Mr. Freedman, do you realize that *even today*, and only *minutes from your front door*, there are people starving to death? There are people shooting black schoolchildren with guns and killing them, and pregnant women smoking crack? You don't even have to go as far away as Alabama, or as far back in time as 1930. I'm serious! I know you don't know about this, or you would be putting your butt on the line for these people instead of criticizing Atticus Finch, who did put his butt on the line for an innocent black man. Of course, he *was* fictional. But then so are your "legal ethics."

Legal Times, March 9, 1992.

CONCLUSION

Professor Freedman's article provoked so much outraged response, similar to R. Mason Barge's rebuttal in the *Legal Times*, that the controversy was covered in the *New York Times* and the *Los Angeles Daily Journal*. Among those responding was the president of the American Bar Association. Finally, on May 18, 1992, Professor Freedman reacted to the criticism in his *Legal Times* column, this time entitled "The Lawyer Mythologized." He opened his column by acknowledging that even though Atticus Finch is fictional, he is mythical, even immortal. He went on to inform the paper's readers of the reaction to his criticism of Atticus, declaring that in the two years of writing his very controversial column, he had never received such outraged objections as he had to the column on Atticus Finch. He concluded by saying that readers of his column, arguing that Atticus Finch was not a good role model for law students, responded as if he were attacking Mother Teresa, Ghandi, God, and Bambi all at once.

STUDY QUESTIONS

1. Consult the chapters on the Scottsboro Case and the civil rights era and write an essay on one of the figures portrayed there as a hero or heroine.
2. Does society's idea of the hero change? Explain.
3. Has your own idea of a particular hero or heroism in general changed? Explain. If so, to what do you attribute any change?
4. In a nutshell, what is Professor Freedman's objection to Atticus as a hero for young lawyers?

TOPICS FOR WRITTEN OR ORAL EXPLORATION

1. Stage a courtroom scene in which Atticus Finch is on trial. Have two people play the roles of prosecuting and defense attorneys and others play characters from the novel who testify for or against Atticus. Add Monroe Freedman to the list of witnesses.
2. Professor Freedman refuses to endorse the tradition of the gentleman as an ideal and virtuous man. Discuss the ideal of the "gentleman" by using the information in Chapter 4 ("Realities and Stereotypes"), *To Kill a Mockingbird*, and Professor Freedman's article.
3. Consider that attorneys Freedman and Barge have submitted their two "briefs" to you, the judge, for an opinion. Compose an opinion (in the manner of Judge James Horton of the Scottsboro case), deciding whether Atticus Finch must relinquish his title of Heroic Lawyer.
4. Write your own definition of a hero, citing examples. How does your definition compare with the character of Atticus Finch?

SUGGESTED READINGS

The following works enlarge on the argument regarding Atticus Finch in the legal community:

Ayer, John D. "Narrative in the Moral Theology of Tom Shaffer." *Journal of Legal Education* 40 (March–June 1990): 173–93.
Carter, Claudia A. "Lawyers as Heroes: The Compassionate Activism of a Fictional Attorney Is a Model We Can Emulate." *Los Angeles Lawyer* 22 (July–August 1988): 13.
D'Alemberte, Talbot. "Remembering Atticus Finch's *Pro Bono* Legacy." *Legal Times*, vol. 14 (April 6, 1992): 26.
Dunn, Timothy. "Atticus Finch De Novo: In Defense of Gentlemen." *New Jersey Law Journal* 130 (April 27, 1992): 15.
Freedman, Monroe. "Finch: The Lawyer Mythologized." *Legal Times*, vol. 14 (May 18, 1992): 25.

Hall, Timothy L. "Moral Character, the Practice of Law, and Legal Education." *Mississippi Law Journal* 60 (Winter 1990): 511–54.

Hodel, Matthew A. "No Hollow Hearts." *American Bar Association Journal* 77 (October 1991): 68, 69.

Margolick, David. "Chipping at Atticus Finch's Pedestal." *New York Times*, February 28, 1992: B1.

Shaffer, Thomas L. "Christian Lawyer Stories and American Legal Ethics." *Mercer Law Review* 33 (Spring 1982): 877–901.

———. *Faith and the Professions*. Salt Lake City: Brigham Young University Press, 1987.

———. "The Moral Theology of Atticus Finch." *University of Pittsburgh Law Review* 42 (1981): 197–204.

———. *On Being a Christian and a Lawyer*. Salt Lake City: Brigham Young University Press, 1981.

6

The Issue of Censorship

To Kill a Mockingbird is one of the most widely read novels of all time. Ever since its publication in 1960, it has also been one of the books most frequently challenged by would-be censors. Objections have been raised to its presence on library shelves and to its use as required reading in schools.

A careful look reveals that most of the elements would-be censors object to can be found in *To Kill a Mockingbird*: (1) references to the sex act, (2) slang and ungrammatical speech, (3) curse words and obscene words, (4) racial slurs, (5) descriptions of rebelliousness or challenges to authority, (6) unfavorable portrayals of the establishment, including organized religion and the government, (7) questioning of absolutes, and (8) the imposition of values. Author Julian Thompson, in categorizing the most frequent objections to literature, cites three main categories that are all pertinent to Harper Lee's novel: (1) vulgar language, (2) references to sexual activity, and (3) expression of anti-establishment attitudes.[1] *To Kill a Mockingbird* has raised objections on all counts.

As students approach the record of controversy over *To Kill a Mockingbird* in Hanover County, Virginia (see the documents that follow), they should be reminded that the impulse to have certain books removed from school reading lists and library shelves is very strong indeed. To grasp the issue clearly, one must consider the arguments that provoke efforts to censor books.

What is the other side of the censorship issue? Who challenges books? Why do these individuals argue that certain materials should not be available in school libraries and classrooms? Studies indicate that the single largest group of censors are parents, but that teachers, school administrators, and other citizens who are not necessarily speaking as parents also challenge books. In addition, there are a number of so-called watchdog organizations that scrutinize school library shelves and textbooks and raise objections to materials. These organizations have on several occasions gone to court in attempts to have materials removed from schools. The "classics" most frequently challenged on moral grounds are *The Scarlet Letter, The Catcher in the Rye, Lord of the Flies, Snow White, The Wizard of Oz, The Grapes of Wrath*, and *Slaughterhouse Five. To Kill a Mockingbird* has also been challenged frequently.

Those who are interested in removing certain books from shelves or classrooms believe students are harmed by reading these materials, that particular books lead students in inappropriate directions. In writing about why parents want to protect their children from reading material they consider offensive or dangerous, R. C. Small, Jr., says that teachers have been telling their students for decades that books are powerful and have the capacity to change lives. Why should anyone be surprised, he writes, when some parents take seriously what they have been taught about the power of books and decide that some books can have the power to harm?

> We have led parents—our former students, after all—to believe that great works contain great truths and that masterpieces are such because of their power to influence. Why should it now be so surprising that parents, discovering curse words, scenes of sexual relations, arguments against the current American social order, questions about the existence of God, believe that we are now pushing ideas as we formerly pushed the ideas in *Silas Marner* and *Julius Caesar*?[2]

One big difference between those who challenge books and those who support the freedom to read (e.g., members of the

American Library Association) is that the former see adolescents as somewhat "passive," as Frances Beck McDonald has written.[3] Would-be censors tend to believe that adolescents are easily influenced and led by what they read, that they are not capable of making independent judgments. The latter assume that adolescents can make judgments and that the more information they receive, the better they will be able to cope with reality.

Judging from hearings in the state of Texas, where parents were permitted to speak out on particular textbooks before they were approved for adoption, the most frequent challenges were made to materials that were "depressing," that revealed people "at their worst," and that showed rebelliousness or lawlessness, which "is not good enough for impressionable young minds!"[4] One powerful group in Texas asked that horror stories be removed from reading lists because they are "conducive to causing emotional instability in young minds."[5] Many books, the group argued, especially those "(1) stressing *change*, (2) *questioning* just about everything, and (3) [making] *no* acknowledgment of anything fixed or *absolute* must, as steady dripping water, gradually indoctrinate students away from traditional, basic, biblical, exact values."[6]

In 1974 a community group in Kanawha County, West Virginia, engaged in a long and violent battle to remove certain textbooks from the classroom and then set out guidelines to be followed in approving books for school use. Only those books would be approved that (1) acknowledged the sanctity of the home as the backbone of American society, (2) did not ask personal questions about the students' feelings or their families, (3) did not contain profanity, (4) did not demean anyone's ethnicity, race, or religion, (5) did not provoke racial hatred, (6) did encourage national loyalty, (7) did not show any other form of government as being better than our own, (8) did not criticize the nation's founders, and (9) did stress conventional English grammar.[7]

Often parents' objections to certain books are met by providing alternative readings for their children. But in a few cases the schools and courts have decided that such children must meet the same requirements demanded of other children, and thus must use the same books even if their parents object. In any case, the substitution of alternative texts is also controversial. Schools sometimes argue that providing alternative materials can mean that some children are being exposed to information very selectively and therefore are not being adequately educated. Parents of such children have argued that schools should accommodate those whose religious beliefs are violated by required readings.

Unfortunately, there is little documented evidence on the objections to *To Kill a Mockingbird*. Objections are usually raised orally in public meetings, which are not widely reported in the press. From records accumulated by the American Library Association, we know that most of the objections to Harper Lee's novel fall into three categories: objections to foul language, to the theme of rape, and to racial slurs. The history of censorship of *To Kill a Mockingbird* is complex; it has been summarized by Jill P. May in an article entitled "Censors as Critics: *To Kill a Mockingbird* as a Case Study" and is continually updated in the American Library Association's *Newsletter on Intellectual Freedom*.[8]

Objections to the use of *To Kill a Mockingbird* in the classroom or its presence on library shelves were made chiefly in the South in the years just after its publication. The most highly publicized case occurred in 1966 in Hanover County, Virginia, where the school board initially decided that the novel would not be on the list of books approved for school use. The chief reason given was that it was immoral. Challenges to the book spread to other parts of the country during the 1970s and 1980s. The reference to rape and the use of obscene and curse words continued to be cited as objections. In Eden Valley, Minnesota, in 1977 the novel was removed from schools because of the use of "damn" and "whore lady," and in the Vernon-Verona-Sherill, New York, school district in 1980 on the grounds that it was a "filthy, trashy novel." In a school in Pennsylvania the novel was removed from shelves on the complaint of a teacher that it contained the word "piss." In Alabama it was challenged by a parent who objected to the word "damn." Language in the novel has also provoked objections in Wisconsin, Washington, West Virginia, and Illinois.

Although all the black characters are sympathetic and the novel exposes racism as abhorrent and white racists as ludicrous and hypocritical, *To Kill a Mockingbird*, like *The Adventures of Huckleberry Finn*, has frequently been challenged by African-American parents chiefly because it contains racial slurs. The American Library Association provides us with a partial list of challenges on these grounds. In Warren, Indiana, in 1981 several citizens found the novel to "represent institutionalized racism under the guise of 'good literature.' " The book was not banned, but three African-American members of a race relations advisory board resigned in protest. In 1984 in Waukegan, Illinois, objections were raised to the novel's use of the word "nigger." In 1985 the novel was challenged in Kansas City and Park Hill, Missouri, and in Casa Grande, Arizona, because it included profanity and racial slurs.

To Kill a Mockingbird does indeed contain racial slurs, spoken from the mouths of some of its characters. But those who would censor it on these grounds should consider the alternative: Would we want a novel about race relations in the South of the 1930s to ignore the language used at the time? to "pretty up" the language of racists? in short, to distort reality and to portray racists as less objectionable than they are?

NOTES

1. "Defending YA Literature against the Pharisees and Censors: Is It Worth the Trouble?" *ALAN Review* 18, no. 2 (1991): 2–5.

2. "Censorship and English: Some Things We Don't Seem to Think about Very Often (But Should)," *Focus* 3 (1978): 18–24.

3. "Appendix B. Freedom to Read: A Professional Responsibility," in Richard Beach and James Marshall, eds., *Teaching Literature in the Secondary School* (New York: Harcourt Brace Jovanovich, 1991).

4. James C. Hefley, *Are Textbooks Harming Your Children?* (Milford, MI: Mott Media, 1979), p. 85.

5. Ibid., p. 85.

6. Ibid., p. 103.

7. Ibid., p. 172.

8. Jill P. May, "Censors as Critics: *To Kill a Mockingbird* as a Case Study," in *Cross-Culturalism in Children's Literature* (New York: Pace University, 1988). The *Newsletter on Intellectual Freedom* is printed bi-monthly in Chicago, Illinois.

A CENSORSHIP ATTEMPT IN HANOVER, VIRGINIA, 1966

This group of documents reflects the history of one very public instance in which *To Kill a Mockingbird* was challenged. The incident began when a prominent physician, W. C. Bosher, the father of a Hanover County student, took a look at the novel his son had brought home to read and decided it was immoral. Dr. Bosher, who was a County Board of Education trustee, was disturbed that his son was reading a book about rape and reported to the school board that the book was "improper for our children to read." On the strength of his motion, the board voted to remove *To Kill a Mockingbird* from the shelves of the Hanover County school libraries.

In the flurry of reportage and exchange of opinions that followed, the board blamed the state, arguing that the County Board had had the novel removed because *To Kill a Mockingbird* had never been on the *state's* list of books approved for state subsidy. When the State Board of Education was challenged about banning the novel, it pointed its finger at the county, saying that the county was free to keep the book on county shelves. The State Board of Education members argued that Harper Lee's novel was not on the approved list solely because no publisher had ever presented *To Kill a Mockingbird* to them for state subsidy. However, it was eventually discovered that thousands of books presented by publishers for places on the approved list had been rejected by the state's censoring board. As in most cases, except for Dr. Bosher's statements to the press, no reason for rejection by county or state was ever given to the public.

The controversy over *To Kill a Mockingbird* is documented in the pages of the Richmond press. Included are news stories reporting the action of the board, editorials, letters to the editor on both sides of the question, and a response from the author, Harper Lee herself. Eventually, the Board backed away from its original decision to take the book out of the library.

MR. BUMBLE AND THE MOCKINGBIRD

The Hanover County School Board last night ordered all copies of Harper Lee's novel, *To Kill a Mockingbird*, removed from the county's school library shelves. In the dim vision of the Hanover board, the novel is "immoral literature." It is "improper for our children to read." And so, by unanimous vote, out it goes—and all other books not on the State Board of Education's approved list are to be taken out of circulation also.

As grown-ups who have been out of Hanover County doubtless are aware, *To Kill a Mockingbird* has become a contemporary classic. It is the tender and moving story of a rape trial in Alabama, and of a white lawyer's effort to obtain justice for a Negro client. A more moral novel scarcely could be imagined. The book was a best-seller; it was made into a notable motion picture; it won the Pulitzer Prize for fiction in 1961; it is read by high school students everywhere else in America but in Hanover County, Virginia.

Fortunately, there exists a remedy for this asinine performance by the Hanover board. Let us now turn to the Beadle Bumble Fund. For some years, we have maintained the fund (named for the famous character in *Oliver Twist*, also an immoral novel) with the sole object of redressing the stupidities of public officials.

Mr. Bumble will gladly purchase and mail a paperbacked copy of *To Kill a Mockingbird* to the first 50 students of Lee-Davis High School who write in. The address is Mr. Bumble, The *News-Leader* Forum, 333 East Grace Street, Richmond.

Editorial Page, *Richmond News-Leader*, Wednesday, January 5, 1966, p. 12.

SOME NOVELS' FATE REMAINS UNCERTAIN

HANOVER SCHOOL BOARD TO USE STATE LIST AS GUIDE

"To Kill a Mockingbird" is dead in Hanover County schools, as far as county school officials are concerned, but the fate of such books as "1984," "Catcher in the Rye," and "Grapes of Wrath" remains in doubt.

The Pulitzer Prize–winning book by Harper Lee will not be used in Hanover County schools because in 1960 it was submitted for inclusion on the state aid book list and rejected, said School Board Chairman B. W. Sadler yesterday.

Under a resolution passed by the county school board Tuesday night, all books taken off the state-approved list must be removed from Hanover schools. The resolution also excludes from county schools books that have been rejected for inclusion on the state list, Sadler said.

The three other widely acclaimed novels also were attacked by W. C. Bosher, the Cold Harbor district school board member who initiated the board's action against "immoral literature."

SON WAS READING

He said the use of "To Kill a Mockingbird" at Lee-Davis High School had come to his attention when he discovered his son, a junior there, reading the book.

"To Kill a Mockingbird," the story of a rape trial in Alabama and of a white lawyer's attempt to obtain justice for a Negro client, is used as supplemental reading by the English department at Lee-Davis, according to the school's principal, B. V. Aylor.

Bosher labeled George Orwell's "1984," depicting the despotism of a regimented society, a "very seductive and suggestive piece of literature."

The books "1984," "Catcher in the Rye," and "Grapes of Wrath" have never been submitted by publishers for inclusion on the state list. J. D. Salinger's "Catcher in the Rye" is about a prep-school youth. John Steinbeck's "Grapes of Wrath" concerns the poverty of Oklahomans in the 1930s. Steinbeck's book was published in the 1930s; "Catcher in the Rye" and "1984" are post–World War II.

All books not appearing on the state aid list, the school board's resolution says, must be approved by a school faculty committee of not fewer than three members including the principal and librarian, if any, before they may be used at a county school.

"We are not censoring any books," declared Sadler. "We are saying in this instance that since the State Department of Education does have a library committee to review those books that are submitted to them, we would make a mockery of the committee, if we disregard their disapproval of books," he said.

Sadler said the school board's resolution was a general policy statement on the selection of books for county schools and would be turned over to school authorities for execution.

A spokesman for the State Department of Education explained that the list compiled by the state does not necessarily attempt to approve or disapprove of books from a moralistic standpoint.

The list is compiled to advise local school boards of books that the state will subsidize the purchase of, the spokesman said. Last year, 4,521 books were submitted by publishers and 3,361 were placed on the approved list.

Aylor, Lee-Davis principal, said he had received no official notification of the school board's action and that he has not attempted to stop the use of "To Kill a Mockingbird" at the school.

English teachers at the school declined comment on the controversy yesterday, as did Bosher.

At no point in the Tuesday meeting did the board consider a general ban of books not on the state-approved list. But Bosher appeared to express the sentiment of the board when he said "there should be a lot of screening" of the books used in our schools.

Richmond Times-Dispatch, Thursday, January 6, 1966, p. 2.

COLLEGE STUDENT DEFENDS MORALITY OF BANNED BOOK

Editor, *News-Leader*:

It is with deep regret that I must announce my ineligibility to request a copy of Harper Lee's immoral novel from Mr. Bumble. Unfortunately, I am now a college student and never resided in Hanover County. That is not to say I have not read the book, nor will consider re-reading it at some future date.

As a matter of fact, I can't think of any book I've ever been afraid of.

I recall my high school days very clearly (a very short time ago, critical elders). They were rich with new literary discoveries—many brought to me by a strongly book-minded mother. From the variety of philosophy consistently handed me, I don't believe she ever attempted to do anything more than make me read.

Ah, but parents so often err—for one day she brought me Harper Lee's story (perhaps she didn't realize that it contained the evil word "rape"). What did it do to me? This horrid piece of trash made me laugh and cry a little inside, forced me to live a life that wasn't mine for some hours, actually had the nerve to make me think of problems I had not yet faced.

It was traumatic.

I'm sure it was even immoral . . . if the good people of Hanover say it is.

Only one thing bothers me—why, if the book were so immoral, didn't I ever commit some criminal act as presented in the indecent tale?

People of the northern county, please learn that your brand of conservatism disgusts those of us with minds.

I tell ya, Mr. Bumble, I don't mind some of the citizens of Hanover County, but I sure wouldn't want my sister to marry one.

Alan Markow

"Forum," *Richmond News-Leader*, January 7, 1966, p. 12.

HIDING "SEAMY SIDE" IS FALSE PROTECTION

Members of the Hanover County School Board are absolutely wrong to ban "To Kill a Mockingbird."

"To Kill a Mockingbird," Mr. Salinger's "Catcher in the Rye," and George Orwell's "1984" are sensitive, frightening, awakening, truthful presentations of what could happen and is happening in our life today. Why hide truth from our young people? We need to teach them right from wrong.

We say "Don't," but fail to explain "Why," which is important whenever anyone is corrected or disciplined. We reinforce learning, even in the smallest toddler, as we correct, then accompany it with simple explanations.

Teach them, show them, but let them make choices whenever possible. Values are formed when one confronts and wrestles with truth. Hiding the "seamy" side of life is false protection. Sound instruction based on free choice of reading material is one way to develop character. We seem to be sadly lacking both at home and school in such instruction.

(Mrs.) Mary Lisle King
Mother of Four

"Voice of the People," *Richmond Times-Dispatch*, January 9, 1966, p. 14-B.

TWO BOOKS BANNED—NO DOUBT

The only thing not open to debate in Hanover County's book-banning battle today was that "To Kill a Mockingbird" and "1984" no longer were on the bookshelves of county schools.

Hanover's top school officials bluntly blamed the State Board of Education for the county school board action banishing the two modern classics from public school libraries.

The state dodged and weaved and disclaimed responsibility. It said even though the books aren't on its approved list, the decision to ban or not to ban is entirely up to local school boards.

. . .

"If we cannot depend on the competence of the state library committee, who can be depended on for guidance as to what books should be in our schools?" asked Hanover's school board chairman, B. W. Sadler.

"The school board or the superintendent of schools doesn't have the time, nor are we competent, to judge the books," Sadler said. "We are simply trying to set standards for books in the county system."

POLICY CHANGE?

"We might change this policy if the state board tells us that their disapproval of any books is not meaningful."

Other books missing from the list, including John Steinbeck's "The Grapes of Wrath" and J. D. Salinger's "The Catcher in the Rye," also will be affected by the school board ruling, Sadler confirmed.

"Voice of the People," *Richmond New-Leader*, January 10, 1966, p. 9.

WHO KILLED THE MOCKINGBIRD?

All of today's Forum is given to the beautiful controversy that has blown up since the Hanover County School Board voted unanimously last Tuesday night to ban Harper Lee's Pulitzer Prize–winning novel, *To Kill a Mockingbird*. While the local board's action has a couple of defenders, the overwhelming bulk of the mail reaching us is critical of the decision.

Yet it has become evident that the criticism is missing its mark—or more accurately, is hitting only one of two appropriate targets. The Hanover School Board exhibited the kind of small-bore stupidity that deserves to be roundly condemned; but the Hanover board was merely following the larger stupidity of the State Board of Education.

News stories have made it clear how the incredible system works. Book publishers submit copies of their books to a committee of the State Board of Education. The committee then recommends that some books be approved and some disapproved. Last year, 3,361 titles won approval; 1,160 were rejected. Because the State extends grant-in-aid funds to local school boards only for purchase of books on its approved list, the effect is to discourage purchase of books not on the approved list.

Miss Lee's novel, widely acclaimed as a contemporary classic, was submitted for approval in 1960, but rejected. George Orwell's great work, *1984*, was approved by the State in 1952, and then removed from the list a year later.

It occurs to us that the fire in this absurd business ought to be shifted from the local board members of Hanover County to the selection committee of the State Board of Education. Who are these dimwitted censors who would deny their sanction to *1984* and *To Kill a Mockingbird*? What credentials, if any, could support such astoundingly bad judgment? Do such broad-gauged men as Lewis Powell and Colgate Darden, members of the State Board of Education, condone this nonsense?

Off and on in recent years, we have detected encouraging signs that Virginia was emerging from the peckerwood provincialism and ingrown "morality" that H. L. Mencken, in a famous phrase, attributed to this Sahara of the Bozart. But if this dimwitted committee of the State Board of Education is fairly representative of the wisdom that prevails in high levels of State education policy, Mencken's old indictment stands reconfirmed today. If Messrs. Powell and Darden would like to start the New Year with a signal public service, perhaps they would take the lead in firing this committee and abolishing the State's Index of Approved Books altogether.

Editorial Page, *Richmond News-Leader*, January 10, 1966, p. 10.

LETTERS AND EDITOR'S COMMENTS FROM "Forum,"
Richmond News-Leader

Editor, *News-Leader*:

Your editorial comments on the action of the Hanover County School Board were very disappointing, to say the least. As a citizen of Hanover and parent of a Lee-Davis student, I am pleased with the action of the Board. Our School Board members and school administrators are interested and concerned with the educational policy for the promotion of the welfare of the children of this county. To establish a reading list of the caliber that would exclude books such as "To Kill a Mockingbird" is an important phase of their welfare. I cannot conceive of this being interpreted as "dim vision," as you termed it.

The book in question is considered as immoral literature and, therefore, is certainly not proper reading for our students. Books on suggested and approved reading lists for high school students should, in my estimation, contribute something or be of some value to a person's education—or why require them to be read? People will always read this type book, but it certainly should never be on a required reading list of a student using his or her time to the best advantage in getting an education for the future. In your defense of the book, you stated it was a best-seller and had been made into a notable movie. This does not give it a stamp of approval. Needless to say, it is read by people everywhere—even Hanover—and more so, now that curiosity has been aroused by publicity. This again does not make it acceptable.

However, this is not the direct cause of my response to your editorial. My reason is to congratulate the Superintendent of Schools, the School Board members, principals and teachers of Hanover County for their efforts and decision in guiding the moral development of our boys and girls. We, as parents, have a tremendous responsibility in the development of our children's moral and spiritual character, as they develop physically. The action taken by our school administrators will have great influence on their moral development. I thank God for them and their vision.

As to your "remedy" of giving 50 copies free to the students of Lee-Davis: I challenge those taking you up on this offer, to write a "Letter to the Editor" and inform us honestly of exactly what the book contributed to their education.

Mrs. L. L. Hollins

BOARD ACTED WISELY IN BANNING OF NOVEL

Editor, *News-Leader*

Our radios and TV screens and newspapers of today are constantly overflowing with news of people who are against one thing or the other, but in Wednesday's paper, on the front page was something almost unheard of! Somebody actually had the courage to dare to say that something was immoral.

That in itself made a newsworthy story, and was correctly placed on the front page. On every hand we are told that indecent pictures are not really indecent—they are actually art in its finest form—and if you don't see it that way—then it is because of your nasty little dirty mind. And so most of us are so brainwashed that we say hesitantly, "Well, maybe we are being too harsh," and fall back into a comfortable listlessness.

Such a stand in favor of morality and possibly the reason for our mass spinelessness, is flustrated [sic] by the news that a school board group stood for something smacking of morality, and the paper's editor gives them "what for" on the editorial page. Dare to stand for something and you're publicly ridiculed! And, of course, plain John Q. Citizen doesn't have a widely circulated newspaper with which to withstand such criticism! It's a bit like slapping the face of a man who has his hands tied behind him, isn't it?

The offer to mail the books to students from the Beadle Bumble Fund was so generous that I would like to offer you, absolutely free, a membership in the "Mind Your Own Business Club," established and maintained by a Hanover citizen. Your generosity to us makes me wonder—when the Catholic Church denounces a book or movie, doesn't the Beadle Bumble Fund get frightfully low in cash?

Mrs. Claude E. Tuck

IMMORAL ACTORS SIDE WITH STUDENTS

Editor, *News-Leader*:

How heartening to know that Harper Lee's novel, "To Kill a Mockingbird," has been removed from school library shelves in Hanover County. It's been a nagging worry to realize that our young people were being exposed to a philosophy which says that innocence must be defended; that legal procedures are preferable to mob violence; that in small, southern communities there are heroic people to whom truth and respect for all men are the cornerstones of character. After all, it's a big, cruel world out there, and what youngster has developed sufficient bigotry to withstand the idea that to hurt a less fortunate fellow is as senseless and sad as killing a mockingbird.

We're also reassured to see that our Hanover officials still move without haste when making such a crucial decision, so that the book's offensiveness became obvious only after five years of availability on these same shelves. Do you suppose there's some sort of memory-erasing machine that could remove injurious impressions from those who have already read it?

There may, of course, be some recalcitrant teen-agers who will insist upon taking Miss Lee's book out behind the fence to read. Since theater people have, through the ages, been notoriously immoral, we offer to these few not only our copy, but the fence as well.

The *News-Leader*, too, is certainly subject to censure for making the Beadle Bumble Fund available to Lee-Davis truants who wish to own paperback editions of the book. But let us not add discrimination to immorality. What about the students at Hanover's second high school, Patrick Henry?

Muriel McAuley, David and Nancy Kilgore
Barksdale Theatre, Hanover C. H.

*Thanks to generous contributions, the Beadle Bumble Fund has been able to extend its benefactions to Patrick Henry High School also. A number of Patrick Henry students already have written for their free copies; and while the supply lasts, all requests from Hanover high school students will be filled.

Editor

ZEALOTS SHIELD STUDENTS FROM GOOD LITERATURE

Editor, *News-Leader*:

Unfortunately, performances such as the Hanover County Board's banning of "To Kill a Mockingbird" are repeated far too often by those over-zealous, self-appointed protectors of our morals.

Such was the case a short time ago when the dramatics department of Thomas Jefferson was almost prevented from using the words "sex-starved cobra" in their production of "The Man Who Came to Dinner."

When are these zealots going to realize that the only thing they are "shielding" the students from is good literature?

I am confident that most students are mature enough to read about the shadier side of life without being permanently perverted.

Michael K. Tobias
N.C. State University

"MOCKINGBIRD" NOT ALONE ON LIST OF
BANNED BOOKS

Editor, *News-Leader*:

I enthusiastically applaud and concur with your comments concerning the removal of "To Kill a Mockingbird" from Hanover County school libraries. I have long held that the only Mockingbird which deserves to be killed is the one which screeches outside my window at some ungodly hour every morning, but the board's move came as no great surprise. Nor would it have surprised anyone who generally reads bulletins posted in Virginia public libraries.

These official guardians of literary morality enshrined on the State Library Board (or whatever it is) have, I am sure, produced some ethical gems in the past. Now they have turned again upon children and really outdone themselves. Among the latest batch ordered removed from circulation in public libraries one will find the Tom Swift series, the Hardy Boys' series, the Uncle Wiggly series, the "Wizard of Oz" (shame on Judy Garland), and, no kidding, "The Bobbsey Twins."

We are informed that these books, among others named, constitute cheap sensationalism. God, what a twisted kid I must have been! I actually enjoyed them! And I still can't even rationalize how they contributed significantly to my complete degeneration. My sympathy to Dick and Jane.

Bruce S. Campbell
Virginia Beach

Richmond News-Leader, January 10, 1966, p. 10.

LETTERS FROM "Forum," *Richmond News-Leader*

SUGGESTS OTHER BOOKS FOR POSSIBLE BANNING

Editor, *News-Leader:*

Regarding the removal of "To Kill a Mockingbird" from the library shelves of the Hanover schools, I suggest the Hanover County School Board check closely into "Rebecca of Sunny Brook Farm." Also, I thought that several passages in "Five Little Peppers and How They Grew" were pretty gamey.

Howard Taylor

IMMORAL LITERATURE IS SIGN OF MORAL DECAY

Editor, *News-Leader:*

I am surprised, shocked, and dismayed to learn that you are not supporting the efforts of our police, school boards, and churches to prevent immoral literature from corrupting our young people. Did not Senator Goldwater warn us in 1964 that its spread is another sign of moral decay in our country?

I would suppose your personal influence and that of your paper would be directed against it, and that you would be among the last to adopt the liberal line of "Anything goes in a work of art."

W. H. Buck
Junction City, Kansas

Richmond News-Leader, January 12, 1966, p. 8.

LETTERS AND COMMENTS FROM *Richmond News-Leader*

Still more reaction has cropped up to the Hanover County school board's banning of two highly praised novels from the county's schools. In developments reported yesterday:

• The county's executive secretary, Rosewell Page, Jr., a former school board member, attacked the board's action and called on members to rescind it.

• The Ashland Ministers Association resolved to ask the General Assembly to clarify the functions of the state library committee's book list. Further, the ministers called for expressed authority to be given to local school boards to select books not on the approved list. (Legally, local boards may do this. But the Hanover board, in ordering removal of "To Kill a Mockingbird" and "1984," based its action on the fact that the former was rejected by the state and the latter removed from the list.)

• Faculties at Lee-Davis and Patrick Henry high schools, the county's two predominantly white secondary schools, declared that they should have been consulted before such a book selection policy was adopted.

Page said it is impossible to rear a child to choose good and evil "if his experience, gained through the reading of books, is to be hampered in such a manner."

The State Department of Education and the Hanover school board "in their wisdom" might consider banning parts of the Old and New Testaments and numerous literary classics, Page said.

(A spokesman for the State Department of Education, in response to a reporter's query, confirmed that the Bible is on the approved state list).

Chairman B. W. Sadler of the Hanover School Board has finally said something close to the heart of the issue in this book-banning fiasco. "The school board or the superintendent of schools has not the time, nor are we competent to judge the books" (*Times-Dispatch*, January 10).

Since both "1984" and "To Kill a Mockingbird" are short and easy to read, it takes little time to read them—probably less time than it takes to defend having banned them. And it is appalling to realize that the men who banned these books refuse to invest that little time that might give them some idea of what they have done.

More appalling, however, and more relevant to the issue, is that, as Sadler says, the School Board is not competent to judge the books. Yet these are two fairly clear and simple works of fiction. If the board members are incompetent to judge the books, can they be competent to set educational policies for the public schools of an entire county? I think not. Most fiction, including "1984" and "To Kill a Mockingbird," is written for general consumption, not for specialized scholars. Anyone who can read can read it; anyone who can reason can judge it. Sadler's statement implies that the Hanover School Board and school superintendent can neither read nor reason. If this is true, steps should be taken to remedy the situation.

(Mrs.) Christina H. Halsted

REASSURED BY BOARD'S DECISION TO BAN BOOK

The Hanover County School Board has taken a firm stand against "slummy" books. When "new English" is accepted as a part of the curriculum along with "new math," "To Kill a Mockingbird" will hardly find a place in any school library. The main characteristic of "new English" is the use of literature from the first grade through high school. Fictionalized court records and case studies in sociology do not meet the established standards for high school fiction, regardless of the fine craftsmanship they illustrate or the prizes they have won.

Literature is used in school to help students develop the right attitude toward life, as well as to improve reading comprehension, build vocabularies, and to supply new ideas. It is doubtful that a judge in a Virginia court would try a case like the one in "To Kill a Mockingbird" with young people in the audience. And, no parent who cares about the character of his son would send him out with the hero of "Catcher in the Rye" to learn the ways of the world. It is true that many of the novels which have stood the test of time and are regarded as classics depict unfavorable scenes and bad characters. But they are plainly labeled as bad and show the disadvantages of unacceptable social behavior. The current books under discussion fail to do this.

. . .

Our selection committee prevents the stocking of library shelves with books purchased with taxpayers' money to discredit the American way of life and the principles of good taste. . . . If this is censorship, I am for it.

(Mrs.) Noral Miller Turman
Parksley School Librarian

Richmond News-Leader, January 14, 1966, p. 6.

LETTER FROM "Voice of the People," *Richmond Times-Dispatch*

NOT ALL "CLASSICS" ARE FIT FOR JUVENILES

As a writer of sixteen published books, including two for children, I heartily support the State Department of Education's policy in withholding state funds from local school authorities for the purchase of books not on the department's approved list. This does not ban the book, since local school boards may acquire any volume they want, provided they use local funds.

The policy, therefore, is not an exercise of censorship, but one of guidance sorely needed in a time when pruriency—occasionally admittedly accompanied by some literary merit—floods the bookstores.

A certain maturity of mind is required for appreciation of genuine literary worth. None at all is needed to produce adolescent snickers or a potentially harmful excitement at the discovery of a phrase or a passage on page so-and-so. Such books, after being awhile in any library, tend to fall open at such well-thumbed pages.

It should be obvious to all Virginians that a measure of restraint or control—call it "guidance" again—must be exercised toward public school library selections. If no line at all were drawn, the titles might conceivably include a new edition of Henry Miller, or "The Memoirs of a Lady of Pleasure," (better known, but not favorably, as "Fanny Hill.")

The fact that a book has become a "classic" does not necessarily make it fit for juvenile reading; the fact that it is on the best-seller list, or has been awarded literary prizes, or made into a motion picture, is even less reason to make it so.

It is true that cheap trash is available to the young, in cheap paperbacks, at too many newsstands and corner drugstores. This problem is out of the hands of all the school authorities, state and local. Here the guidance must come from the parents and the homes.

No one man, in a long lifetime, could possibly read all the good, clean, entertaining and constructive books that have been printed in the five centuries since Gutenberg allegedly invented movable type. Let the parents, then, begin at the ABC stage to inculcate a love for such reading in the minds and hearts of their children. Neither the State Department of Education nor the school librarian can do this.

Allan R. Bosworth
Captain, U.S. Navy (ret.), Roanoke

Richmond Times-Dispatch, January 18, 1966, p. 14.

LETTERS AND EDITOR'S COMMENTS FROM "Forum,"
Richmond News-Leader

AGREES WITH DECISION TO BAN BOOK IN HANOVER

Editor, *News-Leader:*

As a regular reader of your paper I am very disappointed in your recent position regarding a certain book in a Hanover County school. I have not read the book (nor do I intend to do so) but I did see the diabolical movie, which was repulsive enough. No doubt, had I read the book, I should have found a rather detailed and descriptive account of what actually took place in the story.

The decision of our School Board does not deny anyone the right to purchase this controversial book, nor any other book, if he so desires.

In our community, Mr. Bosher is a respected businessman of irreproachable character. Were there more such officials of his caliber in the "driver's seat" of the local, state, and federal government of this nation, the rampant moral decline with which we are currently oppressed might have been avoided.

Someone had the audacity to refer to Mr. Bosher as "ignorant." This term is employed today, often indiscriminately by some folks who attempt to categorize those who disagree with them. All of us are ignorant of various matters.

To put so much emphasis on the fact that the author of "To Kill a Mockingbird" was awarded the Pulitzer Prize does not impress me. Martin Luther King was awarded the Nobel Peace Prize. What irony!

I am thankful that at an early age my parents introduced me to wholesome reading material. Consequently, never having cultivated an appetite for the baser literature (and I use the word "literature" loosely), I have always sought undefiled reading matter.

I don't recall that such a commotion as this came about when an atheist in Maryland carried to the federal courts her protest against the use of prayer in the public schools.

Everyone should be cognizant of the fact that a young mind is a flexible and a vulnerable mind. Therefore, influences such as books, movies, etc. can either elevate or degrade that mind.

It takes a strong back to stand up and be counted. May I say, bravo, Mr. Bosher! Carry on!

Miss Vivian Blake

AUTHOR HARPER LEE COMMENTS ON BOOK-BANNING

Editor, *News-Leader*:

Recently I have received echoes down this way of the Hanover County School Board's activities, and what I've heard makes me wonder if any of its members can read.

Surely it is plain to the simplest intelligence that "To Kill a Mockingbird" spells out in words of seldom more than two syllables a code of honor and conduct, Christian in its ethic, that is the heritage of all Southerners. To hear that the novel is "immoral" has made me count the years between now and 1984, for I have yet to come across a better example of doublethink.

I feel, however, that the problem is one of illiteracy, not Marxism. Therefore I enclose a small contribution to the Beadle Bumble Fund that I hope will be used to enroll the Hanover County School Board in any first grade of its choice.

Harper Lee
Monroeville, Ala.

In most controversies, the lady is expected to have the last word. In this particular discussion, it seems especially fitting that the last word should come from the lady who wrote "To Kill a Mockingbird." With Miss Lee's letter, we call a halt, at least temporarily, to the publication of letters commenting on the book-banning in Hanover County.

Editor

Richmond News-Leader, January 15, 1966, p. 10.

STUDY QUESTIONS

1. Examine the guidelines for book approval proposed by the Texas group and the Kanawha, West Virginia, community as described in the introduction to this section. According to the guidelines, which of your own favorite readings in fiction or nonfiction might be removed from a list of books approved for library or classroom use? Explain.

2. *To Kill a Mockingbird* is not mentioned specifically in the available records from the Texas and West Virginia cases. But if you were to apply the requirements advocated by the two groups mentioned in the introduction to this section, do you think *To Kill a Mockingbird* would be on the approved list? Explain why or why not.

3. Are there books that you would not include in library collections? If so, what are they? Why would you argue for exclusion? How would you support your decision to exclude?

4. Are there books that you would leave on the library shelf but would not approve as required reading? Explain.

5. *To Kill a Mockingbird* has been called both a racist book and a powerful weapon against racism. Which do you think it is? Explain.

6. Outline the arguments presented here for and against taking *To Kill a Mockingbird* off the shelves.

TOPICS FOR WRITTEN OR ORAL EXPLORATION

1. Schools must *select* certain materials to include in the classroom. What is the difference between selecting and censoring?

2. Is there a difference between how and what books will be chosen for a fourth grader and how and what books will be chosen for a tenth grader? At what point do we assume that a student has the maturity and education to handle materials that a child might not have? In short, what does age have to do with how we choose and censor?

3. The question of what constitutes pornography and art is a persistent one in terms of the issue of censorship. How do you define each, and how would you deal with each in the public schools?

4. Play "devil's advocate": carefully consider your own position on the question of removing *To Kill a Mockingbird* from school library shelves, then write an essay making the best defense possible for the opposing point of view.

5. Write another essay presenting your own point of view, showing the superiority of your own point of view and demolishing the other.

6. Stage a hearing before the Board of Education. Assume that one group petitions for the removal of *To Kill a Mockingbird* from a required reading list, and another group argues for its retention. Allow others to "hear" and decide the case on the strength of the argument.

7. From the arguments you have read here of would-be censors of the novel and those arguing for the freedom to read, compose a paper contrasting the basic philosophies that *lie behind* their stances. Consider, for example, their views of human character—of adolescent character in particular; of democratic society; of the nature of education; and so on.

8. The response of the National Education Association to the Kanawha community was that if their guidelines were followed, American history would have to be distorted for the classroom. Consider this controversy. What would happen in the teaching of the Civil War, Watergate, and the Vietnam era, for example? Are there other "problems"?

9. Choose a book that you consider to be truly offensive on social or political grounds—one, for example, that is insulting to women or African-Americans or fundamentalist Christians. Argue for or against its inclusion in library collections.

10. Hold a debate on whether a student who objects to reading *To Kill a Mockingbird* should be allowed to substitute another novel as part of his or her reading requirement.

11. Objections have been raised to certain school materials because they attempt to promote values. The argument is that only parents should teach values. Write a persuasive essay on this issue, considering whether *To Kill a Mockingbird* teaches values and whether or not it should be excluded from use in the classroom if it does.

12. Write a persuasive essay on whether the classroom should be used to re-examine the students' responses to race, gender, or social conventions; or whether, as some would argue, such a teaching method becomes an invasion of the students' privacy.

13. Interview your principal, superintendent, or a member of the school board on the issue of censorship.

SUGGESTED READINGS

The following works are studies of censorship by writers who consider the removal of books from libraries and required reading lists to be dangerous practices:

Burress, Lee, and Edward Jenkinson. *The Student's Right to Know*. Urbana, IL: National Council of Teachers of English, 1982.

Donelson, Ken, "Censorship: Some Issues and Problems." *Theory into Practice* (June 1975): 193.

Egerton, John, "The Battle of the Books." *The Progressive* (June 1976): 13.

Foerstel, Herbert N. *Banned in the U.S.A.: Book Censorship in Schools and Public Libraries*. Westport, CT: Greenwood Press, 1994.

Jenkinson, Edward B. *Censors in the Classroom: The Mind Benders*. Carbondale: Southern Illinois University Press, 1979.

————. "Protecting Holden Caulfield and His Friends from the Censors." In *Teaching Secondary English: Readings and Applications*, ed. Daniel Sheridan, 331–45. New York: Longman, 1993.

McDonald, Frances Beck. "Appendix B. Freedom to Read: A Professional Responsibility." In Richard Beach and James Marshall, *Teaching Literature in the Secondary School*. New York: Harcourt, Brace Jovanovich, 1991. (See this article for a more detailed bibliography of books and articles on censorship.)

Marsh, Dave. *50 Ways to Fight Censorship and Important Facts to Know about Censors*. New York: Thunder's Mouth Press, 1990.

May, Jill P. "Censors as Critics: *To Kill a Mockingbird* as a Case Study." In *Cross-Culturalism in Children's Literature: Selected Papers from the Children's Literature Association*, 91–95. Carleton University, Ottawa, Canada, May 14–17, 1987. New York: Pace University, 1988.

Parker, Barbara, and Stefanie Weiss. *Protecting the Freedom to Learn*. Washington, DC: People for the American Way, 1983.

Parker, Franklin. *The Battle of the Books: Kanawha County*. Bloomington, IN: Phi Delta Kappa Educational Foundation, 1975.

Woods, L. B. *A Decade of Censorship in America: The Threat to Classrooms and Libraries, 1966–1975*. Methuen, NJ: Scarecrow Press, 1979.

Three national organizations collect materials on censorship for distribution: People for the American Way, Washington, DC; American Library Association, whose headquarters is in Chicago, Illinois; and the National Council of Teachers of English, Urbana, Illinois.

The following books are by authors who favor banning certain books from libraries and classrooms:

Hefley, James C. *Textbooks on Trial*. Wheaton, IL: Victor Books, 1976.

La Haye, Tim. *The Battle for the Mind*. Old Tappan, NJ: Fleming Revell, 1980.

————. *The Battle for the Public Schools*. Old Tappan, NJ: Fleming Revell, 1983.

Index

About the Author

CLAUDIA DURST JOHNSON is Professor of English at the University of Alabama, where she chaired the English Department for twelve years. She is the author of the forthcoming volumes in the Greenwood Press "Literature in Context" series, *Understanding The Scarlet Letter* and *Understanding Huckleberry Finn*. She is also author of *To Kill a Mockingbird: Threatening Boundaries* (1994), *American Actress: Perspectives on the Nineteenth Century* (1984), (with Vernon Johnson) *Memoirs of the Nineteenth Century Theatre* (Greenwood, 1982), *The Productive Tension of Hawthorne's Art* (1981), and (with Henry Jacobs) *An Annotated Bibliography of Shakespearean Burlesques, Parodies, and Travesties* (1976), as well as numerous articles on American literature.